Get the eBook FREE!

(PDF, ePub, Kindle, and liveBook all included)

We believe that once you buy a book from us, you should be able to read it in any format we have available. To get electronic versions of this book at no additional cost to you, purchase and then register this book at the Manning website.

Go to https://www.manning.com/freebook and follow the instructions to complete your pBook registration.

That's it!
Thanks from Manning!

grokking
Streaming
Systems

Real-time event processing

Josh Fischer
Ning Wang

MANNING
SHELTER ISLAND

For online information and ordering of this and other Manning books, please visit
www.manning.com. The publisher offers discounts on this book when ordered in quantity.
For more information, please contact

    Special Sales Department
    Manning Publications Co.
    20 Baldwin Road, PO Box 761
    Shelter Island, NY 11964
    Email: orders@manning.com

Manning Publications Co.
20 Baldwin Road
Shelter Island, NY 11964

Development editor: Becky Whitney
Technical development editor: Nick Watts
Review editor: Aleksander Dragosavljević
Production editor: Andy Marinkovich
Copy editor: Christian Berk
Proofreader: Keri Hales
Technical proofreader: Karsten Strøbaek
Typesetter: Dennis Dalinnik
Cover designer: Leslie Hames

ISBN: 9781617297304
Printed and bound by CPI Group (UK) Ltd, Croydon, CR0 4YY

brief contents

contents

4   Stream graph   81

5   Delivery semantics   109

10 Stateful computation   235

preface

A mentor of mine once told me, at the beginning of my tech career, "If there's one thing you can do to better your career, it's contributing to open source." I'd harbored that thought in the back of my mind throughout the years but never had a reason to do so. I thought, "What could I build that would be useful for others?" While working at 1904labs I developed the ECO API for (at the time) Twitter Heron. It came from a client's need—and from a little bit of selfishness; I really wanted to write and contribute that code. Eventually, Twitter donated Heron to the Apache Foundation, and I was invited to be a committer and part of the project management committee for Heron. The project interested me because it was the first open source project I did a deep dive on.

About a year later, from that initial commit on Heron's main branch at about 4 p.m. on a Monday, I received an email with the subject line, "Apache Heron Book or Course Project" from Eleonor Gardner. After a quick read, I almost discarded the email, thinking it was a hoax. After all, why would anyone want me to write a book or teach a course project? Well, how wrong was I? After a discussion with Mike Stephens, Manning's associate publisher, and a few email exchanges with his assistant, Eleonor, I knew I needed some help. I reached out to my friend and fellow Apache Heron committer, Ning Wang, praying that he'd be interested in writing a book with me. Luckily, he was—and that was the start to our long and rewarding journey.

Initially, the conversations about this book were for us to write specifically about Heron. But Ning had some ideas to make the book better. After all, technologies change quickly and breaking changes in software can make a book obsolete quickly. We wanted to write about a topic that would live beyond individual streaming frameworks. We agreed to write a framework-agnostic book to teach the core concepts in a way that would allow readers to be able to jump into any streaming framework's documentation and hit the ground running.

So, we started writing the book using only words and then Ning and I were "gently" guided to try another approach. Again. And again. And again. And again. We learned that diagrams make the content of a book much easier for readers to absorb. We created our first diagrams on paper with pen, and they were dismal:

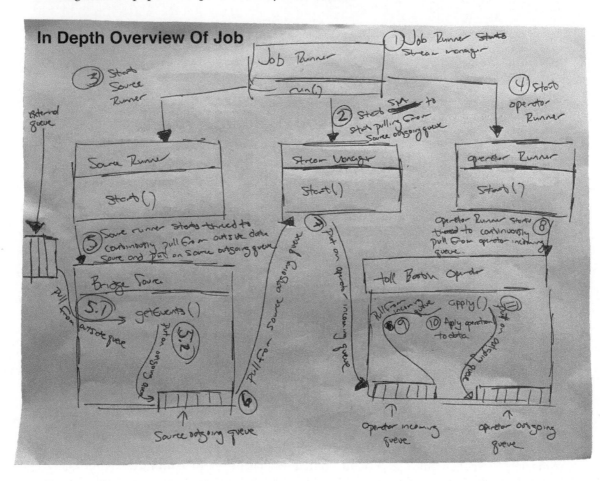

Over the course of writing the book, our primitive-looking, scrawled creations evolved into the diagrams you now see in the book. Ning and I designed and developed all of these diagrams ourselves. We are extremely proud of what we have created, and we hope that you see value in this book.

—Josh Fischer, November 2021

acknowledgments

First, I must thank my kids and my ever-so-wonderful partner, Melissa. She is the most patient and fabulous person anyone could ever ask for. She has helped me endure all the tough spots of life while writing this book. My kids—Aiden, Wes, Hollyn, Oliver, Declan, and Dylan—have been patient, and often self-entertaining, on the late nights or early mornings while I took time to write.

Thank you, Ning, for sticking with me through the process of writing. Learning from you has been one of the greatest benefits of writing this book.

I must thank Dan Tumminello, Dave Lodes, Laura Stobie, Jim Towey, Steve Willis, Mike Banocy, Sean Walsh, Pavan Veeramachineni, Robert McMillan, Chad Storm, Karthik Ramasamy, and Chandra Shekar. All of them have been a great influence on me personally and professionally.

Last but not least, I want to thank Bert Bates. He is without a doubt the most patient, forgiving, and all-around fantastic teacher I have ever had. Becky Whitney always participated in conversations that may have been tough, but kept us on track to deliver for Manning. Thank you, Mike Stephens, for giving me a chance. Eleonor Gardner set up our initial conversations, and, finally, Andy Marinkovich and Keri Hales, who put the finishing touches on the book.

To all the reviewers, Andres Sacco, Anto Aravinth, Anupam Sengupta, Apoorv Gupta, Beau Bender, Brent Honadel, Brynjar Smári Bjarnason, Chris Lundberg, Cicero Zandona, Damian Esteban, Deepika Fernandez, Fernando Antonio da Silva Bernardino, Johannes Lochmann, Kent R. Spillner, Kumar Unnikrishnan, Lev Andelman, Marc Roulleau, Massimo Siani, Matthias Busch, Miguel Montalvo, Sebastián Palma, Simeon Leyzerzon, Simon Seyag, and Simon Verhoeven: your comments, questions, and concerns have all made this a better book. Thank you.

—Josh Fischer, November 2021

Two years! I have lost count of how many people I need to thank. This book wouldn't be possible without any of the people listed here, as well as many others not listed.

Firstly, it wouldn't be possible for me to complete this book without my daughter's understanding and support. I owe you two years of weekends, Xinyi! It has also been more than two years since I visited my parents, Jili Wang and Shujun Liu, and my sister, Feng Wang, in China. I miss them very much.

Many thanks to my co-author, Josh. What a ride it has been! It wouldn't have been possible without your creativity and excellent ideas.

I believe in the power of data processing, and I feel so grateful that I have the chance to work with many great engineers. Many of the things I have learned from you are critical for this book: thank you to Maosong Fu, Neng Lu, Huijun Wu, Dmitry Rusakov, Xiaoyao Qian, Yao Li, Zhenxiao Luo, Hao Luo, Mainak Ghosh, Da Cheng, Fred Dai, Beinan Wang, Chunxu Tang, Runhang Li, Yaliang Wang, Thoms Cooper, and Faria Kalim of the Real-Time Compute team at Twitter; Pavan Patibandla, Farshad Rostamabadi, Kurt Norwood, Julien Dubeau, Cathy Nam, Leo Zhang, Neha Bhambhani, Nick Wu, Robyn Nason, Zachery Miranda, Jeffrey Wang, and Nirmal Utwani of the Data Pipeline team at Amplitude; and many others in the Apache Heron community.

As a first-time writer (and in English!), it would be a mission impossible for me without all the help I received from the hardworking Manning editors. Thank you so much Bert Bates, Becky Whitney, Jennifer Houle, Matthew Spaur, and the many other editors and reviewers who contributed. I have learned so much from you!

—Ning Wang, November 2021

about this book

Grokking Streaming Systems helps you unravel what streaming systems are, how they work, and whether they're right for your business. Because they're written to be tool-agnostic, you'll be able to apply what you learn no matter which framework you choose. You'll start with the key concepts and then work your way through increasingly complex examples, including tracking a real-time count of IoT sensor events and detecting fraudulent credit card transactions in real time. You'll even be able to easily experiment with your own streaming system by downloading the custom-built and super-simplified streaming framework designed for this book. By the time you're done, you'll be able to assess the capabilities of streaming frameworks and solve common challenges that arise when building streaming systems.

Who should read this book?

We have written this book for developers who have at least a couple of years of experience and who are looking to improve their knowledge and expertise. If you've been building web clients, APIs, batch jobs, etc., and are wondering what's next, then this book is for you.

How this book is organized: A road map

This book has a simple setup—just 11 chapters split into two parts; after you work your way through chapters 1 through 5 in order, you should be able to work through the remaining chapters in any order you choose. Here's the rundown:

- Chapter 1 introduces readers to streaming systems from a 1,000-foot view and compares them against other typical computer systems.

- Chapter 2 delves into the fundamental ways in which streaming systems work.

- Chapter 3 discusses parallelization, data grouping, and how streaming jobs can scale.

- Chapter 4 covers stream graphs and how streaming jobs can be represented.

- Chapter 5 walks you through delivery semantics, such as how a developer can use a streaming system to reliably deliver events (or not).

- Chapter 6 reviews the core concepts and offers a preview of later chapters.

- Chapter 7 discusses windows—how these systems can help you slice up endless streams of data.

- Chapter 8 describes streaming joins, or bringing data together in real time.

- Chapter 9 tells you all about how streaming systems handle failures.

- Chapter 10 lets you know how streaming systems deal with stateful operations in real time.

- Chapter 11 wraps up the later chapters and offers our advice on where to go next with your interest in streaming systems.

About the code

We've provided code for chapters 2, 3, 4, 5, 7, and 8. You can download it from https://github.com/nwangtw/GrokkingStreamingSystems. In addition, the source code can be downloaded free of charge from the Manning website at https://www.manning.com/books/grokking-streaming-systems. To run the examples, you will need Java 11, Apache Maven 3.8.1, and the command-line tool Netcat, or NMap.

This book contains many examples of source code, both in numbered listings and in line with normal text. In both cases, source code is formatted in a `fixed-width font` to separate it from ordinary text. Sometimes code is also shown in bold to indicate that it has changed from previous steps in the chapter, such as when a new feature adds to an existing line of code. In many cases, the original source code has been reformatted; we've added line breaks and reworked indentation to accommodate the available page space in the book. In rare cases, even this was not enough, and listings include line-continuation markers (➥). Additionally, comments in the source code have often been removed from the listings when the code is described in the text. Code annotations accompany many of the listings, highlighting important concepts.

liveBook discussion forum

Purchase of *Grokking Streaming Systems* includes free access to liveBook, Manning's online reading platform. Using liveBook's exclusive discussion features, you can attach comments to the book globally or to specific sections or paragraphs. It's a snap to make notes for yourself, ask and answer technical questions, and receive help from the author and other users. To access the forum, go to https://livebook.manning.com/book/grokking-streaming-systems/discussion/. You can also learn more about Manning's forums and the rules of conduct at https://livebook. manning.com/#!/discussion.

Manning's commitment to our readers is to provide a venue where a meaningful dialogue between individual readers and between readers and the author can take place. It is not a commitment to any specific amount of participation on the part of the authors, whose contribution to the forum remains voluntary (and unpaid). We suggest you try asking them some challenging questions lest their interest stray! The forum and the archives of previous discussions will be accessible from the publisher's website as long as the book is in print.

about the authors

Josh Fischer, currently a team lead at 1904labs, has worked with moving large datasets in real time for other organizations, such as Monsanto and Bayer.

Ning Wang is a software engineer at Amplitude who builds real-time data pipelines. He was a key contributor to Apache Heron on Twitter's Real-time Compute team.

Both authors are Apache committers and are part of the project management committee for the Apache Heron distributed stream processing engine.

Part 1
Getting started with streaming

Part 1 of this book drops you head-first into the world of streaming systems. It can help you answer questions, such as "Why do streaming systems work this way?" and "Why would I ever use them?" Chapter 1 describes the high-level differences in what sets streaming systems apart from others. Chapter 2 is the *hello world* of streaming, where we walk you through the fundamentals of how these streaming systems work. Chapter 3 describes how to scale out these systems, and chapter 4 shows you how data can traverse streaming jobs. Chapter 5 spells out how these systems can help you reliably deliver data in real time, and chapter 6 recaps the important points from each chapter. By the end of part 1, you will have the knowledge necessary to jump into any streaming framework of your choice and hit the ground running.

In this chapter

- an introduction to stream processing

- differentiating between stream processing systems
  and other systems

> 66 *If it weren't for the rocks in its bed, the stream* 99
> *would have no song.*
>
> —CARL PERKINS

In this chapter, we will try to answer a few basic questions about streaming systems, starting with "what is stream processing?" and "what are these stream processing systems, or streaming systems, used for?" The objective is to cover some basic ideas that will be discussed in later chapters.

What is stream processing?

Stream processing has been one of the most popular technologies in the recent years in the big data domain. Streaming systems are the computer systems that process continuous event streams.

A key characteristic of stream processing is that the *events* are processed as soon as (or almost as soon as) they are available. This is to minimize the latency between the original event's entrance into the streaming system and the end result from processing the event. In most cases, the latency varies from a few milliseconds to seconds, which can be considered real-time or near real-time; hence, stream processing is also called *real-time processing*. From the usage point of view, stream processing is typically used for analyzing different types of events. As a result, the terms *real-time analytics*, *streaming analytics*, and *event processing* might also be used to reference stream processing systems in different scenarios. In this book, *stream processing* is the chosen term, which is well-adopted by the industry.

Examples of events:

Here are a few examples of events:

- The mouse clicks on a computer
- The taps and swipes on a cell phone
- The trains arriving at and leaving a station
- The messages and emails sent out by a person
- The temperatures collected by sensors in a laboratory
- The interactions on a website (page views, user logins, clicks, and so on) from all users
- The logs generated by computer servers in a data center
- The transactions of all accounts in a bank

Note that, typically, there isn't a predetermined ending time for the events processed in streaming systems. You can think of them as never-ending; hence, the events are often considered *continuous* and *unbounded*. Events are everywhere—literally. We are living in the information age. A lot of data is generated, collected, and processed all the time.

> **Think about it**
>
> Stream processing systems are the computer systems designed to process continuous event streams.

Streaming system examples

Let's look at two examples:

- The first example is a temperature-monitoring system in a laboratory. Many sensors are installed in different locations to collect temperature data every second. The streaming system is built to process the collected data and display the real-time information in a dashboard. It can also trigger alerts when any anomaly is detected. Laboratory administrators use the system to monitor all the rooms and make sure the temperature is in the right range.

- The second example is the monitoring and analyzing systems that process user interactions, such as page views, user logins, or button clicks on a website. When you visit a website, it is common that a lot of events are logged. These raw events often have many fields, so it is not efficient to digest directly. Also, some of the fields are not human-readable and need to be translated before consuming. Streaming systems are very helpful for converting the raw events data into more useful information, such as number of requests, active users, views on each page, and suspicious user behaviors, in this context.

In the examples above, a huge number of events can be processed by streaming systems to dig out useful information hidden in the data in real time. Streaming systems are very useful because there is a lot of useful information hidden in these events, and real time is critical in many cases.

Streaming systems and *real time*

A streaming system refers to a system that extracts useful information from continuous streams of events. More specifically, as we mentioned at the beginning of this section, we would like streaming systems to process the events and generate results as soon as possible after the events are collected. This is desirable because it allows the results to be available with minimal delays and the proper reactions to be performed in time. Their *real-time* nature makes streaming systems very useful in many scenarios, such as the laboratory and the website, where low-latency results are desired.

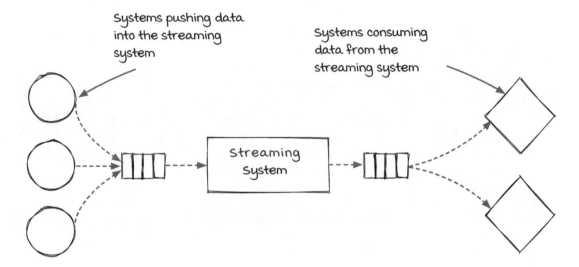

In the laboratory, the monitoring system can trigger alerts, start backup devices automatically, and notify the administrators, when necessary. If failed equipment is not repaired or replaced in time and the temperature is not under control, the temperature-sensitive devices and samples could be affected or damaged. Some ongoing experiments may be interrupted as well. For a website, in addition to monitoring issues, charts and dashboards generated by streaming systems could be helpful for developers to understand how users engage with the website so they can improve their products accordingly.

How a streaming system works

After seeing some examples of events and streaming systems, you should now have some ideas about what streaming systems are. The next few pages will show you how streaming systems work from a very high level by comparing them with other types of systems.

Comparison of four typical computer systems

You'll find that stream processing systems and other computer systems have many things in common. After all, a streaming system is still a computer system. Below are a few typical systems we chose to compare:

- Applications
- Backend services
- Batch processing services
- Stream processing services

Applications

An *application* is a computer program that users interact with directly. Programs installed on your computer and apps installed on your smartphone are applications. For example, the calculator, text editor, music and video players, messenger, web browser, and games installed on a computer or smartphone are all applications. They are everywhere! Users interact with computers via all kinds of applications.

Users use applications to perform tasks. You can create a note or a book in a text editor and save it in a file. If you have a video file, you can use a video player application to open and play it. You can use a web browser to search for information, watch videos, and shop on the internet.

Inside an application

Applications will vary a lot. A command-line tool, a text editor, a calculator, a photo processor, a browser, and a video game look and feel significantly different from each other. Have you ever thought of them to be the same type of software? Internally, they are even more different. A simple calculator can be implemented with a few lines of code, while a web browser or a game has millions of lines in its code base.

Despite all the differences, the basic process in most applications are similar: there is a starting point (when the application is opened), an ending point (when the application is closed), and a loop (the main loop) of the following three steps:

1. Get user input
2. Execute logic
3. Show results

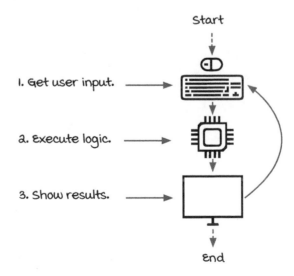

Backend services

A *backend service* is a computer program that runs *behind the scenes*. Different from an application, a backend service doesn't interact with users directly. Instead, it responds to requests and performs specific tasks accordingly. A service is normally a long-running process, and it waits for incoming requests all the time.

Let's look at a simple web service as an example. When a request is received, the program parses the requests, performs tasks accordingly, and, finally, responds. After a request is handled, the program waits for the next request again. The web service is often not working alone. It works with other services together to serve the requests. Services can handle requests from each other, and each one is responsible for a specific task. The figure below shows a web service and a storage service working together to serve a page request.

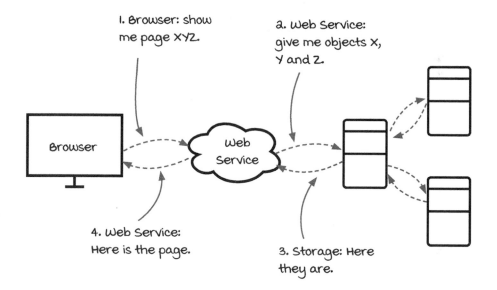

Inside a backend service

Inside a backend service, there is a main loop, too, but it works differently, because the requests processed by a service are quite different from the user inputs in an application. Because an application is normally used by a single user, checking the user input at the beginning of the main loop is normally sufficient, but in a backend service, many requests can arrive at the same time, and the requests can arrive at any moment. To handle the requests promptly, *multi-threading* is an important technique for this use case. A thread is a subtask executed within a process; multiple threads can exist within the context of one process. Multiple threads share the process's resources like memory, and they can be executed concurrently.

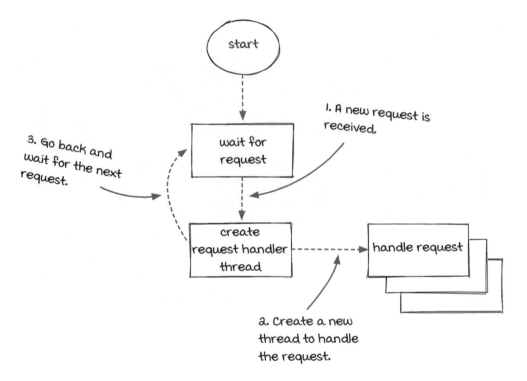

A typical service looks like the previous diagram. When a request is received, the request handler creates a new thread to perform the real logic, and it returns immediately without waiting for the results. The time-consuming calculation (the real logic) is then performed concurrently on its own thread. This way, the main loop runs very quickly, so the new incoming requests can be accepted as soon as possible.

Batch processing systems

Both applications and backend services are designed to serve clients (human users or remote requests) as soon as possible. Batch processing systems are different. They are not designed to respond to any input. Instead, they are designed to execute tasks at scheduled times or when resources permit.

You can see real-life examples of batch processing systems fairly often. For example, in a post office, mail is collected, sorted, transported, and delivered at scheduled times because it is more efficient this way. It would be hard to imagine a system in which someone accepts your handwritten letter, runs out the door, and tries to deliver the letter to the recipient immediately. Well, it could work, but it would be super inefficient, and you would need a really good excuse to justify the effort.

Nowadays, huge amounts of data, such as articles, emails, user interactions, and the data collected from services and devices, are generated every second. It is critical and challenging to process the data and find useful information. Batch processing systems are designed for this use case.

> *Look!*
>
> Batch processing systems are designed to process huge amounts of data efficiently.

Inside a batch processing system

In a typical batch processing system, the whole process is broken into multiple steps, or stages. The stages are connected by storages that store intermediate data.

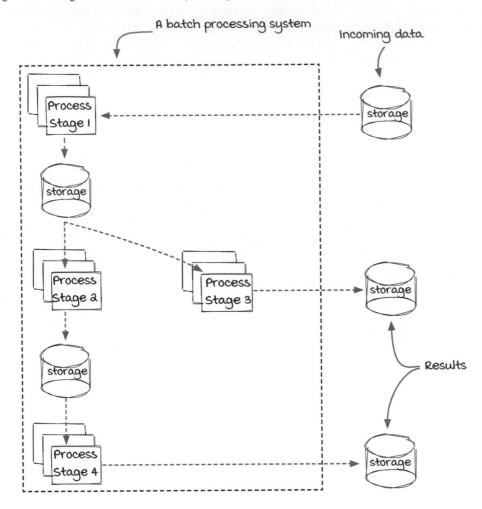

In our example, the incoming data is processed in batches (an example could be user interaction data for each hour on a website). When new data is available (the whole batch is received and ready to be processed), stage 1 is started to load the data and execute its logic. The results are persisted in the intermediate storage for the following stages to pick up and process. After all the data in the batch is processed by the stage, the stage is shut down and the next stage (stage 2 in the diagram above) is started to execute on the intermediate results generated by stage 1. The processing is completed after the batch is processed by all the stages.

Stream processing systems

The batch processing architecture is a very powerful tool in the big data world. However, batch processing systems have one major limitation: *latency*.

Batch processing systems require data to be collected and stored as batches at regular intervals, such as hourly or daily before starting. Any events collected in a particular time window need to wait until the end of the window to be processed. This could be unacceptable in some cases, such as for the monitoring system in a laboratory, where alerts will be triggered in the following hour with a batch processing system. In these cases, it could be more desirable for data to be processed immediately after it is received— in other words, to get the results in real time. Stream processing systems are designed for these more real-time use cases. In a stream processing system, data events are processed as soon as possible once they are received.

We have used the post office as our real-world example of a batch processing system. In this system, mail is collected, transported, and delivered a few times a day at scheduled times. A real-world example of a stream processing system could be an assembly line in a factory. The assembly line has multiple steps, too, and it keeps running to accept new parts. In each step, an operation is applied to one product after another. At the end of the assembly line, the final products come out one by one.

> *Look!*
>
> Stream processing systems are designed to process huge amounts of data with low latency.

Inside a stream processing system

A typical stream processing system architecture looks similar to the batch processing systems. The whole process is broken into multiple steps called *components*, and data keeps flowing from component to component until the processing steps have completed.

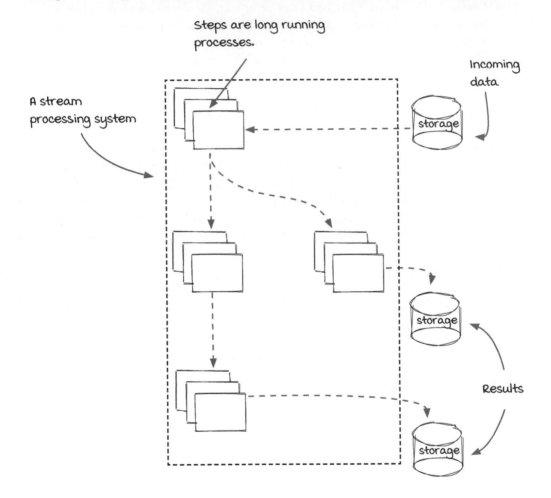

The major difference between stream processing systems and batch processing systems is that the components are *long running* processes. They keep running and accepting new data to process. Each event will be processed immediately by the next component after it is processed by the previous component. Therefore, the final results will be generated shortly after an event is received by the streaming system.

The advantages of multi-stage architecture

Both batch and stream processing systems have a multi-stage architecture. This architecture has a few advantages that make it suitable for data processing use cases:

- *More flexible*—Developers can add or take away stages to their jobs as they see fit.

- *More scalable*—Stages are connected, but each of them is independent from each other. If one stage becomes the bottleneck of the whole process with the existing instances (instances 1 through 3 in the diagram below), it is easy to bring up more instances (instances 4 and 5) to increase the throughput.

- *More maintainable*—Complicated processes can be composed with simple operations, which are easier to implement and maintain.

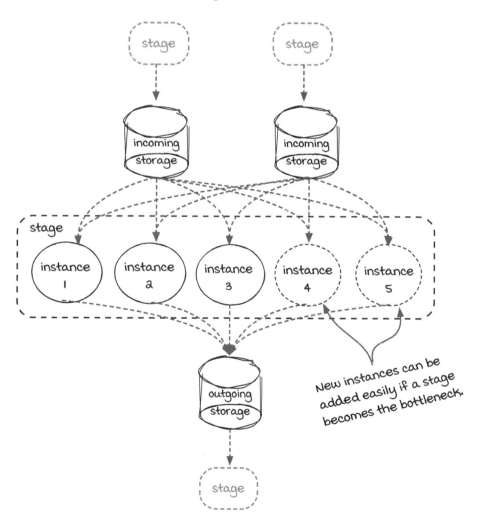

The multi-stage architecture in batch and stream processing systems

Batch processing systems

In batch processing systems, stages run independently of each other, and instances in the same stage also run independently of each other. This means they are not all running at the same time. All the instances in the system can be executed one by one or batch by batch, as long as the execution order is correct. As a result, you can build a batch processing system to process a huge (we really mean it) amount of data with very limited resources (though it will take more time to process with fewer resources). To compensate for the overhead of persistence of intermediate data, normally it is more efficient to process events in bigger batches. For example, hourly or daily are common batching windows. The events happening at the beginning of a window have to wait for the whole hour or day to be closed before being processed. This is the cause of the high latency.

One major advantage is that failure handling is easy with batch processing systems. In case an issue happens, such as a computer crashing or failing to read or write data, the failing step can simply be rescheduled on another machine and rerun.

Stream processing systems

On the streaming side of things, all the steps are long running processes. Events are transferred from one to another continuously. As a result, we don't have the ability to stop stages when they are not working properly anymore, and failure handling becomes more complicated. However, events are being processed as soon as possible, so we can get real-time results.

Compare the systems

Let's compare the systems we have introduced in this section to have a better idea how different types of computer systems work.

Application	Backend service	Batch processing system	Stream processing system
Process user inputs	Process requests	Process data	Process data
Interact with users directly	Interact with clients and other services directly. Interact with users indirectly.	Apply operations on data. The results can be consumed by users directly or indirectly.	Apply operations on data. The results can be consumed by users directly or indirectly.
Applications are started and stopped by users.	Instances of a service are long running processes.	Instances in the system are scheduled to start and stop.	Instances in the system are long running processes.
Single main loop	Single main loop with threads	Multi-stage process	Multi-stage process

One thing to keep in mind is that these examples are just typical architectures for typical use cases. Real-world systems could be architected in many different ways to fulfill their own requirements.

A model stream processing system

After looking at a few different systems, let's focus on stream processing systems. From the previous section, you have learned that a streaming system consists of multiple long running component processes.

The answer to the question depends on the systems you want to build. What do you want to do? How big is the traffic? How many resources do you have? How will you manage these resources? How will you recover from a failure? How will you make sure the results are correct after the recovery? There are many questions to consider when building a stream processing system. So, the answer seems to be a *yes*?

Well, yes, streaming systems can be fairly complicated, but they are *not* that hard to build either. In the next chapters, we are going to learn how to build streaming systems and how they work internally. Are you ready?

Summary

In this chapter, we learned that stream processing is a data processing technology that processes continuous events to get real-time results. We also studied and compared typical architectures of four different types of computer systems to understand how stream processing systems differ from the others:

- Applications
- Backend services
- Batch processing systems
- Stream processing systems

Exercise

1. Can you think of more examples of applications, services, batch processing systems, and stream processing systems?

Hello, streaming systems! | 2

In this chapter

- learning what events are in streaming systems

- understanding the different streaming components

- assembling a job from streaming components

- running your code

First, solve the problem. Then, write the code.

—JOHN JOHNSON

The chief needs a fancy tollbooth

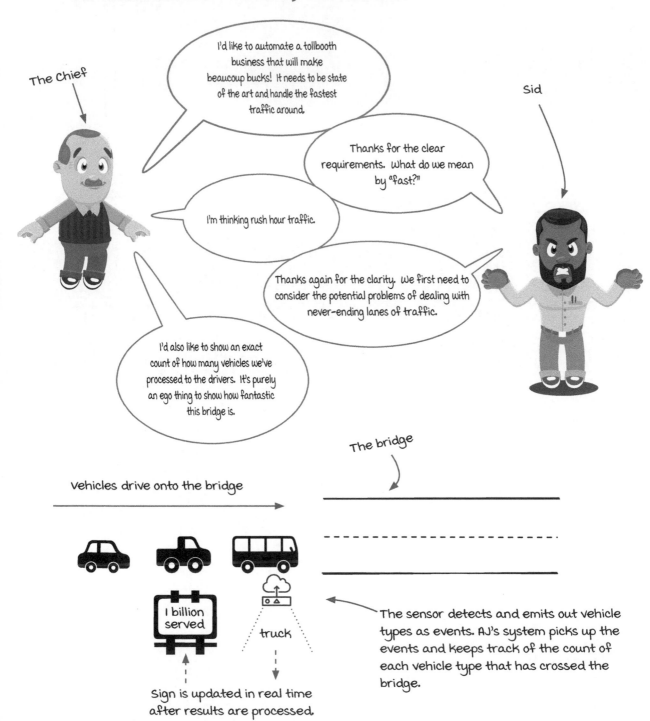

The Chief

I'd like to automate a tollbooth business that will make beaucoup bucks! It needs to be state of the art and handle the fastest traffic around.

Sid

Thanks for the clear requirements. What do we mean by "fast?"

I'm thinking rush hour traffic.

Thanks again for the clarity. We first need to consider the potential problems of dealing with never-ending lanes of traffic.

I'd also like to show an exact count of how many vehicles we've processed to the drivers. It's purely an ego thing to show how fantastic this bridge is.

The bridge

Vehicles drive onto the bridge

I billion served

truck

The sensor detects and emits out vehicle types as events. AJ's system picks up the events and keeps track of the count of each vehicle type that has crossed the bridge.

Sign is updated in real time after results are processed.

It started as HTTP requests, and it failed

As technology has quickly advanced over the years, most of the manual parts of tollbooths have been replaced with IoT (Internet of Things) devices. When a vehicle enters the bridge, the system is notified of the vehicle type by the IoT sensor. The first version of the system is to count the total number of vehicles by type (cars, vans, trucks, and so on) that have crossed the bridge. The chief would like the result to be updated in real time, so every time a new vehicle passes, the corresponding count should be updated immediately.

AJ, Miranda, and Sid, as usual, started out with the tried and true backend service design that used HTTP requests to transfer data. But it failed.

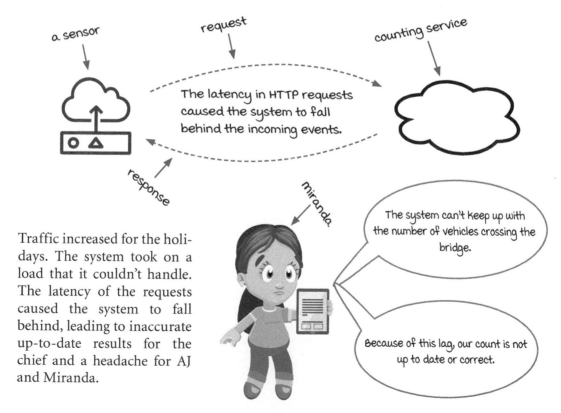

Traffic increased for the holidays. The system took on a load that it couldn't handle. The latency of the requests caused the system to fall behind, leading to inaccurate up-to-date results for the chief and a headache for AJ and Miranda.

AJ and Miranda take time to reflect

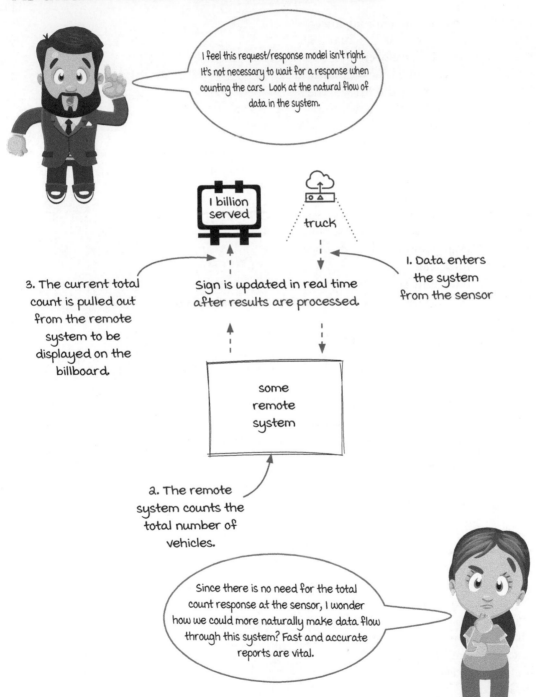

AJ ponders about streaming systems

Without getting too far into the details of networking and packet exchanges, there is a difference in how streaming systems communicate over systems that use the http back-end service architecture. The main difference in the backend service design is that a client will send a request, wait for the service to do some calculations, then get a response. In streaming systems, a client will send a request and not wait for the request to be processed before sending another. Without the need to wait for data to be processed, systems can react much more quickly.

Still a little unclear? We will get you more details step by step as we continue in this chapter.

Comparing backend service and streaming

Backend service: A synchronous model

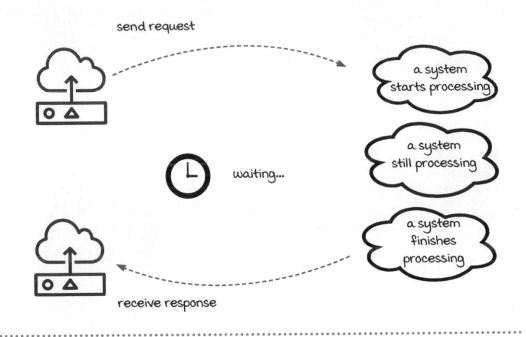

Streaming: An asynchronous model

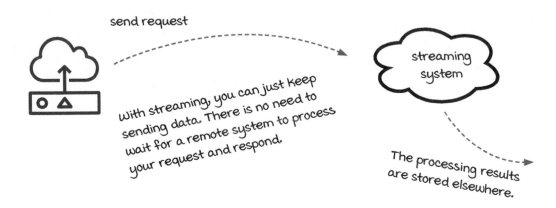

How a streaming system could fit

At a high level, AJ gets rid of the request/response model and decouples the process into two steps. The diagram below shows how a streaming system would fit in the scenario of counting vehicles that cross the bridge. We will cover the details in the rest of the chapter.

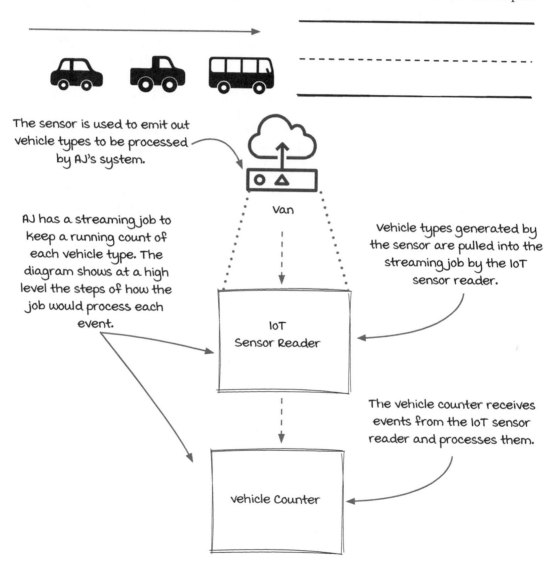

The sensor is used to emit out vehicle types to be processed by AJ's system.

AJ has a streaming job to keep a running count of each vehicle type. The diagram shows at a high level the steps of how the job would process each event.

Van

Vehicle types generated by the sensor are pulled into the streaming job by the IoT sensor reader.

IoT Sensor Reader

The vehicle counter receives events from the IoT sensor reader and processes them.

Vehicle Counter

Queues: A foundational concept

Before moving forward, let's take a particular look at a data structure: a *queue*. It is heavily used in all streaming systems.

Traditional distributed systems typically communicate via the *request/response* model—also known as the synchronous model. With streaming systems this is not the case, as the request/response model introduces unneeded latency when working with *real-time* data (technically speaking, *near real-time* could be more accurate, but streaming systems are often considered to be *real-time* systems). At a high level, distributed streaming systems keep a long running connection to components across the system to reduce data transfer time. This long running connection is for continually transferring data, which allows the streaming systems to react to events as they occur.

All distributed systems have some form of process running under the hood to transfer data for you. Among all the options, a queue is very useful to simplify the architecture for streaming use cases:

- Queues can help decouple modules in a system so that each part can run at its own pace without worrying about the dependencies and synchronization.

- Queues can help systems process events in order, since they are a FIFO (first in first out) data structure.

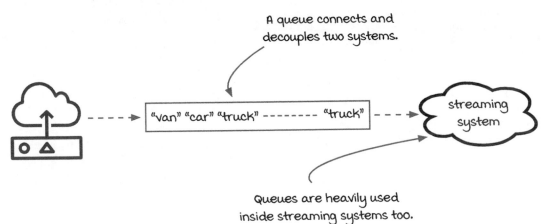

A queue connects and decouples two systems.

Queues are heavily used inside streaming systems too.

However, using queues to order continually transferring data is not all rainbows and sunshine. There can be many unexpected pitfalls when guaranteeing how data is processed. We will cover this topic in chapter 5.

Data transfer via queues

Take a minute or two to understand the diagram below. It shows two components and the intermediate queue of events between them, as well as the queues to the upstream and the downstream components. This transferring of data from one component to the next creates the concept of a *stream,* or continuously flowing data.

> ### Process and thread
>
> In computers, a *process* is the execution of a program, and a *thread* is an execution entity within a process. The major difference between them is that multiple threads in the same process share the same memory space, while processes have their own memory spaces. Both of them can be used to execute the data operation processes in the diagram that follows. Streaming systems might choose either one (or a combination of both) according to their requirements and considerations. In this book, to avoid confusion, *process* is the chosen term (unless explicitly stated otherwise) to represent independent sequence of execution no matter which one is really in the implementation.

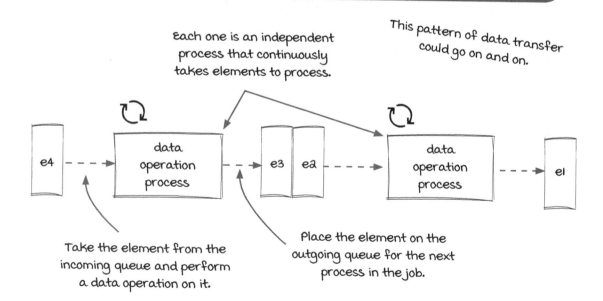

Our streaming framework (the start of it)

During the initial planning phases for writing this book, several discussions took place on how to teach streaming concepts without tight coupling to a specific streaming technology for its examples. After all, it's known that technology is advancing every day, and keeping the book up to date with ever-changing technology would have been extremely challenging. We feel that a lightweight framework, which we creatively named the *Streamwork*, will help introduce the basic concepts in streaming systems in a framework-agnostic way.

The Streamwork framework has an overly simplified engine that runs locally on your laptop. It can be used to build and run simple streaming jobs, which can hopefully be helpful for you to learn the concepts. It is limited in terms of functionality that is supported in widely used streaming frameworks, such as Apache Heron, Apache Storm, or Apache Flink, which stream data in real time across multiple physical machines, but it should be easier to understand.

One of the most interesting aspects (in our opinion) of working with computer systems is that there's not a single *correct* way to solve all problems. In terms of functionality, streaming frameworks, including our Streamwork framework, are similar to each other, as they share the common concepts, but internally, the implementations could be very different because of considerations and tradeoffs.

> **Think about it!**
>
> It would be a lot of work to build streaming systems from scratch. Frameworks take care of the heavy lifting, so we can focus on the business logic. However, sometimes it is important to know how frameworks work internally.

The Streamwork framework overview

Generally, streaming frameworks have two responsibilities:

- Provide an application programing interface (API) for users to hook up customer logic and build the job

- Provide an engine to execute the streaming job

We will see the API later. It should be understood that the goal of this book is not to teach you how to use the Streamwork API. The framework is used only as a framework-agnostic tool. Let's look at the engine first. The following diagram attempts to describe at a high level all of the moving pieces in the Streamwork framework. It should be understood that there is another process that starts each of the executors, and each executor starts a data source or a component. Each executor is standalone and does not stop or start other executors.

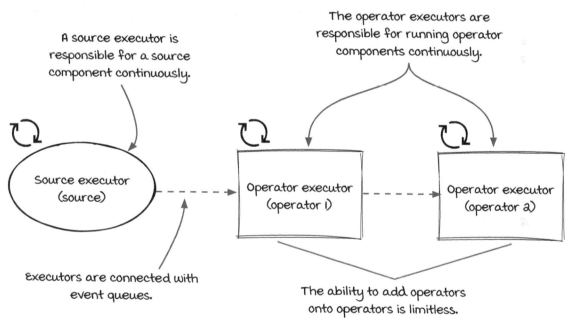

The framework is very simple in this chapter. However, all the components mentioned are comparable to real streaming frameworks components. The Streamwork framework will evolve in later chapters when more functionality is added.

Zooming in on the Streamwork engine

We are going to zoom in to show in detail how executors apply user logic on events.

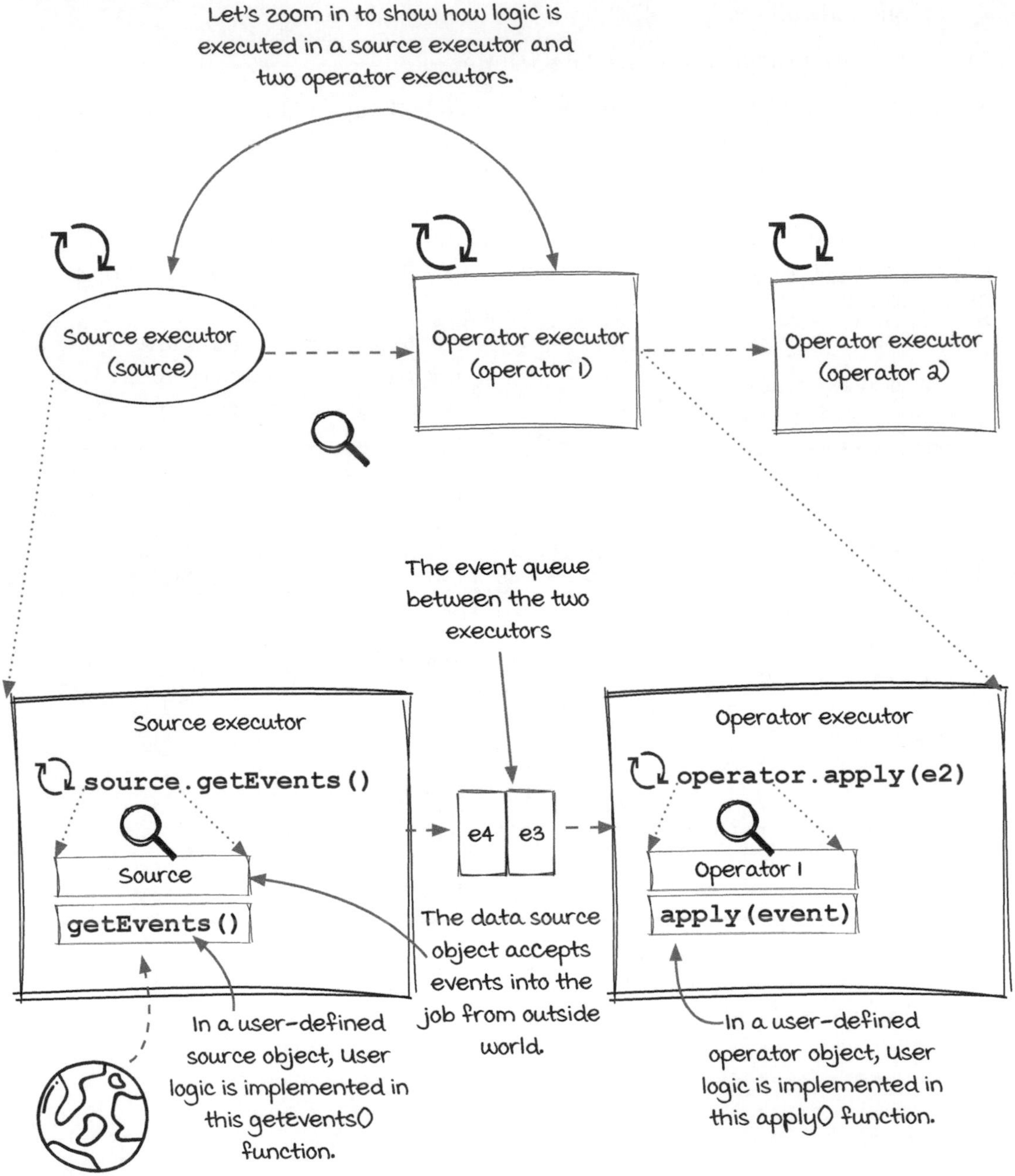

Let's zoom in to show how logic is executed in a source executor and two operator executors.

Source executor
(source)

Operator executor
(operator 1)

Operator executor
(operator 2)

The event queue
between the two
executors

Source executor

`source.getEvents()`

Source

`getEvents()`

e4 e3

The data source object accepts events into the job from outside world.

In a user-defined source object, user logic is implemented in this getEvents() function.

Operator executor

`operator.apply(e2)`

Operator 1

`apply(event)`

In a user-defined operator object, user logic is implemented in this apply() function.

Core streaming concepts

There are five key concepts in most streaming systems: *event, job, source, operator,* and *stream*. Keep in mind that these concepts apply to most streaming systems with a one-to-one mapping.

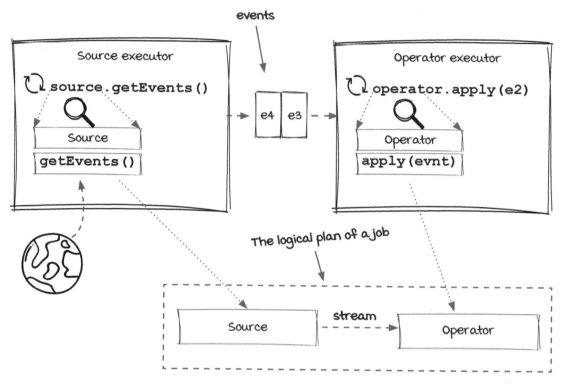

If we ignore the executors and only look at user-defined objects, we get a new diagram to the right, which is a cleaner (more abstract) view of the streaming system without any details. This diagram (we call it a *logical plan*) is a high-level abstraction that shows the components and structure in the system and how data can logically flow through them. From this diagram, we can see how the source object and the operator object are connected via a stream to form a streaming job. It should be known that a stream is nothing more than a continuous transfer of data from one component to another.

More details of the concepts

The diagram below shows the five key concepts, *event*, *job*, *source*, *operator*, and *stream*, with more details.

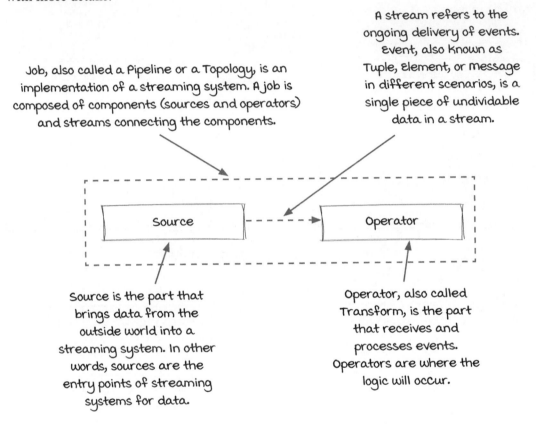

Job, also called a Pipeline or a Topology, is an implementation of a streaming system. A job is composed of components (sources and operators) and streams connecting the components.

A stream refers to the ongoing delivery of events. Event, also known as Tuple, Element, or message in different scenarios, is a single piece of undividable data in a stream.

Source is the part that brings data from the outside world into a streaming system. In other words, sources are the entry points of streaming systems for data.

Operator, also called Transform, is the part that receives and processes events. Operators are where the logic will occur.

We will cover how the concepts are used in a streaming system as we walk through the different parts of your first streaming job. For now, make sure the five key concepts are crystal clear.

The streaming job execution flow

With the concepts we have learned in the last two pages, you can now visualize this vehicle count streaming job of two components and one stream between them to look like the image on the right.

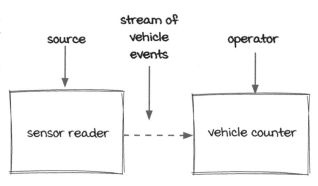

- The sensor reader brings data in from the sensor and stores the events in a queue. It is the source.

- The vehicle counter is responsible for counting vehicles that pass through the stream. It is an operator.

- The continuous moving of data from the source to the operator is the stream of vehicle events.

The sensor reader is the start of the job, and the vehicle counter is the end of the job. The edge that connects the sensor reader (source) and the vehicle counter (operator) represents the stream of vehicle types (events) flowing from the sensor reader to the vehicle counter.

In this chapter, we are going to dive into the system above. It will run on your local computer with two terminals: one accepts user input (the left column), and the other one shows the outputs of the job (the right column).

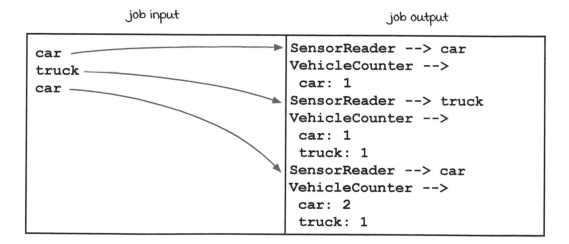

Your first streaming job

Creating a streaming job using the Streamwork API is straightforward with the following steps:

1. Create an event class.

2. Build a source.

3. Build an operator.

4. Connect the components.

Your first streaming job: Create your event class

An *event* is a single piece of data in a stream to be processed by a job. In the Streamwork framework, the API class Event is responsible for storing or wrapping user data. Other streaming systems will have a similar concept.

In your job, each event represents a single vehicle type. To keep things simple for now, each vehicle type is just a string like car and truck. We will use VehicleEvent as the name of the event class, which is extended from the Event class in the API. Each VehicleEvent object holds vehicle information that can be retrieved via the get-Data() function.

The internal string for vehicles

```java
public class VehicleEvent extends Event {
  private final String vehicle;

  public VehicleEvent(String vehicle) {
    this.vehicle = vehicle;
  }

  @Override
  public String getData() {
    return vehicle;
  }
}
```

The constructor that takes vehicle as a string and stores it

Gets vehicle data stored in the event

Your first streaming job: The data source

A *source* is the component that brings data from the outside world into a streaming system. The earth icon is a representation of data that would be outside of your job. In your streaming job the sensor reader accepts vehicle type data from a local port into the system.

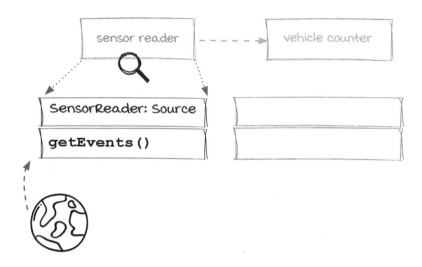

All streaming frameworks have an API that gives you the ability to write the logic that only you care about for data sources. All data source APIs have some type of *lifecycle hook* that will be called to accept data in from the outside world. This is where your code would be executed by the framework.

What is a lifecyle hook?

Lifecycle hooks in software frameworks are methods that are called in some type of repeatable pattern by the framework in which they reside. Typically, these methods allow developers to customize how their application behaves during a life cycle phase of a framework they are building their application in. In the case of the Streamwork framework we have a lifecycle hook (or method) called `getEvents()`. It is called continuously by the framework to allow you to pull data in from the outside world. Lifecyle hooks allow developers to write the logic they care about and to let the framework take care of all the heavy lifting.

Your first streaming job: The data source (continued)

In your job the sensor reader will be reading events from the sensor. In this exercise you will simulate the bridge sensor by creating the events yourself and sending them to the open port on your machine that the streaming job is listening to. The vehicle types you send to the port will be picked up by the sensor reader and emitted into the streaming job to show what it's like to process an infinite (or unbounded) stream of events.

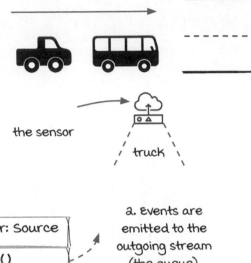

the sensor

truck

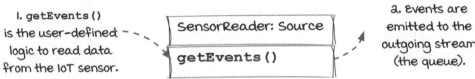

l. getEvents()
is the user-defined
logic to read data
from the IoT sensor.

SensorReader: Source

getEvents()

a. Events are
emitted to the
outgoing stream
(the queue).

The Java code for the SensorReader class looks like:

```java
public class SensorReader extends Source {
    private final BufferedReader reader;
    public SensorReader(String name, int port) {
        super(name);
        reader = setupSocketReader(port);
    }

    @Override
    public void getEvents(List<Event> eventCollector) {
        String vehicle = reader.readLine();
        eventCollector.add(new VehicleEvent(vehicle));
        System.out.println("SensorReader --> " + vehicle);
    }
}
```

The lifecycle hook of the
streaming system to
execute user defined logic

Read one vehicle
type from input.

Emit the string into
the collector.

Your first streaming job: The operator

Operators are where the user processing logic will occur. They are responsible for accepting events from upstream to process and generating output events; hence, they have both input and output. All of the data processing logic in your streaming systems will typically go into the operator components.

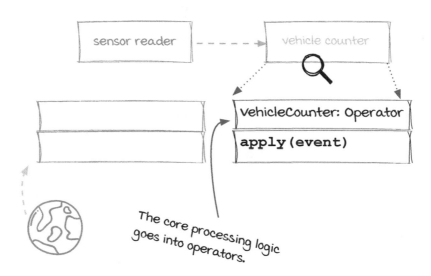

To keep your job simple, we have only one source and one operator in it. The current implementation of the vehicle counter is to just count the vehicles and then to log the current count in the system. Another, and potentially better, way to implement the system is for the vehicle counter to emit vehicles to a new stream. Then, logging the results can be done in an additional component that would follow after the vehicle counter. It is typical to have a component that has only one responsibility in a job.

By the way, Sid is the CTO. He is kind of old-fashioned sometimes, but he is very smart and interested in all kinds of new technologies.

Your first streaming job: The operator (continued)

Inside the `VehicleCounter` component, a `<vehicle, count>` map is used to store vehicle type counts in memory. It is updated accordingly when a new event is received.

In this streaming job, the vehicle counter is the operator that counts vehicle events. This operator is the end of the job, and it doesn't create any output to the downstream operators.

Key(vehicle)	value(count)
car	2
truck	1
van	1

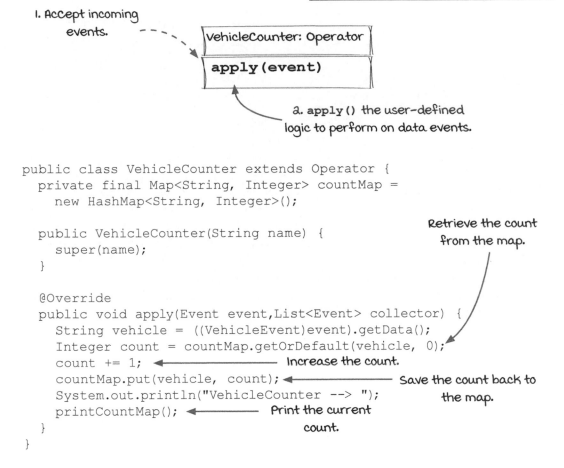

1. Accept incoming events.

VehicleCounter: Operator

apply(event)

2. `apply()` the user-defined logic to perform on data events.

```java
public class VehicleCounter extends Operator {
  private final Map<String, Integer> countMap =
    new HashMap<String, Integer>();

  public VehicleCounter(String name) {
    super(name);
  }

  @Override
  public void apply(Event event,List<Event> collector) {
    String vehicle = ((VehicleEvent)event).getData();
    Integer count = countMap.getOrDefault(vehicle, 0);
    count += 1;                              Increase the count.
    countMap.put(vehicle, count);            Save the count back to
    System.out.println("VehicleCounter --> ");   the map.
    printCountMap();                         Print the current
  }                                                count.
}
```

Retrieve the count from the map.

Your first streaming job: Assembling the job

To assemble the streaming job, we need to add both the `SensorReader` source and the `VehicleCounter` operator and connect them. There are a few hooks in the `Job` and `Stream` classes we built for you:

- `Job.addSource()` allows you to add a data source to the job.

- `Stream.applyOperator()` allows you to add an operator to the stream.

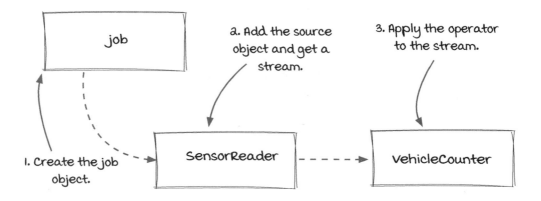

The following code matches the steps outlined in the previous image:

```
public static void main(String[] args) {
    Job job = new Job();          ←———————— Create the job object.
    Stream bridgeOut=job.addSource(new SensorReader()); ←┐
                                                          │
                        Add the source object and get a stream.

    bridgeOut.applyOperator(newVehicleCounter()); ←— Apply the operator
                                                       to the stream.

    JobStarter starter = new JobStarter(job);
    starter.start();←——————— Start the job.
}
```

Executing the job

All you need to execute the job is a Mac, Linux, or Windows machine with access to a *terminal* (*command prompt* on Windows). You will also need a few tools to compile and run the code: git, Java development kit (JDK) 11, Apache Maven, Netcat (or Nmap on Windows). After all the tools are installed successfully, you can pull the code down and compile it:

```
$ git clone https://github.com/nwangtw/GrokkingStreamingSystems.git
$ cd GrokkingStreamingSystems
$ mvn package
```

The mvn command above should generate the following file: target/gss.jar. Finally, to run the streaming job, you'll need two terminals: one for running your job and the other for sending data for your job to ingest.

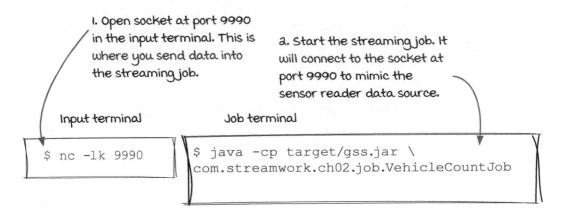

1. Open socket at port 9990 in the input terminal. This is where you send data into the streaming job.

2. Start the streaming job. It will connect to the socket at port 9990 to mimic the sensor reader data source.

Input terminal

```
$ nc -lk 9990
```

Job terminal

```
$ java -cp target/gss.jar \
com.streamwork.ch02.job.VehicleCountJob
```

Open a new terminal (the input terminal), and run the following command. (Note that nc is the command on Mac and Linux; on Windows, it is ncat). This will start a small server at port 9990 that can be connected to from other applications. All user inputs in this terminal will be forwarded to the port.

```
$ nc -lk 9990
```

Then, in the original terminal (the job terminal) that you used to compile the job, run the job with the following command:

```
$ java -cp target/gss.jar com.streamwork.ch02.job.VehicleCountJob
```

Inspecting the job execution

After the job is started, type car into the *input terminal,* and hit the return key, then the count will be printed in the *job terminal.*

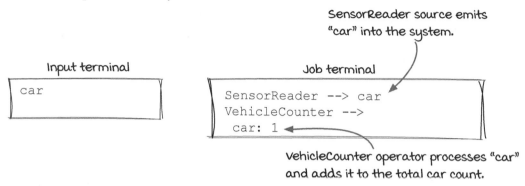

Now if you continue typing in truck in the input terminal, the counts of car and truck will be printed in the job terminal.

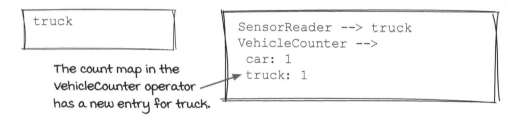

You can keep typing in different type of vehicles (to make it more interesting, you can prepare a bunch of vehicles in a text editor first and copy/paste them into the input terminal), and the job will keep printing the running counts, as in the example below, until you shut down the job. This demonstrates that as soon as data enters the system your streaming job takes action on it without delay.

```
car
car
.
.
.
```

```
SensorReader --> car
VehicleCounter -->
 car: 2
 truck: 1
SensorReader --> car
VehicleCounter -->
 car: 3
 truck: 1
```

Look inside the engine

You have learned how the components and the job are created. You also observed how
the job runs on your computer. During the job execution, you've hopefully noticed the
events automatically move from the sensor reader object to the vehicle counter object
without you needing to implement any additional logic. Fancy, right?

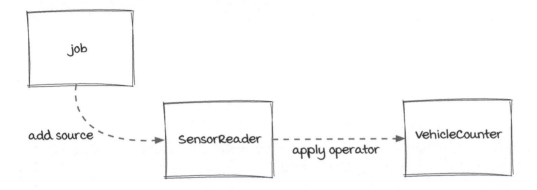

Your job or components don't run by themselves. They are driven by a streaming engine.
Let's take a look under the hood and inspect how your job is executed by the Streamwork
engine. There are three moving parts (at the current state), and we are going to look into
them one by one: *source executor*, *operator executor*, and *job starter*.

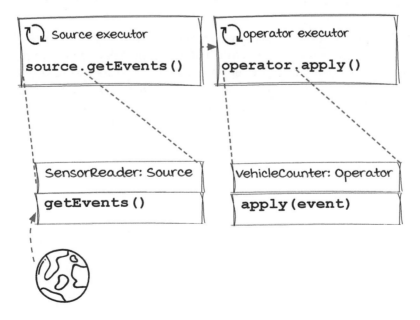

Look inside the engine: Source executors

In the Streamwork we've built for you, the source executor continuously runs data sources by executing over infinite loops that pull data in from the outside world to be placed on an outgoing queue within the streaming job. Even though there is a *yes* decision on *Exit*, yes will never be reached.

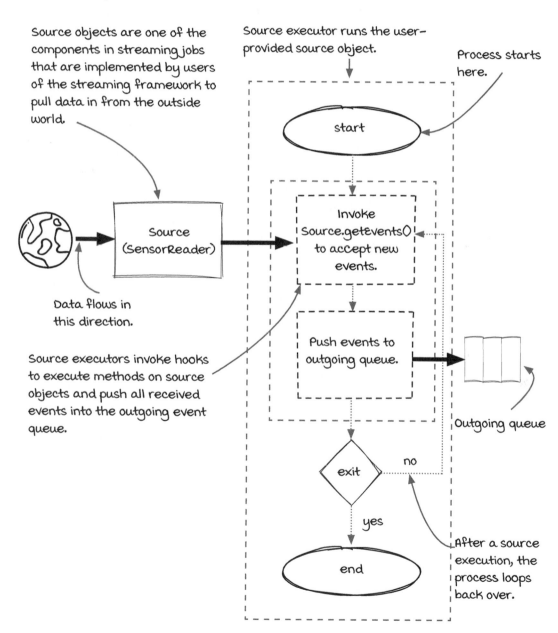

Source objects are one of the components in streaming jobs that are implemented by users of the streaming framework to pull data in from the outside world.

Source executor runs the user-provided source object.

Process starts here.

start

Source (SensorReader)

Data flows in this direction.

Source executors invoke hooks to execute methods on source objects and push all received events into the outgoing event queue.

Invoke Source.getEvents() to accept new events.

Push events to outgoing queue.

Outgoing queue

exit

no

yes

end

After a source execution, the process loops back over.

Look inside the engine: Operator executors

In the Streamwork, the operator executor works in a similar way to the source executor. The only difference is that it has an incoming event queue to manage. Even though there is a *yes* decision on *Exit*, yes will never be reached.

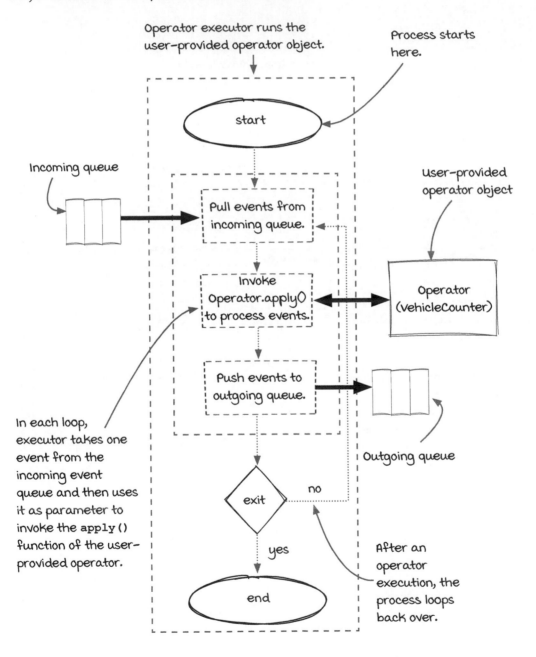

Look inside the engine: Job starter

The `JobStarter` is responsible for setting up all the moving parts (executors) in a job and the connections between them. Finally, it starts the executors to process data. After the executors are started, events start to flow through the components.

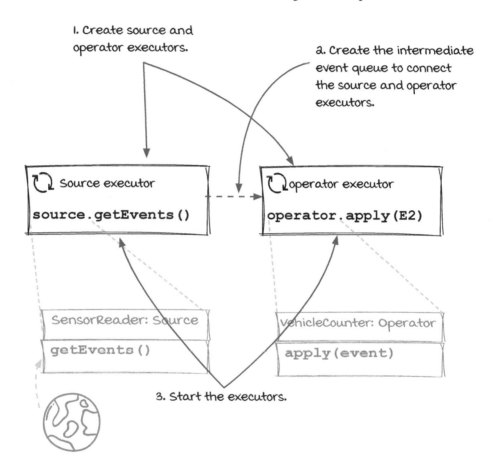

1. Create source and operator executors.

2. Create the intermediate event queue to connect the source and operator executors.

Source executor

`source.getEvents()`

operator executor

`operator.apply(E2)`

SensorReader: Source

`getEvents()`

VehicleCounter: Operator

`apply(event)`

3. Start the executors.

> *Remember!*
>
> Keep in mind that this is the architecture of a typical streaming engine, and an attempt to generalize how frameworks work at a high level. Different streaming frameworks may work in different ways.

Keep events moving

Let's zoom out to look at the whole engine and its moving parts, including the user-defined components of the actual job.

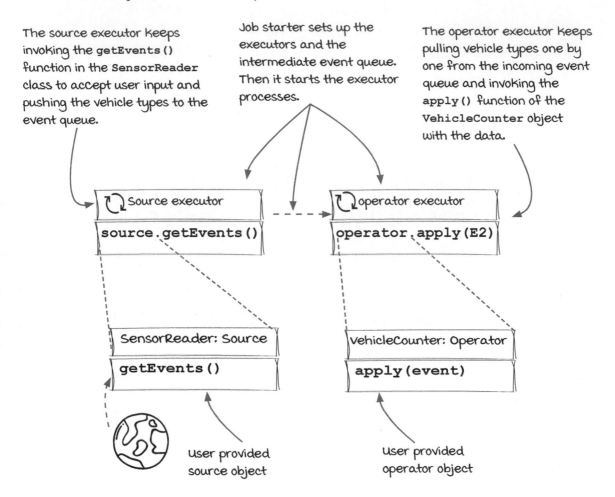

The source executor keeps invoking the getEvents() function in the SensorReader class to accept user input and pushing the vehicle types to the event queue.

Job starter sets up the executors and the intermediate event queue. Then it starts the executor processes.

The operator executor keeps pulling vehicle types one by one from the incoming event queue and invoking the apply() function of the VehicleCounter object with the data.

After our job is started, all the executors start running concurrently or, in other words, at the same time!

The life of a data element

Let's discuss a different aspect of streaming systems and take a look at the life of a single event. When you input *car* and press the enter key in the input terminal, the event will travel through the streaming system, as explained in the following diagram.

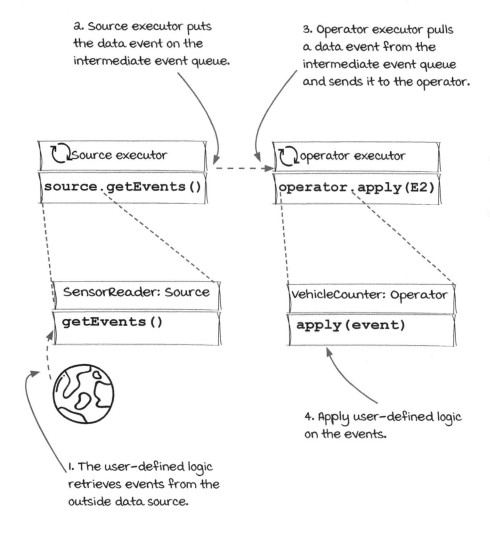

2. Source executor puts the data event on the intermediate event queue.

3. Operator executor pulls a data event from the intermediate event queue and sends it to the operator.

Source executor

source.getEvents()

operator executor

operator.apply(E2)

SensorReader: Source

getEvents()

VehicleCounter: Operator

apply(event)

4. Apply user-defined logic on the events.

1. The user-defined logic retrieves events from the outside data source.

Reviewing streaming concepts

Congratulations on finishing your first streaming job! Now, let's take a few minutes to step back and review the key concepts of streaming systems.

Job, also known as a Pipeline or a Topology, is an implementation of a streaming system. A job is composed of components (sources and operators) and streams connecting the components.

A stream refers to the ongoing delivery of events. Event, also known as Tuple, Element, or Message in different scenarios, is a single piece of undividable data in a stream.

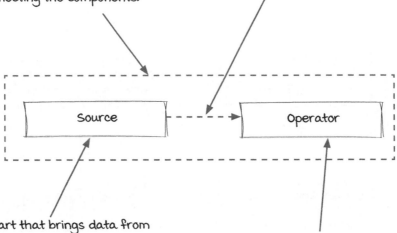

Source is the part that brings data from the outside world into a streaming system. In other words, sources are the entry points for data in streaming systems.

Operator, also called Transform, is the part that receives and processes events. Operators are where the logic will occur.

Summary

A streaming job is a system that processes events in real time. Whenever an event happens, the job accepts it into the system and processes it. In this chapter, we have built a simple job that counts vehicles entering a bridge. The following concepts have been covered:

- Streams and events
- Components (sources and operators)
- Streaming jobs

In addition, we looked into our simple streaming engine to see how your job is really executed. Although this engine is overly simplified, and it runs on your computer instead of a distributed environment, it demonstrates the moving parts inside a typical streaming engine.

Exercises

1. What are the differences between a source and an operator?

2. Find three examples in real life that can be simulated as streaming systems. (If you let us know, they might be used in the next edition of this book!)

3. Download the source code and modify the `SensorReader` source to generate events automatically.

4. Modify your `VehicleCounter` logic to calculate the collected fees in real time. You can decide how much to charge for each vehicle type.

5. The `VehicleCounter` operator in the first job has two responsibilities: counting vehicles and printing the results, which is not ideal. Can you change the implementation and move the printing logic to a new operator?

Parallelization and data grouping | 3

In this chapter

- parallelization

- data parallelism and task parallelism

- event grouping

> 66 *Nine people can't make a baby in a month.* 99
>
> —FREDERICK P. BROOKS

In the previous chapter, AJ and Miranda tackled keeping a real-time count of traffic driving over the bridge using a streaming job. The system she built is fairly limited in processing heavy amounts of traffic. Can you imagine going through a bridge and tollbooth with only one lane during rush hour? Yikes! In this chapter, we are going to learn a basic technique to solve a fundamental challenge in most distributed systems. This challenge is scaling streaming systems to increase throughput of a job or, in other words, process more data.

The sensor is emitting more events

In the previous chapter, AJ tackled keeping a real-time count of traffic driving over the chief's bridge using a streaming job. Detecting traffic with one sensor emitting traffic events was acceptable for collecting the traffic data. Naturally, the chief wants to make more money, so he opted to build more lanes on the bridge. In essence, he is asking for the streaming job to scale in the number of traffic events it can process at one time.

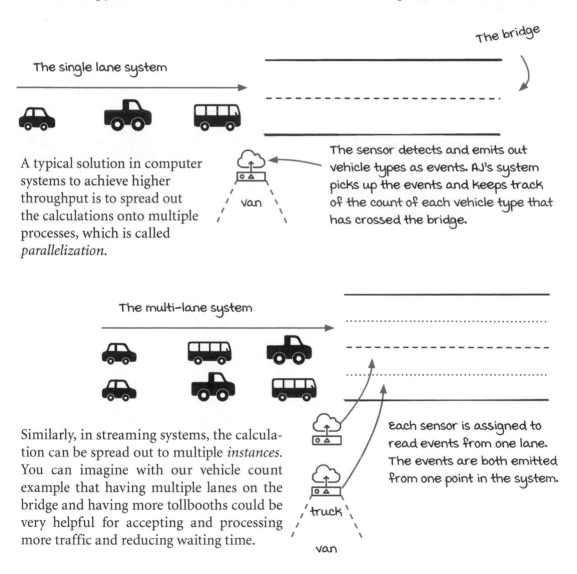

The bridge

The single lane system

The sensor detects and emits out vehicle types as events. AJ's system picks up the events and keeps track of the count of each vehicle type that has crossed the bridge.

van

A typical solution in computer systems to achieve higher throughput is to spread out the calculations onto multiple processes, which is called *parallelization*.

The multi-lane system

Each sensor is assigned to read events from one lane. The events are both emitted from one point in the system.

truck

van

Similarly, in streaming systems, the calculation can be spread out to multiple *instances*. You can imagine with our vehicle count example that having multiple lanes on the bridge and having more tollbooths could be very helpful for accepting and processing more traffic and reducing waiting time.

Even in streaming, real time is hard

Increasing lanes caused the job to fall behind

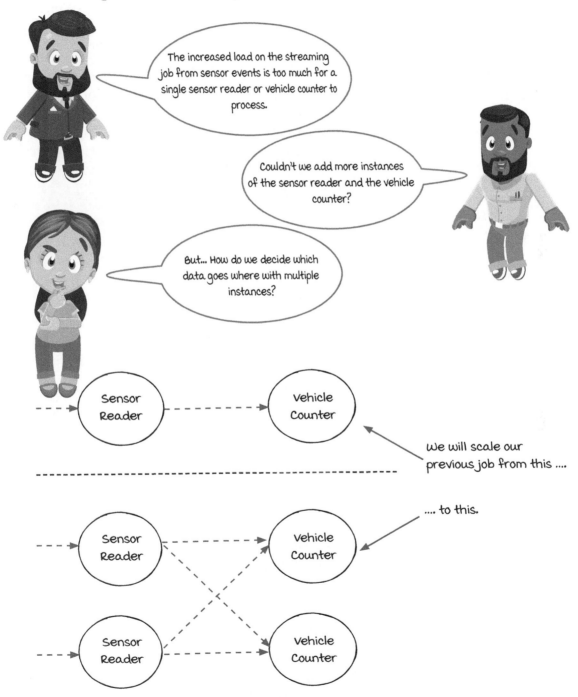

New concepts: Parallelism is important

Parallelization is a common technique in computer systems. The idea is that a time-consuming problem can often be broken into smaller sub-tasks that can be executed concurrently. Then, we can have more computers working on the problem cooperatively to reduce the total execution time greatly.

Why it's important

Let's use the streaming job in the previous chapter as an example. If there are 100 vehicle events waiting in a queue to be processed, the single vehicle counter would have to process all of them one by one. In the real world, there could be millions of events every second for a streaming system to process. Processing these events one by one is not acceptable in many cases, and parallelization is critical for solving large-scale problems.

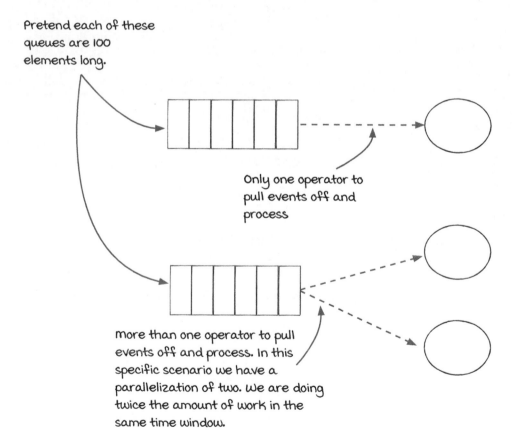

Pretend each of these queues are 100 elements long.

Only one operator to pull events off and process

more than one operator to pull events off and process. In this specific scenario we have a parallelization of two. We are doing twice the amount of work in the same time window.

New concepts: Data parallelism

It is not fast enough to solve the counting problem with one computer. Luckily, the chief has multiple computers on hand—because what tollbooth IT operation center doesn't? It is a reasonable idea to assign each vehicle event to a different computer, so all the computers can work on the calculation in parallel. This way you would process all vehicles in one step instead of processing them one by one in 100 steps. In other words, the throughput is 100 times greater. When there is more data to process, more computers instead of one *bigger* computer can be used to solve the problem faster. This is called *horizontal scaling*.

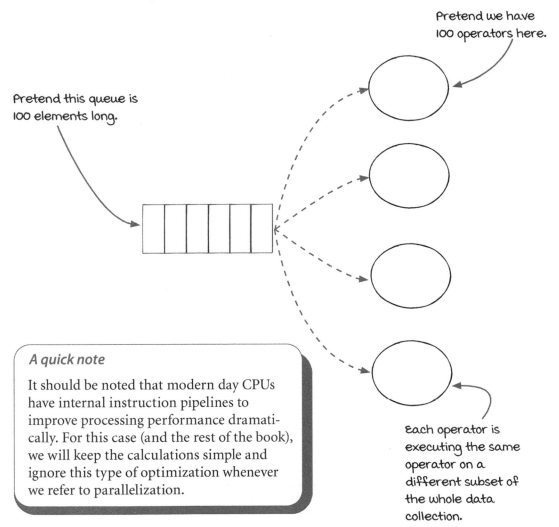

Pretend we have 100 operators here.

Pretend this queue is 100 elements long.

Each operator is executing the same operator on a different subset of the whole data collection.

> ### A quick note
>
> It should be noted that modern day CPUs have internal instruction pipelines to improve processing performance dramatically. For this case (and the rest of the book), we will keep the calculations simple and ignore this type of optimization whenever we refer to parallelization.

New concepts: Data execution independence

Say the phrase *data execution independence* out loud, and think about what it could mean. This is quite a fancy term, but it isn't as complex as you think.

Data execution independence, in regards to streaming, means the end result is the same no matter the order of the calculations or executions being performed across data elements. For example, in the case of multiplying each element in the queue by 4, they will have the same result whether they are done at the same time or one after another. This independence would allow for the use of data parallelism.

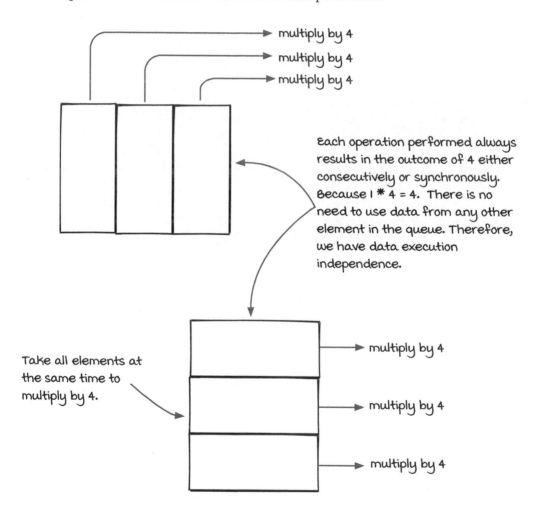

multiply by 4
multiply by 4
multiply by 4

Each operation performed always results in the outcome of 4 either consecutively or synchronously. Because 1 * 4 = 4. There is no need to use data from any other element in the queue. Therefore, we have data execution independence.

Take all elements at the same time to multiply by 4.

multiply by 4

multiply by 4

multiply by 4

New concepts: Task parallelism

Data parallelism is critical for many big data systems as well as general distributed systems because it allows developers to solve problems more efficiently with more computers. In addition to data parallelism, there is another type of parallelization: *task parallelism*, also known as function parallelism. In contrast to data parallelism, which involves running the same task on different data, task parallelism focuses on running different tasks on the same data.

A good way to think of task parallelism is to look at the streaming job you studied in chapter 2. The sensor reader and vehicle counter components keep running to process incoming events. When the vehicle counter component is processing (counting) an event, the sensor reader component is taking a different, new event at the same time. In other words, the two different tasks work concurrently. This means an event is emitted from the sensor reader, then it is processed by the vehicle counter component.

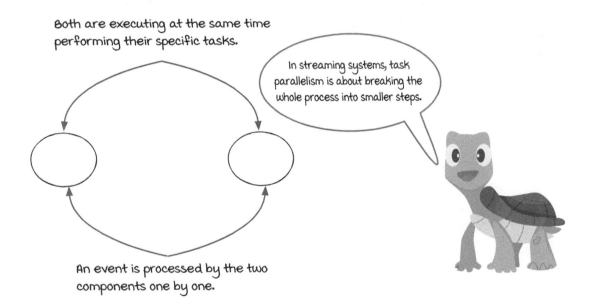

Data parallelism vs. task parallelism

Let's recap:

- Data parallelism represents that the same task is executed on different event sets at the same time.
- Task parallelism represents that different tasks are executed at the same time.

Data parallelism is widely used in distributed systems to achieve horizontal scaling. In these systems, it would be relatively easy to increase parallelization by adding more computers. Conversely, with task parallelism, it normally requires manual intervention to break the existing processes into multiple steps to increase parallelization.

Streaming systems are combinations of data parallelism and task parallelism. In a streaming system, data parallelism refers to creating multiple instances of each component, and task parallelism refers to breaking the whole process into different components to solve the problem. In the previous chapter, we have applied the task parallelism technique and broken the whole system into two components. In this chapter, we are going to learn how to apply the data parallelism technique and create multiple instances of each component.

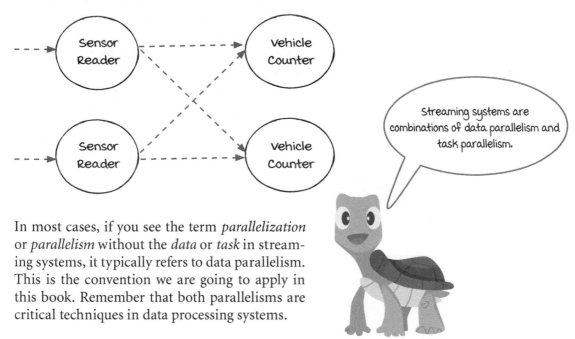

Streaming systems are combinations of data parallelism and task parallelism.

In most cases, if you see the term *parallelization* or *parallelism* without the *data* or *task* in streaming systems, it typically refers to data parallelism. This is the convention we are going to apply in this book. Remember that both parallelisms are critical techniques in data processing systems.

Parallelism and concurrency

Is there a difference?

This paragraph could easily start a contentious tech uproar, potentially as easily as writing a paragraph to justify the use of tabs over spaces. During the planning sessions of this book, these concepts came up several times. Typically, these conversations would always end up with us asking ourselves which term to use.

Parallelization is the term we've decided to use when explaining how to modify your streaming jobs for performance and scale. More explicitly in the context of this book, parallelism refers to the number of instances of a specific component. Or you could say parallelism is the number of instances running to complete the same task. *Concurrency*, on the other hand, is a general word that refers to two or more things happening at the same time.

It should be noted that we are using threads in our streaming framework to execute different tasks, but in real-world streaming jobs you would typically be running multiple physical machines somewhere to support your job. In this case you could call it parallel computing. Some readers may question whether parallelization is the accurate word when we are only referring to code that is running on a single machine. This is yet another question we asked ourselves. Is this correct for us to write about? We have decided not to cover this question. After all, the goal of this book is that, by the end, you can comfortably talk about topics in streaming. Overall, just know that parallelization is a huge component of streaming systems, and it is important for you to get comfortable talking about the concepts and understanding the differences well.

Parallelizing the job

This is a good time to review the state of the last streaming job we studied. You should have a traffic event job that contains two components: a sensor reader and a vehicle counter. As a refresher, the job can be visualized as the below image.

This implementation has worked for the previous chapter. However, we will now introduce a new component we decided to call the *event dispatcher*. It will allow us to route data to different instances of a parallelized component. With the `eventDispatcher` the chapter 2 job structure will look like the following. The image below is an end result of reading through this chapter and working through the steps to build up the job. By the end of this chapter, you will have added two instances of each component and understand how the system will decide to send data to each instance.

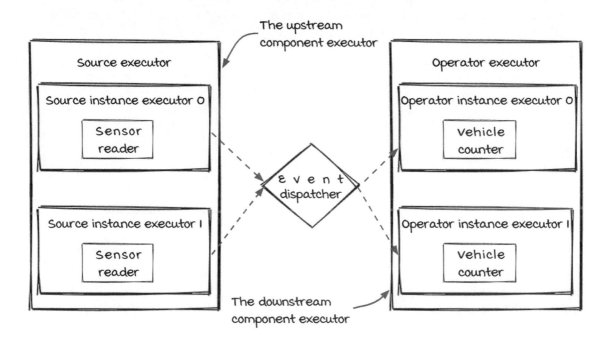

Parallelizing components

The following image shows the end goal of how we want to parallelize the components in the streaming job. The event dispatcher will help us distribute the load across downstream instances.

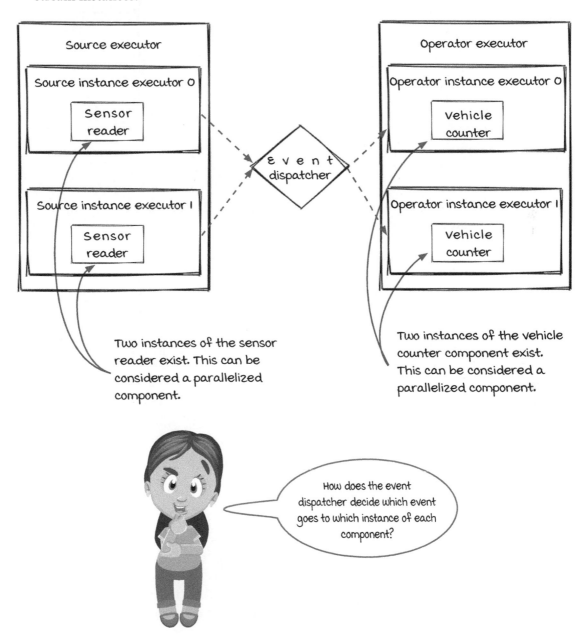

Parallelizing sources

First, we are only going to parallelize the data sources in the streaming job from one to two. To simulate a parallelized source, this new job will need to listen on two different ports to accept your input. The ports we will use are 9990 and 9991. We have updated the engine to support parallelism, and the change in the job code is very straightforward:

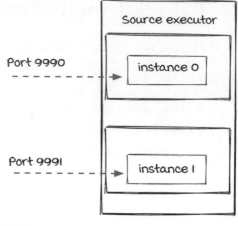

```
Stream bridgeStream = job.addSource(
  new SensorReader("sensor-reader", 2, 9990)
);
```

To run the job, you need to first create two input terminals and execute the command with different ports:

Input terminal 1

```
$ nc -lk 9990
```

Input terminal 2

```
$ nc -lk 9991
```

Then, you can compile and execute the sample code in a separate *job* terminal:

```
$ mvn package
$ java -cp target/gss.jar \
  com.streamwork.ch03.job.ParallelizedVehicleCountJob1
```

At this point you should have three terminals open to run your job: input terminal 1, input terminal 2, and the job terminal. Input terminals 1 and 2 are where you will be typing vehicle events to be picked up by the streaming job. The next page will show some sample output.

> **Networking FYI**
>
> Due to limitations of networking, we cannot have more than one process, thread, or compute instance listening on the same port. Since we have two of the same sources running on the same machine for our learning purposes, we have to run the extra instance of source on a different port.

Viewing job output

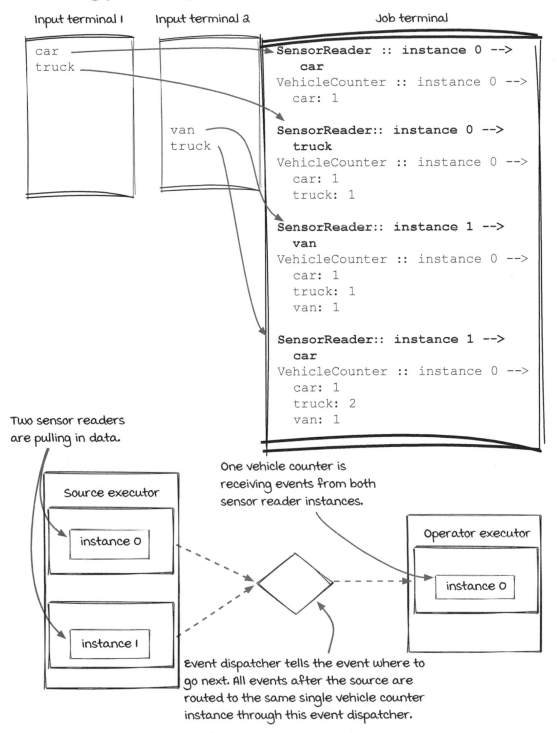

Input terminal 1   Input terminal 2   Job terminal

```
car
truck
```

```
van
truck
```

```
SensorReader :: instance 0 -->
    car
VehicleCounter :: instance 0 -->
    car: 1

SensorReader:: instance 0 -->
    truck
VehicleCounter :: instance 0 -->
    car: 1
    truck: 1

SensorReader:: instance 1 -->
    van
VehicleCounter :: instance 0 -->
    car: 1
    truck: 1
    van: 1

SensorReader:: instance 1 -->
    car
VehicleCounter :: instance 0 -->
    car: 1
    truck: 2
    van: 1
```

Two sensor readers
are pulling in data.

One vehicle counter is
receiving events from both
sensor reader instances.

Source executor

instance 0

instance 1

Operator executor

instance 0

Event dispatcher tells the event where to
go next. All events after the source are
routed to the same single vehicle counter
instance through this event dispatcher.

Parallelizing operators

Running the new job

Now, let's parallelize the `VehicleCounter` operator:

```
bridgeStream.applyOperator(
  new VehicleCounter("vehicle-counter", 2));
```

Keep in mind we are using two parallelized sources, so we will need to execute the same `netcat` command as we did before in two separate terminals. For a refresher, each command tells Netcat to listen for connections on the ports specified in each command.

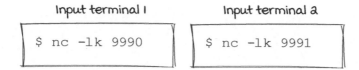

Input terminal 1	Input terminal 2
`$ nc -lk 9990`	`$ nc -lk 9991`

Then, you can compile and execute the sample code in a third, separate *job* terminal:

```
$ mvn package
$ java -cp gss.jar \
    com.streamwork.ch03.job.ParallelizedVehicleCountJob2
```

This job that runs will have two sources and operators. It can be represented by the diagram below. The job output follows.

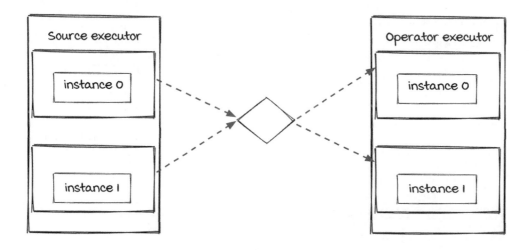

Viewing job output

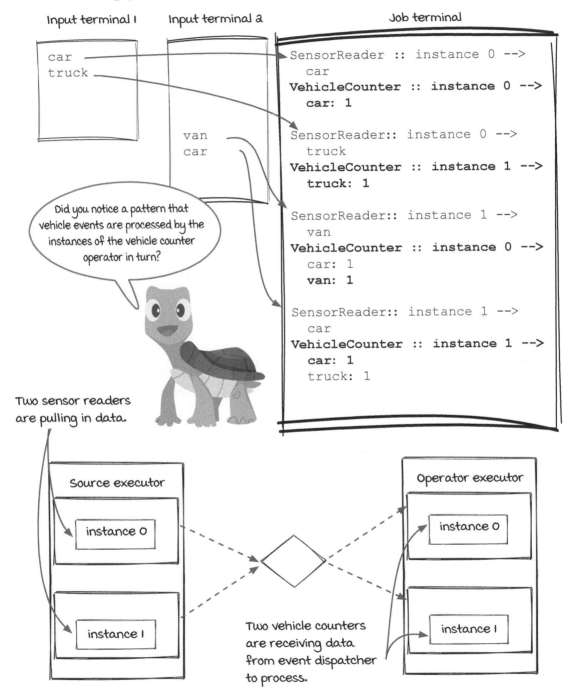

Input terminal 1   Input terminal 2   Job terminal

car

truck

van
car

Did you notice a pattern that vehicle events are processed by the instances of the vehicle counter operator in turn?

```
SensorReader :: instance 0 -->
   car
VehicleCounter :: instance 0 -->
   car: 1

SensorReader:: instance 0 -->
   truck
VehicleCounter :: instance 1 -->
   truck: 1

SensorReader:: instance 1 -->
   van
VehicleCounter :: instance 0 -->
   car: 1
   van: 1

SensorReader:: instance 1 -->
   car
VehicleCounter :: instance 1 -->
   car: 1
   truck: 1
```

Two sensor readers are pulling in data.

Source executor

instance 0

instance 1

Operator executor

instance 0

instance 1

Two vehicle counters are receiving data from event dispatcher to process.

Events and instances

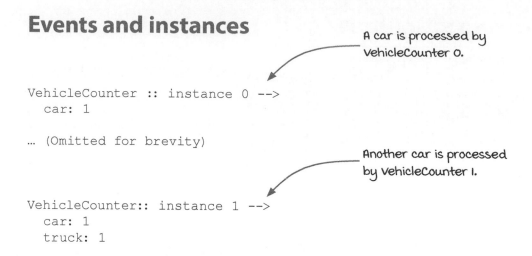

A car is processed by
VehicleCounter 0.

```
VehicleCounter :: instance 0 -->
  car: 1

... (Omitted for brevity)


VehicleCounter:: instance 1 -->
  car: 1
  truck: 1
```

Another car is processed
by VehicleCounter 1.

If you take a close look at the results of the vehicle counter instances, you will see that both of them receive a different car event. Depending on how the system is set to run this type of behavior, it may not be desirable for a streaming job. We will study the new concept of *event grouping* later to understand the behavior and how to improve the system. For now, just understand that any vehicle can be processed by either of the two tollbooth instances.

Another important concept you need to understand here is *event ordering*. Events have their order in a stream—after all, they all reside in queues, typically. How do you know if one event will be processed before another? Generally, two rules apply:

- Within an instance, the processing order is *guaranteed* to be the same as the original order (the order in the incoming queue).

- Across instances, there is *no guarantee* about the processing order. It is possible that a later event can be processed and/or finished earlier than another event that arrived earlier, if the two events are processed by different instances.

A more concrete example follows.

Event ordering

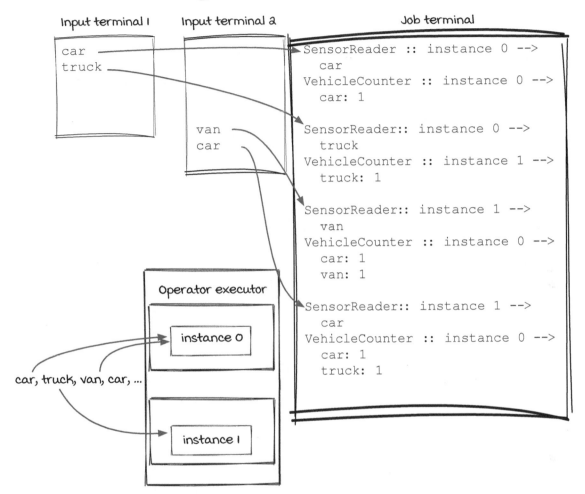

Let's look at the four vehicle events that were entered in the input terminals. The first and third vehicles are car and van, and they are sent to VehicleCounter instance 0, while the second and the fourth events truck and car are routed to VehicleCounter instance 1.

In the Streamwork engine, the two operator instances are executed independently. Streaming engines normally guarantee that the first and the third vehicles are processed in their incoming order because they are processed in the same instance. However, there is no guarantee that the first vehicle car is processed before the second vehicle truck, or the second vehicle truck is processed before the third vehicle van because the two operator processes are independent of each other.

Event grouping

Up until now your parallelized streaming job had vehicle counter instances that were getting events *randomly* (really, pseudorandomly) routed to the vehicle counter instances.

A car is processed by
VehicleCounter 0.

The streaming job has
no predictable behavior
of how it will route
data to either
vehicleCounter 0 or
vehicleCounter 1.

```
SensorReader:: instance 0 -->
  car
VehicleCounter :: instance 0 -->
  car: 1

... (Omitted for brevity)

SensorReader:: instance 1 -->
  car
VehicleCounter:: instance 1 -->
  car: 1
  van: 1
```

Another car is processed by
VehicleCounter 1.

This pseudorandom routing is acceptable in many cases, but sometimes you may prefer to predictably route events to a specific downstream instance. This concept of directing events to instances is called *event grouping*. *Grouping* may not sound very intuitive, so let us try to explain a bit: all the events are divided into different groups, and each group is assigned a specific instance to process. There are several event grouping strategies. The two most commonly used are:

- *Shuffle grouping*—Events are pseudorandomly distributed to downstream components,

- *Fields grouping*—Events are predictably routed to the same downstream instances based on values in specified fields in the event.

Normally, event grouping is a functionality baked into streaming frameworks for reuse by developers. Flip through the next few pages to go a little deeper into how these two different grouping strategies work.

Shuffle grouping

Shuffle grouping defined in few words is the random distribution of data elements from a component to a downstream operator. It allows for a relatively even distribution of load to downstream operators.

Round robin is the way to perform a shuffle grouping in many frameworks. In this grouping strategy, downstream instances (aka the incoming queues) are picked in equal portions and in circular order. Compared to a shuffle grouping based on random numbers, the distribution can be more even, and the calculation can be more efficient. The implementation is similar to the diagram below. Note that in the diagram the two `truck` vehicles are counted by two different `VehicleCounter` instances.

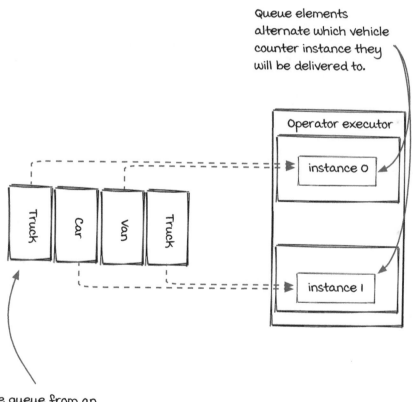

Shuffle grouping: Under the hood

To make sure that events are routed evenly across instances, most streaming systems use the round robin method for choosing the next destination for their event.

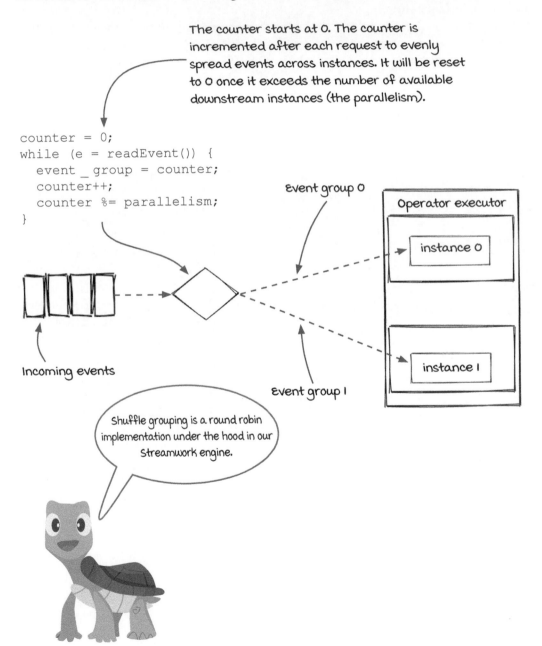

The counter starts at 0. The counter is incremented after each request to evenly spread events across instances. It will be reset to 0 once it exceeds the number of available downstream instances (the parallelism).

```
counter = 0;
while (e = readEvent()) {
  event _ group = counter;
  counter++;
  counter %= parallelism;
}
```

Event group 0

Operator executor

instance 0

instance 1

Incoming events

Event group 1

Shuffle grouping is a round robin implementation under the hood in our Streamwork engine.

Fields grouping

Shuffle grouping works well for many use cases. However, if you needed a way to predictably send elements, shuffle grouping won't work. *Fields grouping* is a good candidate to assist with a predictable routing pattern for your data processing needs. It works by making a decision on where to route data based on fields out of the streamed event element (usually designated by the developer). Field grouping is also called *group by* or *group by key* in many scenarios.

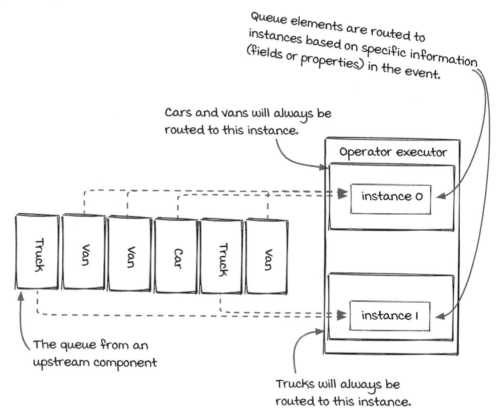

Queue elements are routed to instances based on specific information (fields or properties) in the event.

Cars and vans will always be routed to this instance.

Operator executor

instance 0

instance 1

The queue from an upstream component

Trucks will always be routed to this instance.

In this chapter's streaming job, we take each vehicle that comes in from the bridge and send them to either vehicle counter 0 or vehicle counter 1 based on the vehicle type, so the same type of vehicle is always routed to the same vehicle counter instance. By doing this, we keep the count of individual vehicle types by instance (and more accurately).

Fields grouping: Under the hood

To make sure the same vehicle events are always assigned to the same group (routed to the same instance), typically a technique called hashing is used. *Hashing* is a widely used type of calculation that takes a large range of values (such as strings) and maps them onto a smaller set of values (such as integer numbers).

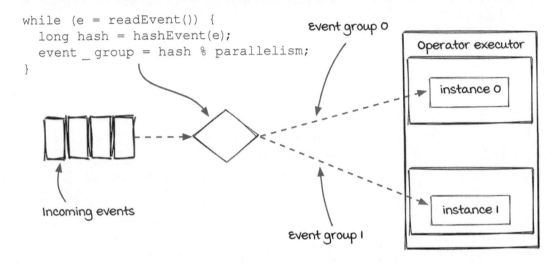

```
while (e = readEvent()) {
  long hash = hashEvent(e);
  event _ group = hash % parallelism;
}
```

The most important property of hashing is that for the same input, the result is always the same. After we get the hashing result (usually some large integer, such as 98216, called the *key*), we perform this calculation:

```
key % parallelism
```

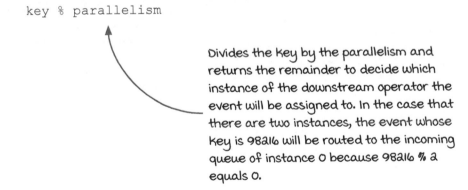

Divides the key by the parallelism and returns the remainder to decide which instance of the downstream operator the event will be assigned to. In the case that there are two instances, the event whose key is 98216 will be routed to the incoming queue of instance 0 because 98216 % 2 equals 0.

Event grouping execution

The event dispatcher is a piece of the streaming system that sits between component executors and executes the event grouping process. It continuously pulls events from its designated incoming queue and places them on its designated outgoing queues based on the key returned from the grouping strategy. Keep in mind that all streaming systems have their own way of doing things. This overview is specific to the Streamwork framework we provided for you.

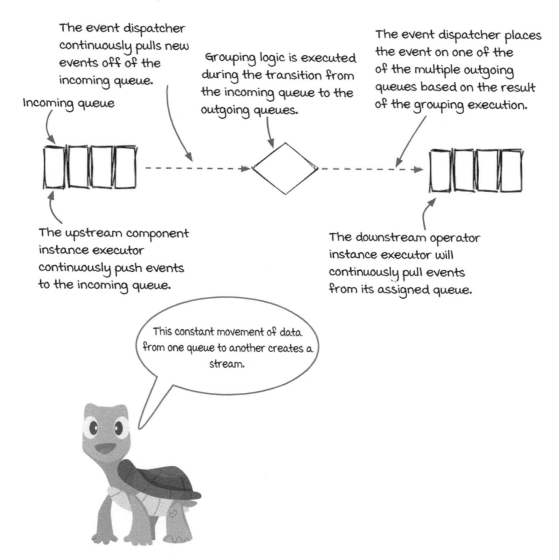

Look inside the engine: Event dispatcher

The event dispatcher is responsible for accepting events from the upstream component executor, applying the grouping strategy, and emitting the events to the downstream component.

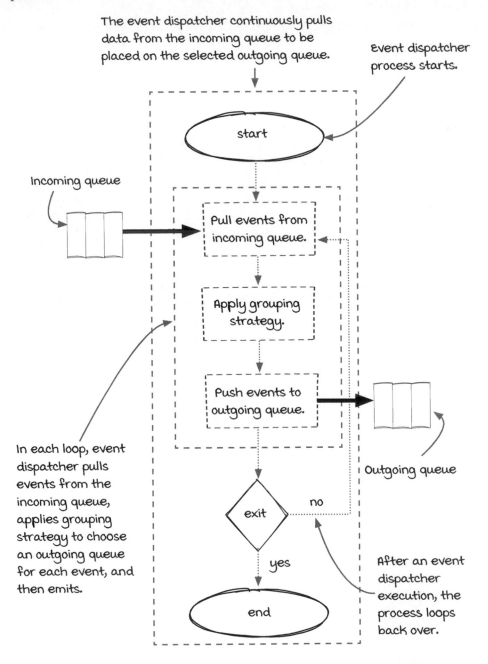

The event dispatcher continuously pulls data from the incoming queue to be placed on the selected outgoing queue.

Event dispatcher process starts.

Incoming queue

Pull events from incoming queue.

Apply grouping strategy.

Push events to outgoing queue.

Outgoing queue

In each loop, event dispatcher pulls events from the incoming queue, applies grouping strategy to choose an outgoing queue for each event, and then emits.

exit

no

yes

end

After an event dispatcher execution, the process loops back over.

start

Applying fields grouping in your job

By applying fields grouping to your job, it will be much easier to keep an aggregated count of different vehicle types, as each vehicle type will always be routed to the same instance. With the Streamwork API, it is easy to enable fields grouping:

```
bridgeStream.applyOperator(
  new VehicleCounter("vehicle-counter", 2, new FieldsGrouping())
);
```

Apply fields grouping.

The only thing you need to do is to add an extra parameter when you call the `apply-Operator()` function, and the Streamwork engine will handle the rest for you. Remember that streaming frameworks help you focus on your business logic without worrying about how the engines are implemented. Different engines might have different ways to apply fields grouping. Typically, you may find the function with the name of `groupBy()` or `{operation}ByKey()` in different engines.

To run the example code, it is the same as before. First, you need to have two input terminals with the following commands running, so you can type in vehicle types. Then, you can compile

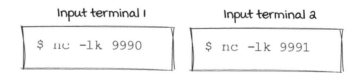

Input terminal 1

```
$ nc -lk 9990
```

Input terminal 2

```
$ nc -lk 9991
```

and execute the sample code in a third, separate *job* terminal:

```
$ mvn package
$ java -cp target/gss.jar \
  com.streamwork.ch03.job.ParallelizedVehicleCountJob3
```

Event ordering

If you run the above commands, the job terminal will print an output similar to the
following.

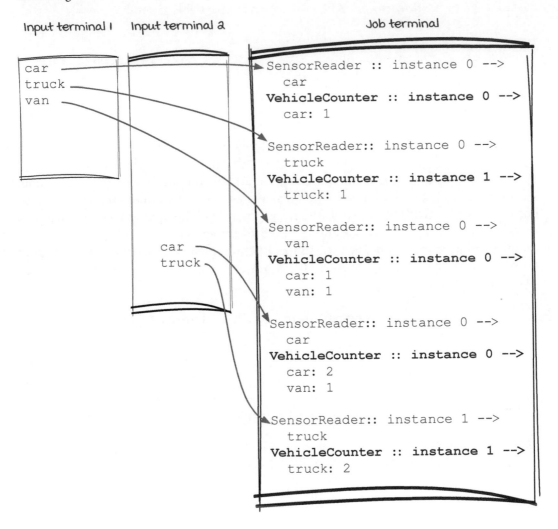

Comparing grouping behaviors

Let's put the shuffle and grouping job outputs side by side and view the differences in behavior with the same job input. It doesn't really matter which terminal the input is from, so we combine them into one. See if you can identify the differences in how each job output differs.

Job Input: car truck van car truck ...

Shuffle Grouping Job Output	Fields Grouping Job Output
| ```
SensorReader :: instance 0 ->
  car
VehicleCounter :: instance 0 ->
  car: 1

SensorReader:: instance 0 ->
  truck
VehicleCounter :: instance 1 ->
  truck: 1

SensorReader:: instance 0 ->
  van
VehicleCounter :: instance 0 ->
  car: 1
  van: 1

SensorReader:: instance 0 ->
  car
VehicleCounter :: instance 1 ->
  car: 1
  truck: 1

SensorReader:: instance 1 ->
  truck
VehicleCounter:: instance 0 ->
  car: 1
  truck: 1
  van: 1
``` | ```
SensorReader :: instance 0 ->
  car
VehicleCounter :: instance 0 ->
  car: 1

SensorReader:: instance 0 ->
  truck
VehicleCounter :: instance 1 ->
  truck: 1

SensorReader:: instance 0 ->
  van
VehicleCounter :: instance 0 ->
  car: 1
  van: 1

SensorReader:: instance 0 ->
  Car
VehicleCounter :: instance 0 ->
  car: 2
  van: 1

SensorReader:: instance 1 ->
  truck
VehicleCounter:: instance 1 ->
  truck: 2
``` |

Summary

In this chapter, we've read about the fundamentals of scaling streaming jobs. Scalability is one of the major challenges for all distributed systems, and parallelization is a fundamental technique for scaling them up. We've learned how to parallelize components in a streaming job and about the related concepts of data and task parallelisms. In streaming systems, if the term *parallelism* is used without *data* and *task*, it normally refers to *data parallelism*.

When parallelizing components, we also need to know how to control or predict the routing of events with event grouping strategies to get the expected results. We can achieve this predictability via shuffle grouping or fields grouping. In addition, we also looked into the Streamwork streaming engine to see how parallelization and event grouping are handled from a conceptual point of view to prepare for the next chapters and real-world streaming systems.

Parallelism and event grouping are critical because they are useful for solving a critical challenge in all distributed systems: throughput. If a bottleneck component can be identified in a streaming system, you can scale it horizontally by increasing its parallelism, and the system is capable of processing events at a faster speed.

Exercises

1. Why is parallelization important?

2. Can you think of any other grouping strategy? If you can think of one, can you implement it in Streamwork?

3. The field grouping in the example is using the hash of the string. Can you implement a different field grouping that uses the first character instead? What are the advantages and disadvantages of this new grouping strategy?

In this chapter

- stream fan-out

- stream fan-in

- graph and DAG (directed acyclic graph)

> 66 *Bad programmers worry about the code. Good programmers worry about data structures and their relationships.* 99
>
> —LINUS TORVALDS

In the previous chapters, AJ has built a streaming job and then scaled it up. It works well for monitoring vehicles on the bridges. However, the structure of the job is quite simple, as the job is pretty much a list of operators. In this chapter, we are going to learn how to build more complicated streaming systems to solve additional problems in the real world.

A credit card fraud detection system

Sid has been impressed by the vehicle counting system AJ built, and he is thinking of new problems to solve with stream processing technology now. The one he is mostly interested in is a fraud detection problem, but he has one concern: the new system will be more complicated and requires very low latency. Can it be solved with a streaming system?

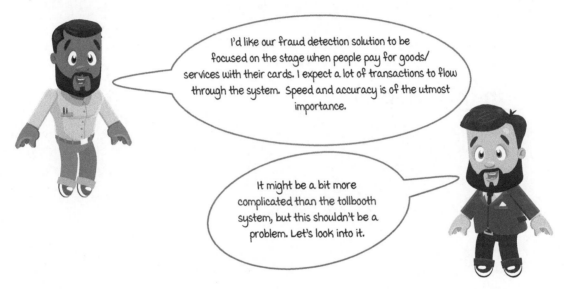

I'd like our fraud detection solution to be focused on the stage when people pay for goods/services with their cards. I expect a lot of transactions to flow through the system. Speed and accuracy is of the utmost importance.

It might be a bit more complicated than the tollbooth system, but this shouldn't be a problem. Let's look into it.

The streaming job built in the previous two chapters is limited in capability. Every data element that enters the job is required to pass through both components in a fixed order: the sensor reader and then the vehicle counter. There is no conditional routing of data for edge cases or errors that could occur in streaming systems. You could visualize the path of the data elements in your streaming job as a straight line.

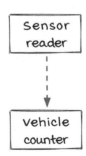

More about the credit card fraud detection system

In this chapter, we are going to build a credit card fraud detection system. It will be more complicated than the tollbooth problem we had before.

If I understand the requirements correctly, we want a system with multiple rule-based analyzer operators that evaluate the transactions and score the risks. At the end we will need a classifier that combines all the scores from each analyzer and makes a decision.

In the past, all of our jobs have executed sequentially; this could be a bottleneck for us with heavy load. How could we execute the fraud detection operations more efficiently?

The analyzers apply rules to evaluate the risks of the transactions. All the risk scores are combined at the end as one result. We can start from a few simple rules for now.

The fraud detection business

The card network sits between the stores and the banks. As transactions enter the card network, logic is performed to give the paying banks as much information as possible. This helps them make the decision to pay a transaction or not.

Brick and mortar locations, online businesses, and even mobile devices can all take credit card payments.

The card network routes transactions to be paid to the correct bank after collecting as much information as it can to help banks make a decision to pay for the charges. The fraud detection system lives here to generate risk scores.

Banks make a decision to allow the transaction to go through based on information gathered by the card network.

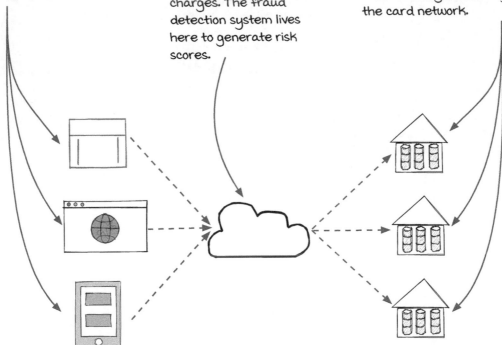

Streaming isn't always a straight line

We can build the system like the tollbooth system. First, the transaction source component is responsible for accepting transaction events from external systems. Then, the analyzers are applied one by one, and risk scores are added into the events. Finally, a score aggregator makes a final decision from the scores.

The solution works, but it is not ideal. New analyzers will be added in the future, the list will grow, and the end-to-end latency will increase. Plus, the job could be harder to maintain when there are many analyzers.

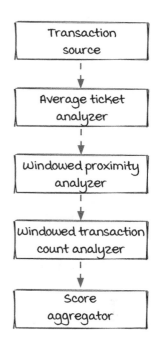

The first solution was not ideal. Every analyzer we added increased latency.

Another option is to build the system like the diagram below. All three analyzers connect to the transaction source and run independently. The score aggregator collects results from them and aggregates the scores to make a final decision. In this solution, the end-to-end latency won't increase when more analyzers are added.

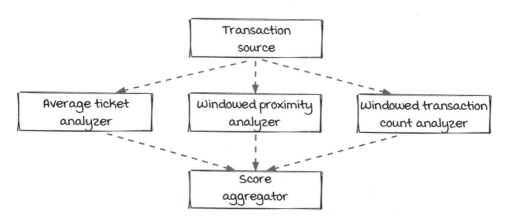

Zoom into the system

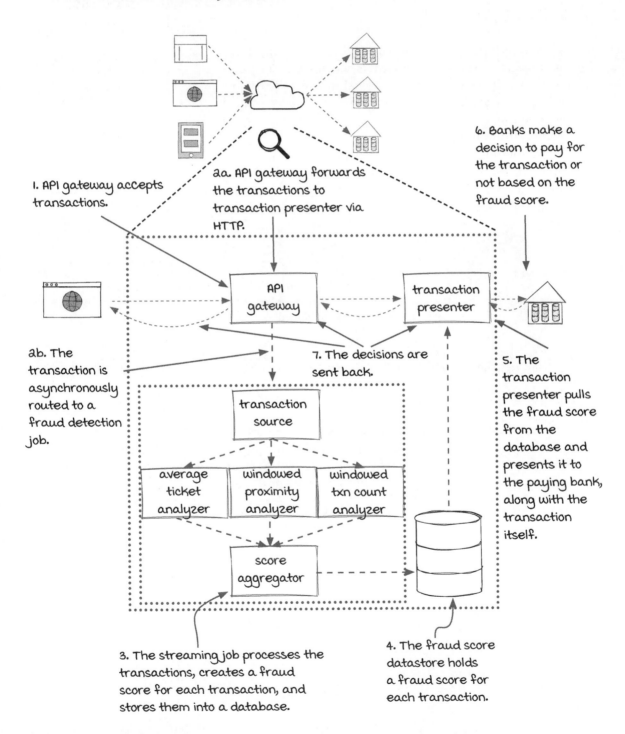

1. API gateway accepts transactions.

2a. API gateway forwards the transactions to transaction presenter via HTTP.

6. Banks make a decision to pay for the transaction or not based on the fraud score.

2b. The transaction is asynchronously routed to a fraud detection job.

7. The decisions are sent back.

5. The transaction presenter pulls the fraud score from the database and presents it to the paying bank, along with the transaction itself.

3. The streaming job processes the transactions, creates a fraud score for each transaction, and stores them into a database.

4. The fraud score datastore holds a fraud score for each transaction.

The fraud detection job in detail

Let's take a deeper look into the fraud detection job and see each component's responsibility.

> **How do we know if a transaction is potentially fraudulent?**
>
> Fraud scores can range from 0–3. A score of 0 means no fraud is detected by any analyzer, and a score of 3 means fraud is detected by all analyzers. Each analyzer will add a point to the score. We can consider a transaction potentially fraudulent with a score of 2 or greater.

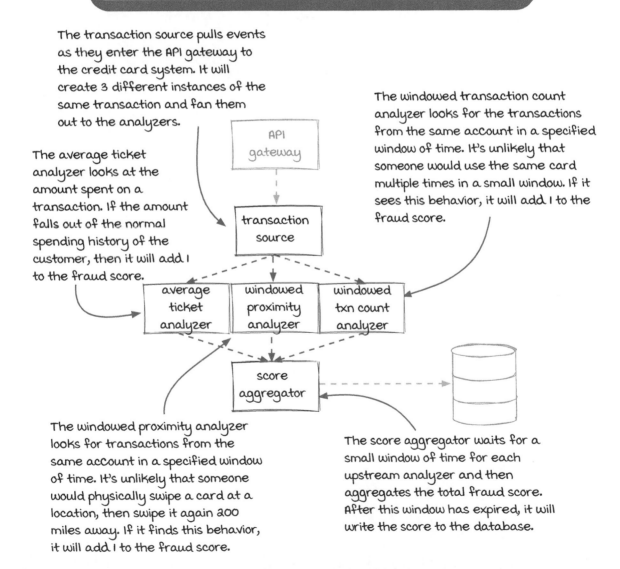

The transaction source pulls events as they enter the API gateway to the credit card system. It will create 3 different instances of the same transaction and fan them out to the analyzers.

The average ticket analyzer looks at the amount spent on a transaction. If the amount falls out of the normal spending history of the customer, then it will add 1 to the fraud score.

The windowed transaction count analyzer looks for the transactions from the same account in a specified window of time. It's unlikely that someone would use the same card multiple times in a small window. If it sees this behavior, it will add 1 to the fraud score.

The windowed proximity analyzer looks for transactions from the same account in a specified window of time. It's unlikely that someone would physically swipe a card at a location, then swipe it again 200 miles away. If it finds this behavior, it will add 1 to the fraud score.

The score aggregator waits for a small window of time for each upstream analyzer and then aggregates the total fraud score. After this window has expired, it will write the score to the database.

New concepts

In chapter 2, you learned the moving parts in a streaming system, the data sources and the operators, and the connections. We also looked at how the underlying engine handles them. These are all very important concepts that we will keep using through the whole book.

In this chapter, we are going to look into streaming jobs that have more complicated structures. The new diagram looks more complicated than the old straight-line diagram. This is correct, but there is nothing to worry about.

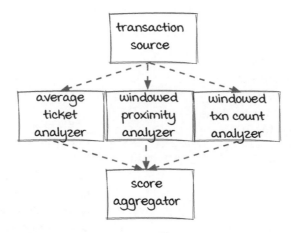

Before moving forward, let's look at a few new concepts we can learn from this new diagram:

- Upstream and downstream components
- Stream fan-out
- Stream fan-in
- Graph and DAG (directed acyclic graph)

With these new concepts, we can construct more complicated streaming systems to solve more general problems.

Upstream and downstream components

Let's start with two new concepts: *upstream components* and *downstream components*. They are pretty simple and straightforward.

Overall, a streaming job looks like a series of events flowing through components. For each component, the component (or components, as we will discuss later) directly in front is its upstream component, and the component directly behind is its downstream component. Events flow from an upstream component to a downstream component. If we look at the diagram of the streaming job we built in the previous chapter, events flow from the sensor reader to the vehicle counter. Therefore, the sensor reader is the upstream component, and the vehicle counter is the downstream component.

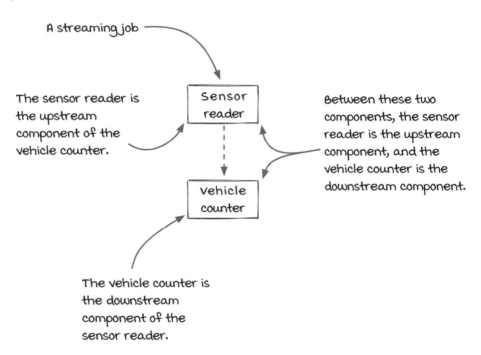

Stream fan-out and fan-in

Now, let's look at the new diagram proposed by AJ. It looks quite different from the previous job overall. The major difference is that one component may have more than one upstream or downstream component.

The transaction source component has three downstream components connected to it. This is called *stream fan-out*. Similarly, the score aggregator has three upstream components (we can also say that the three analyzers have the same downstream component). This is called *stream fan-in*.

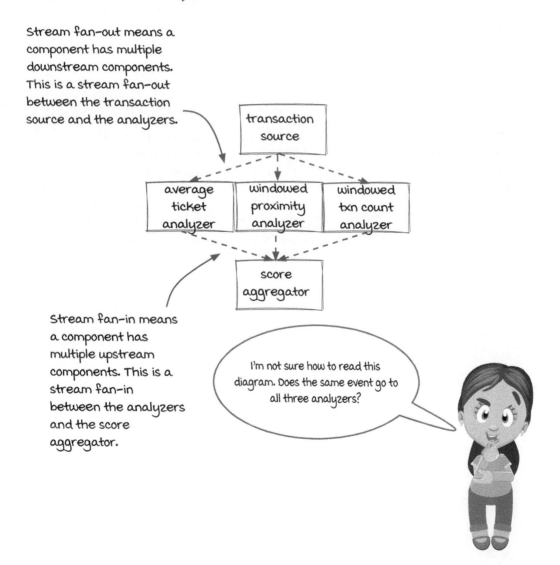

Stream fan-out means a component has multiple downstream components. This is a stream fan-out between the transaction source and the analyzers.

Stream fan-in means a component has multiple upstream components. This is a stream fan-in between the analyzers and the score aggregator.

I'm not sure how to read this diagram. Does the same event go to all three analyzers?

Graph, directed graph, and DAG

The last three concepts we will cover in this chapter are *graph*, *directed graph*, and *DAG*.

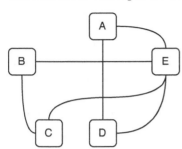

First of all, a graph is a data structure that consists of a set of *vertices* (or *nodes*) and *edges* (also known as *connections* or *lines*) that connect pairs of vertices. Two data structures used by developers, tree and list, are examples of graphs.

If every edge in a graph has a direction (from one vertex to another one), this graph is called a *directed graph*. The diagram to the right is an example of directed graph with five vertices and seven directed edges.

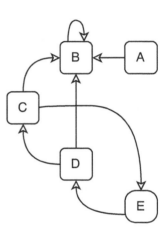

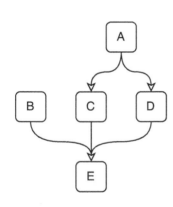

A special type of directed graph is a *directed acyclic graph*, or a DAG. A DAG is a directed graph that has no directed cycles, which means that in this type of graph, there is no way to start from a vertex and loop back to it following directed edges.

The diagram to the left is a DAG because from any of the vertices, no path can be found to loop back to itself. In the directed graph diagram, vertices C, D, and E form a cycle; hence, this graph is not a DAG. Note that there is another cycle on vertex B because it has an edge looping back to itself directly.

Most streaming jobs can be presented as DAGs.

DAG in stream processing systems

DAG is an important data structure in computer science and in stream processing systems. We won't jump into too much mathematical detail here, but it is important to know that DAG is a common term in the streaming world.

It is convenient to represent how events flow through a system with a directed graph. A loop in a directed graph means that events can be looped back and reprocessed in the same component again. It needs to be handled very carefully because of the extra complexity and risks. In some cases, loops could be necessary, but they are relatively rare. Most stream processing systems don't have loops; hence, they can be presented as DAGs.

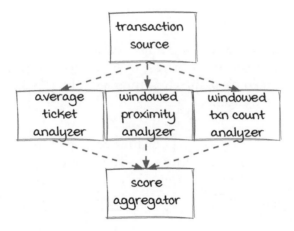

Note that, from this chapter forward, when we draw a job diagram, we are going to draw a DAG. It will only include the logical components of the job without the engine objects, such as the executors and event dispatchers (unless they are necessary), like in the diagram above, so we can focus on the business logic without worrying about the details in the engine layer. Parallelism is not included either because it is not business logic related.

All new concepts in one page

We have talked about quite a few concepts in this chapter. Let's put them together in one page, so it is easier to distinguish the relationships between them.

Events flow from the transaction source to the analyzers. The transaction source is the upstream component and the analyzers are the downstream components. The transaction source has multiple downstream components connected to it. This is called "stream fan-out."

```
              transaction
                source

  average        windowed       windowed
   ticket        proximity      txn count
  analyzer       analyzer       analyzer

                 score
              aggregator
```

Similarly, the score aggregator component has multiple upstream components. This is called "stream fan-in."

In general, a streaming job can be presented as a graph, more specifically, a directed acyclic graph (DAG), because there are no directed cycles in the directed graph. The vertices are the components, and the edges are the connections between the components.

Stream fan-out to the analyzers

It is time to jump into our system now, starting from the stream fan-out part. The stream fan-out in the fraud detection system is between the source component and the analyzer operators. With the Streamwork API, it is straightforward to link the stream coming from the source component to the evaluators. We can connect the source and evaluators, as in the code below.

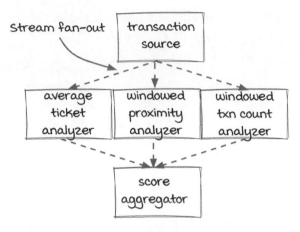

```
Job job = new Job();
Stream transactionOut = job.addSource(new TransactionSource());
Stream evalResults1 = transactionOut.applyOperator(new
AvgTicketAnalyzer());
Stream evalResults2 = transactionOut.applyOperator(new
WindowedProximityAnalyzer());
Stream evalResults3 = transactionOut.applyOperator(new
WindowedTransactionAnalyzer());
```

multiple operators are applied to the same stream.

Basically, multiple operators, in this case the evaluators, can be applied to the same transaction stream from the source component. In the runtime, every event emitted from the source component will be duplicated three times and sent to the three evaluators.

> A stream fan-out is one component with multiple downstream components.

Look inside the engine

The real work happens inside the engine. In the Streamwork engine, when a new operator is hooked up to a stream, a new queue is created between the operator's event dispatcher and the instance executors of the component that generates the stream. In other words, one instance executor can push events into multiple outgoing queues.

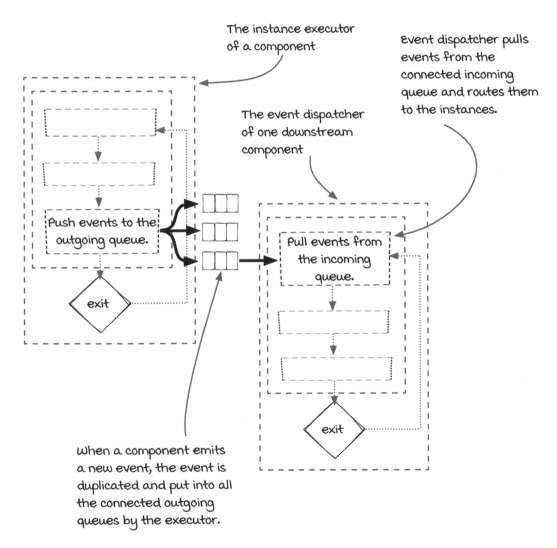

The instance executor of a component

Event dispatcher pulls events from the connected incoming queue and routes them to the instances.

The event dispatcher of one downstream component

Push events to the outgoing queue.

exit

Pull events from the incoming queue.

exit

When a component emits a new event, the event is duplicated and put into all the connected outgoing queues by the executor.

There is a problem: Efficiency

Now, every evaluator should have a copy of the transaction events, and they can apply their evaluation logic. However, this solution is not very efficient.

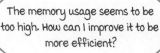

The memory usage seems to be too high. How can I improve it to be more efficient?

Each event is a transaction record. It contains a lot of the information about the transaction, such as merchandise id, transaction id, transaction time, amount, user account, merchandise categories, customer location, and so on. As a result, events are relatively large in size:

```
class TransactionEvent extends Event {
  long transactionId;
  float amount;
  Date transactionTime;
  long merchandiseId;
  long userAccount;
  ......
}
```

In the current solution, every event is duplicated multiple times because they are pushed to different queues. Because of the different queues, different analyzers are able to process each event asynchronously. These fat events are transferred through the network and loaded and handled by the analyzers. In addition, some analyzers don't need or can't process some of the events, but these events are still transferred and processed. As a result, the memory and network resource usage are not efficient and can be improved, which could be important when event traffic is high.

Stream fan-out with different streams

In stream fan-out, different outgoing queues don't need to be the same as each other. The word *different* has two meanings here:

- An emitted event could be pushed into some outgoing queues but skip others.
- Furthermore, events in different outgoing queues toward different downstream components could have different data structures.

As a result, only the necessary events with necessary fields are sent to each evaluator.

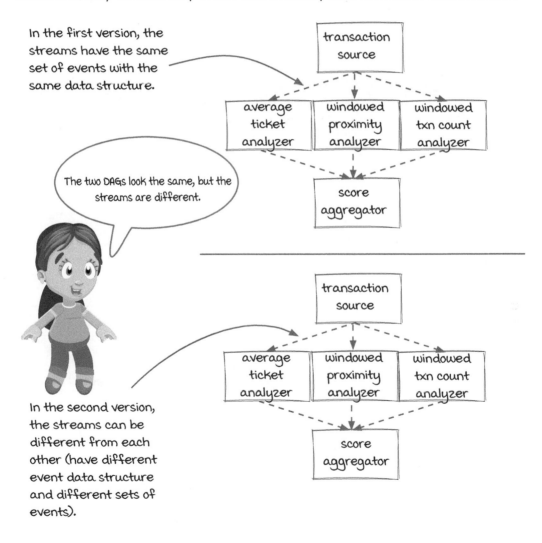

In the first version, the streams have the same set of events with the same data structure.

The two DAGs look the same, but the streams are different.

In the second version, the streams can be different from each other (have different event data structure and different sets of events).

Look inside the engine again

We have learned that one component executor can have multiple outgoing queues. Previously, the executor just pushed the same event to all the outgoing queues connected to the event dispatchers of the downstream components. Now, to support multiple streams, the executor needs to take the events emitted from each component and puts them into the correct outgoing queues.

The component object provides this information via channels. Different events are emitted into different channels, and the downstream components can choose which channel to receive events from.

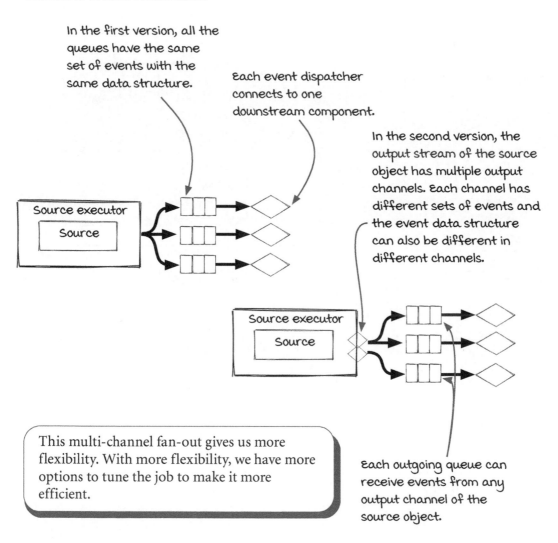

In the first version, all the queues have the same set of events with the same data structure.

Each event dispatcher connects to one downstream component.

In the second version, the output stream of the source object has multiple output channels. Each channel has different sets of events and the event data structure can also be different in different channels.

This multi-channel fan-out gives us more flexibility. With more flexibility, we have more options to tune the job to make it more efficient.

Each outgoing queue can receive events from any output channel of the source object.

Communication between the components via channels

To support this new type of stream fan-out, the component and the executor need to be updated:

- The component needs to be able to emit events into different channels.

- The executor needs to take events from each channel and push them into the right outgoing queues.

- The last piece is that the downstream component needs to be able to select a specific channel when connecting to it via applyOperator().

The output of the component was a list of events before. Now it is a map of channel names to a list of events:

```
default: [......]
amount_only: [......]
location_related: [......]
```

When a component is added into the job (apply to the output stream of its upstream component), it can select a specific channel and register to it, for example:

```
"location_related"
```

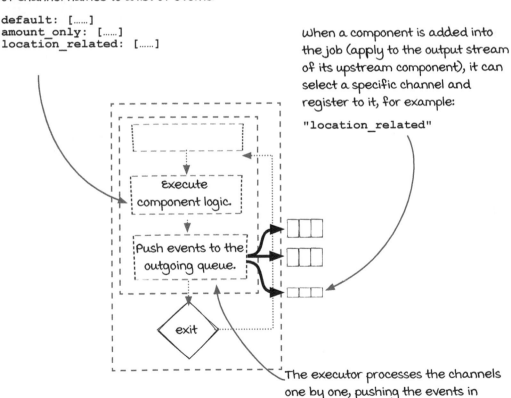

Execute component logic.

Push events to the outgoing queue.

exit

The executor processes the channels one by one, pushing the events in each channel to the outgoing queues that are registered to the channel.

Multiple channels

With multichannel support, the fan-out in the
fraud detection system can be modified to send
only necessary fields in events to the evaluators. Firstly, in the `TransactionSource`
class, channel information can be specified
when events are emitted. Note that the same
incoming event can be converted into different events in different channels.

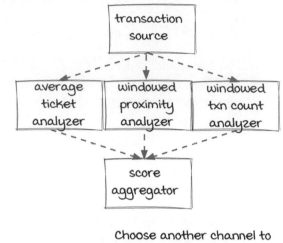

The event is emitted into
the default channel.

Choose another channel to
push events into.

```
eventCollector.add(new DefaultEvent(transactionEvent));
eventCollector.add("location _ based",
            new LocationalEvent(transactionEvent);
```

The events in this channel have
different data structures.

Then, when an evaluator is added into the streaming job via the `applyOperator()`
function, a channel can be specified first.

```
Job job = new Job();
Stream transactionOut = job.addSource(new TransactionSource());
```

A default channel is used when no channel
is selected to apply the operator.

```
Stream evalScores1 = transactionOut
    .applyOperator(new AvgTicketAnalyzer());
Stream evalScores2 = transactionOut
    .selectChannel("location _ based")
    .applyOperator(new WindowedProximityAnalyzer());
Stream evalScores3 = transactionOut
    .applyOperator(new WindowedTransactionAnalyzer());
```

A specific channel is
selected to apply
the operator.

Stream fan-in to the score aggregator

The evaluators receive transaction events and perform their own evaluations. The output of each evaluator is a *risk score* for each transaction. In our system, the risk scores of each transaction are sent to the *score aggregator* component to make the decision. If fraud is detected, an alert is written into a fraud transaction database.

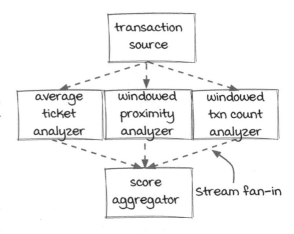

You can see from the diagram that the *score aggregator* operator takes input from multiple upstream components— the evaluators. You can also think of it in a different way: the output streams from the evaluators are merged, and the events in all of them are sent to the *score aggregator* operator in the same way. This is a *stream fan-in*.

One thing worth mentioning is that, in the *score aggregator* operator, events from different streams are treated in the same way. Another case is that the events in different incoming streams could have different data and need to be used differently. This second case is a more complicated stream fan-in that could be the focus of a full chapter. At the moment, let's focus only on the simple case.

```
Stream evalScores1 = ......
Stream evalScores2 = ......
Stream evalScores3 = ......

Operator aggregator = new ScoreAggregator(
    "aggregator", 2, new GroupByTransactionId());
Streams.of(evalScores1, evalScores2, evalScores3)
    .applyOperator(aggregator);
```

multiple streams are merged into one `Streams` object.

The `ScoreAggregator` operator is applied on the `Streams` object. Note that `GroupByTransactionId` is a subclass of `FieldsGrouping` to make sure the scores for a specific transaction are sent to the same aggregator instance.

Stream fan-in in the engine

Stream fan-in is straightforward in the Streamwork engine. The incoming queue of a component (connected to its event dispatcher) can be used by multiple upstream components. When an event is emitted by any of the upstream components (in fact, by an instance of the component), the event will be put in the queue. The downstream component pulls events from the queue and processes them. It doesn't distinguish between who pushed the events into the queue.

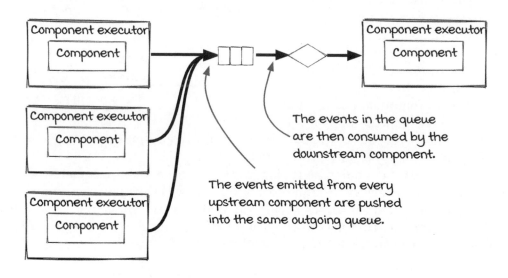

The events in the queue are then consumed by the downstream component.

The events emitted from every upstream component are pushed into the same outgoing queue.

As we discussed before, the queue decouples the upstream and downstream components.

A brief introduction to another stream fan-in: Join

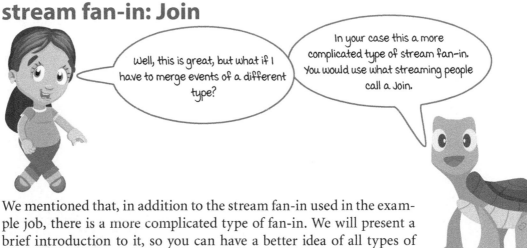

We mentioned that, in addition to the stream fan-in used in the example job, there is a more complicated type of fan-in. We will present a brief introduction to it, so you can have a better idea of all types of fan-ins and fan-outs.

In the simple stream fan-in, all incoming events have the same data structure and are treated the same way. In other words, the incoming streams are the same. What if the incoming streams are different from each other and need to be combined together? If you have ever used any databases, you should have some idea of an operation on multiple tables: *join*. If you don't know it, or you have forgotten it (we all know how reliable human memory is), no need to worry—it is not a prerequisite.

In databases, the join operation is used to combine columns from multiple tables. For example, a table of `user-id` and `name` and another table of `user-id` and `phone-number` can be joined to create a new table of `user-id`, `name` and `phone-number` by matching the `user-id` column in the two original tables. In the streaming world, the basic purpose of the join operation is similar: joining fields from multiple data sources.

However, relative to database tables, streams are much more dynamic. Events are accepted and processed continuously, and matching fields from multiple continuous data sources requires a lot more considerations. We are going to stop here on the basic concept of *join* and leave further exploration of this topic to its own chapter.

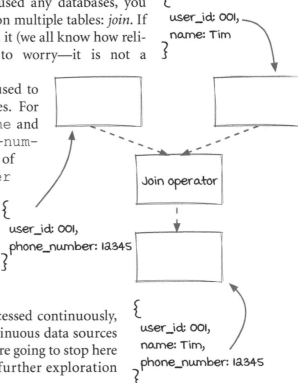

```
{
  user_id: 001,
  name: Tim
}
```

```
{
  user_id: 001,
  phone_number: 12345
}
```

Join operator

```
{
  user_id: 001,
  name: Tim,
  phone_number: 12345
}
```

Look at the whole system

Now that we have discussed stream fan-out and fan-in one by one in the previous sections, let's put them together and zoom out to take another look at the whole system. From a high level, the job can be represented as the graph below; sometimes we call it the *logical plan*. It represents the logical structure (components and their connections) of the job.

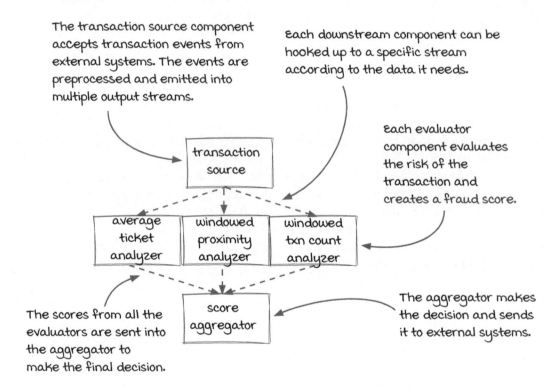

The transaction source component accepts transaction events from external systems. The events are preprocessed and emitted into multiple output streams.

Each downstream component can be hooked up to a specific stream according to the data it needs.

Each evaluator component evaluates the risk of the transaction and creates a fraud score.

transaction source

average ticket analyzer

windowed proximity analyzer

windowed txn count analyzer

score aggregator

The scores from all the evaluators are sent into the aggregator to make the final decision.

The aggregator makes the decision and sends it to external systems.

In the real world, fraud detection systems will evolve continuously, and new evaluators will be introduced from time to time. With the Streamwork framework, or other stream processing frameworks, adding, removing, and replacing evaluators is pretty simple and straightforward.

Graph and streaming jobs

With the support of stream fan-out and fan-in, now we can build streaming systems in more complicated and general graph type structures. This is a very important step forward because with this new structure, we can cover more real-world problems.

Here are the DAGs of two example streaming systems. Can you try to imagine what kind of systems they might be?

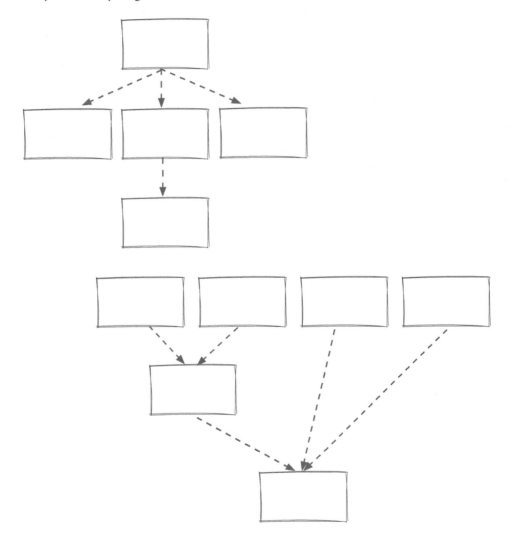

The example systems

The truth is, these graphs can be so many things! Here are potential answers for the two diagrams.

The first diagram could be a simple traffic monitoring system. The events collected by the traffic sensors are sent to three core processors: an accident detector, a congestion detector, and a junction optimizer. The congestion detector has a location-based aggregator as a preprocessor.

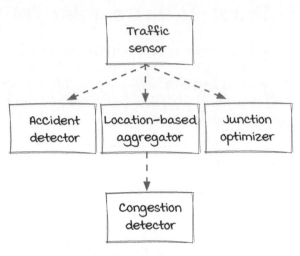

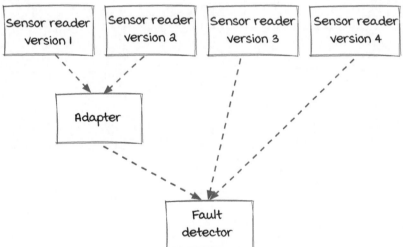

The second diagram could be a fault detection system that processes events from sensor readers in multiple versions. The events generated from the first two versions are not compatible with the detector; hence, an adapter is needed for them. In the system, all the sensor readers can work together seamlessly, and it is easy to add new versions or deprecate old versions.

After all, stream jobs are not very complicated. The example systems are significantly simplified compared to the real-world systems. Nevertheless, hopefully you have a better idea of what streaming systems can do now. In their simplest form, streaming jobs are components and their connections. Once a streaming job is set up and running, events flow through the components along the connections *forever*.

Summary

In this chapter, we moved forward from the list type system structure we discussed in previous chapters to a more general type of system structure: the graph. Because events flow through systems from the sources to the operators, in most cases a streaming job can be presented as a directed acyclic graph (DAG). Most jobs in the real world have graph architecture; hence, this is a critical step.

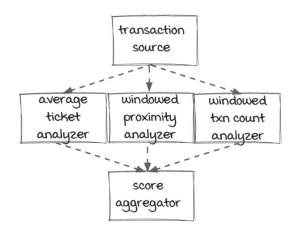

Different from the components in the list type system structure, in a job graph, a component can link to multiple upstream components and downstream components. These types of connections are called stream fan-in and fan-out. The streams coming into a component or going out of it could have the same types of events or different types.

In addition, we also looked at the Streamwork framework a little bit to see how the engine handles the connections. Hopefully, this will be helpful for your understanding of how streaming systems work in general.

Exercises

1. Can you add a new evaluator to the fraud detection job?

2. Currently, each evaluator takes a transaction event from the transaction source component and creates a score. Now two evaluators have the same type of calculation at beginning of their evaluation. Could you change the job for this case? The result will look like the graph below:

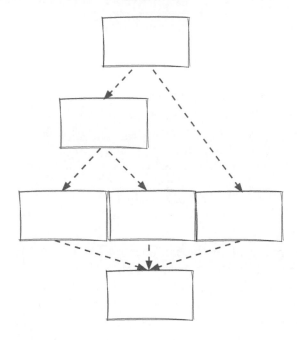

In this chapter

- introducing delivery semantics and their impact

- at-most-once delivery semantic

- at-least-once delivery semantic

- exactly-once delivery semantic

> " *There's never enough time to do it right, but there's always enough time to do it over.* "
>
> —Jack Bergman

Computers are pretty good at performing accurate calculations. However, when computers work together in a distributed system, like many streaming systems, accuracy becomes a little bit more (I mean, a lot more) complicated. Sometimes, we may not want 100% accuracy because other more important requirements need to be met. "Why would we want wrong answers?" you might ask. This is a great question, and it is the one that we need to ask when designing a streaming system. In this chapter, we are going to discuss an important topic related to accuracy in streaming systems: *delivery semantics.*

The latency requirement of the fraud detection system

In the previous chapter, the team built a credit card fraud detection system which can make a decision within 20 milliseconds for each transaction and store the result in a database. Now, let's ask an important question when building any distributed system: what if any failure happens?

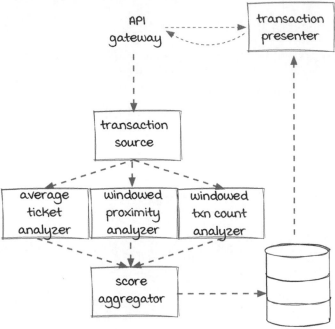

Low latency is critical for the system. Looks like our system can finish the process under 20 milliseconds for each transaction. Everything looks good, right?

We will need to account for failure handling by sacrificing accuracy to meet the requirement when things go wrong.

Sounds good... Wait. Sacrifice accuracy?!! What do you mean?

Revisit the fraud detection job

We are going to use the fraud detection system from the previous chapter as our example in this chapter to discuss the topic of delivery semantics. So let's look at the system and the fraud detection job briefly to refresh your memory first.

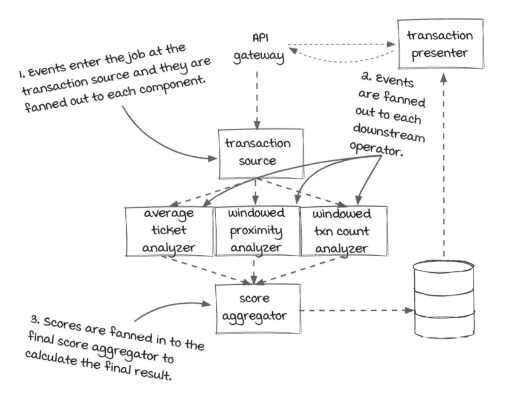

The fraud detection job has multiple analyzers working in parallel to process the transactions that enter the card network. The fraud scores from these analyzers are sent to an aggregator to calculate the final results for each transaction, and the results are written to the database for the transaction presenter.

The 20-millisecond latency threshold is critical. If the decision is not made in time, the transaction presenter won't be able to provide the answer for the transaction to the bank, which would be bad. Ideally, we would like the job to run smoothly and meet the latency requirement all the time. But, you know, stuff happens.

About accuracy

We make lots of tradeoffs in distributed systems. A challenge in any streaming system is to reliably process events. Streaming frameworks can help keep the job running reliably as often as possible, but you need to know what you really need. We are used to seeing accurate results with computers; hence, it is important to understand that accuracy is not absolute in streaming systems. When necessary, it might need to be sacrificed.

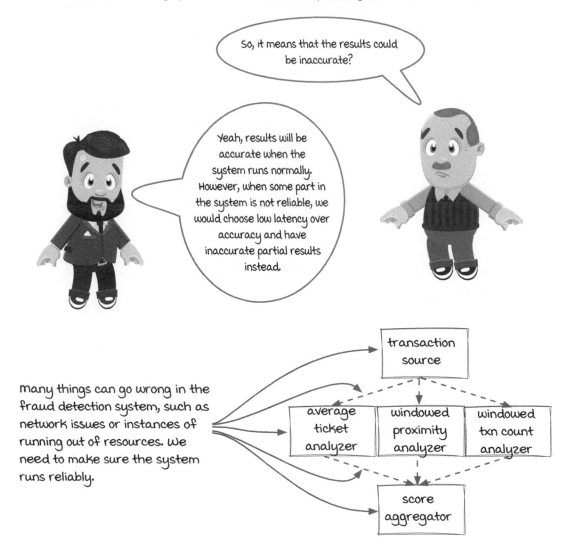

Don't panic! In the next few pages we will look at solutions with these types of results.

Partial result

A partial result is a result of incomplete data; hence, we can't guarantee its accuracy. The following figure is an example of partial result when the average ticket analyzer has temporary issues.

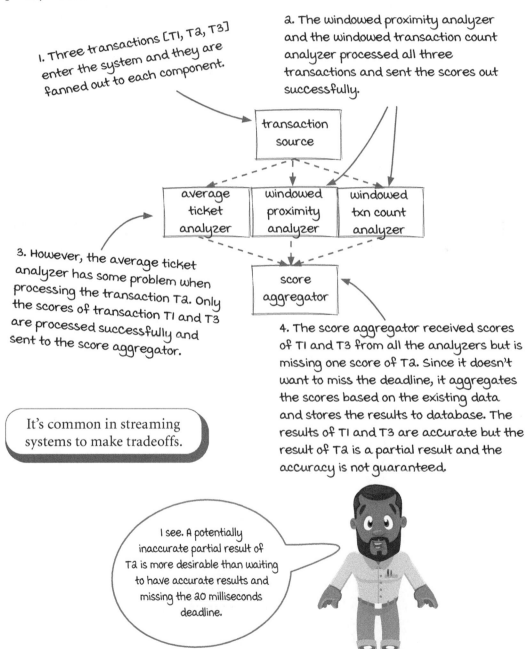

1. Three transactions [T1, T2, T3] enter the system and they are fanned out to each component.

2. The windowed proximity analyzer and the windowed transaction count analyzer processed all three transactions and sent the scores out successfully.

3. However, the average ticket analyzer has some problem when processing the transaction T2. Only the scores of transaction T1 and T3 are processed successfully and sent to the score aggregator.

4. The score aggregator received scores of T1 and T3 from all the analyzers but is missing one score of T2. Since it doesn't want to miss the deadline, it aggregates the scores based on the existing data and stores the results to database. The results of T1 and T3 are accurate but the result of T2 is a partial result and the accuracy is not guaranteed.

It's common in streaming systems to make tradeoffs.

I see. A potentially inaccurate partial result of T2 is more desirable than waiting to have accurate results and missing the 20 milliseconds deadline.

A new streaming job to monitor system usage

Now that we have seen the requirements of the fraud detection job, to better understand different delivery semantics, we want to introduce another job that has different requirements to compare. The fraud detection system has been a hit in the credit card processing business. With the speed of system operations, other credit card companies are becoming interested in this idea, and with interest increasing, the team decided to add another streaming job into the system to help monitor system usage. The job tracks key information, such as how many transactions have been processed.

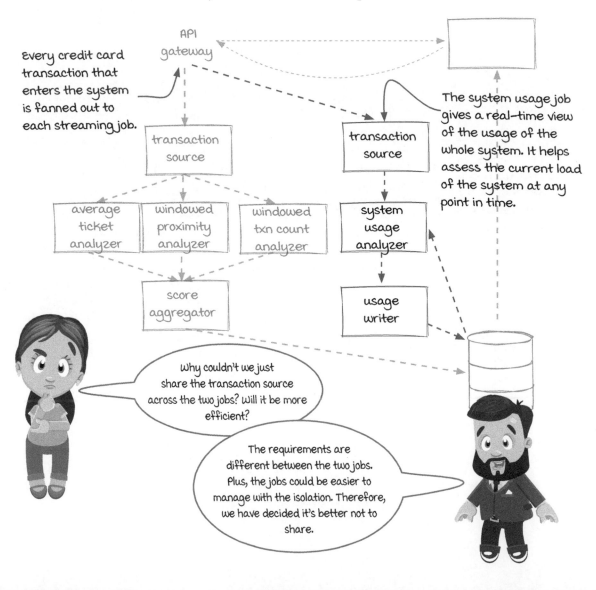

The new system usage job

The new system usage job is used internally to monitor the current load of the system. We can start with two critical numbers that we are interested in first:

- How many transactions have been processed? This number is important for us to understand the trend of the overall amount of data the fraud detection job is processing.

- How many suspicious transactions have been detected? This number could be helpful for us to understand the number of new records created in the result database.

The counting logic is in the `SystemUsageAnalyzer` operator:

```
class SystemUsageAnalyzer extends Operator {
  private int transactionCount = 0;
  private int fraudTransactionCount = 0;

  public void apply(Event event, EventCollector collector) {        Count the
    String id = ((TransactionEvent)event).getTransactionId();       transaction.
    transactionCount++;

    Thread.sleep(20);          Pause for 20 milliseconds for
                               the fraud detection job to
                               finish its process.

                                        Read the detection result of the
    boolean fraud = fraudStore.getItem(id);  transaction from database. This
                                             operation may fail if the database is not
                                             available, and an exception will be thrown.

    if (fraud) {
      fraudTransactionCount++;
    }                                Count the fraud transaction if
                                     the result is true.
    collector.emit(new UsageEvent(
    transactionCount, fraudTransactionCount));
  }
}
```

The operator looks very simple:

- For every transaction, the value of `transactionCount` increases by one.

- If the transaction is a detected fraud transaction, the value of `fraudTransactionCount` increases by one.

However, the `getItem()` call in the function could fail. How the job behaves when failures happen is a key difference between different *delivery semantics*.

The requirements of the new system usage job

Before worrying about the failures, we have a few more things to talk about. First, let's look at the requirements of the job. As an internal tool, the latency and accuracy requirements can be quite different from the fraud detection job:

- *Latency*—The 20-millisecond latency requirement of the fraud detection job is not necessary in the system usage job, since the results are not used by the presenter service to generate decisions for the banks. We humans can't read the results that quickly anyway. Moreover, a small delay when something goes wrong could be totally acceptable.

- *Accuracy*—On the other hand, accurate results could be important for us to make the right decision.

In the system usage job, accuracy is more important. We need to configure the system to give us the accurate results even if something goes wrong.

Is there a way to configure accuracy settings in our streaming engine?

Yes, there is a critical configuration widely supported by most engines. It's known as delivery semantics or delivery guarantees.

We will walk you through the most common delivery semantics to get you started in your stream-processing journey. Along the way we will discuss the different ways you can use streaming systems to guarantee how transactions will be processed and why you would want to use them.

New concepts: (The number of) times delivered and times processed

To understand what delivery semantics really means, the concepts of *times processed* and *times delivered* will be very helpful:

- Times processed can refer to the number of times an event was processed by a component.
- Times delivered can refer to the number of times the result was generated by a component.

The two numbers are the same in most cases, but not always. For example, in the flow chart of the logic in the SystemUsageAnalyzer operator below, it is possible that the *get detection result* step can fail if the database is having issues. When the step fails, the event is processed once (but not successfully), and no result is generated. As a result, the times processed would be 1, and the times delivered would be 0. You may also consider times delivered as times *successfully processed*.

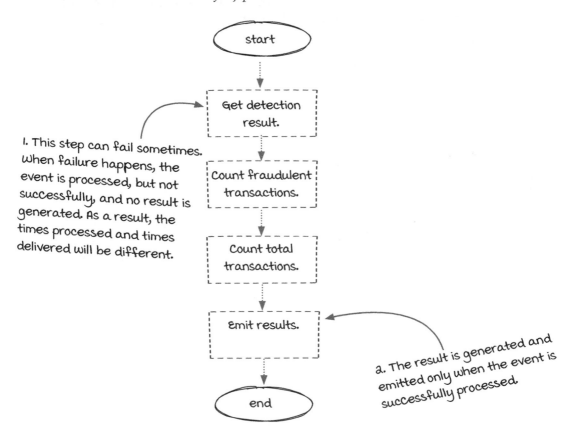

1. This step can fail sometimes. When failure happens, the event is processed, but not successfully, and no result is generated. As a result, the times processed and times delivered will be different.

2. The result is generated and emitted only when the event is successfully processed.

New concept: Delivery semantics

Here comes the key topic of this chapter: *delivery semantics*, also known as *delivery guarantees* or *delivery assurances*. It is a very important concept to understand for streaming jobs before we move on to more advanced topics.

Delivery semantics concerns how streaming engines will guarantee the delivery (or successful processing) of events in your streaming jobs. There are three main buckets of delivery semantics to choose from. Let's introduce them briefly here and look at them one by one in more detail later.

- *At-most-once*—Streaming jobs guarantee that every event will be processed no more than one time, with no guarantees of being successfully processed at all.

- *At-least-once*—Streaming jobs guarantee that every event will be successfully processed at least one time with no guarantees about the number of times it is processed.

- *Exactly-once*—Streaming jobs guarantee that every event will be successfully processed once and only once (at least it looks this way). In some frameworks, it is also called *effectively-once*. If you feel that this is too good to be true because exactly-once is extremely hard to achieve in distributed systems, or the two terms seem to be controversial, you are definitely not alone. We will talk about what exactly-once really is later in its own section.

Choosing the right semantics

You may ask whether it is true that exactly-once is the go-to semantic for everything. The advantage is pretty obvious: the results are guaranteed to be accurate, and the correct answer is better than an incorrect answer.

With exactly-once, the streaming engine will do everything for you and there is nothing to worry about. What are the other two options for? Why do we need to learn about them? The fact is, all of them are useful because different streaming systems have different requirements.

Here is a simple table for the tradeoffs to begin with. We will revisit the table later after more discussion.

Delivery semantics	At-most-once	At-least-once	Exactly-once
Accuracy	• No accuracy guarantee because of missing events	• No accuracy guarantee because of duplicated events	• (Looks like) accurate results are guaranteed
Latency (when errors happen)	• Tolerant to failures; no delay when errors happen	• Sensitive to failures; potential delay when errors happen	• Sensitive to failures; potential delay when errors happen
Complexity	• Very simple	• Intermediate (depends on the implementation)	• Complex

> We will choose at-most-once for the fraud detection job because we need to have low process latency, and exactly-once for the system usage job to have better accuracy.

Let's continue to learn how the delivery semantics are actually handled in streaming systems. Then, you should be able to understand the tradeoffs better. Note that in the real world, each framework could have its own architecture and handle delivery semantics very differently. We will try to explain in a framework agnostic manner.

At-most-once

Let's start from the simplest semantic: *at-most-once*. Inside the jobs with this semantic, events are not tracked. Engines will do their best to process each event successfully, but if any error occurs along the way, the engines will forget the events and carry on processing others. The diagram below shows how events are handled in the Streamwork engine for at-most-once jobs.

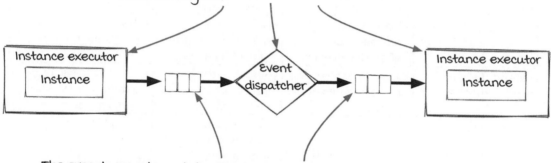

The executors and event dispatchers blindly transfer events to the downstream processes. By this we mean that it does not keep a ledger anywhere of what goes where. They just pick up and move events as fast as they can.

The executors and event dispatchers blindly transfer events to the downstream processes. By this we mean that it does not keep a ledger anywhere of what goes where. They just pick up and move events as fast as they can.

It might be hard for some people to believe, but many real-life systems would accept the temporarily inaccurate results to keep them simple.

Since the engines don't track events, the whole job can run very efficiently without much overhead. And since the job will just continue running without the need of recovering from the issues, the latency and higher throughput won't be affected by the errors. In addition, the job will also be easier to maintain because of the simplicity. On the other hand, the effect of losing events when the system is having issues is that the results could be temporarily inaccurate.

The fraud detection job

Let's look back at the fraud detection job with the at-most-once semantic. The fraud detection job is responsible for adding up fraud scores on each transaction that enters the card network, and it must generate the results within 20 milliseconds.

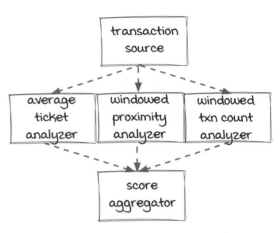

The good

With the at-most-once guarantee, the system is simpler and processes transactions with lower latency. When something goes wrong in the system, such as a transaction failing to process or transport, or any instance is temporarily unavailable, the affected events will simply be dropped and the score aggregator will just process with the available data, so the critical latency requirement is met.

Low resource and maintenance costs is the other main motivation to choose the at-most-once semantic. For example, if you have a huge amount of data to process in real time with limited resources, the at-most-once semantic could be worth your consideration.

The bad

Now, it is time to talked about the catch: inaccuracy. It is definitely an important factor when choosing the at-most-once semantic. At-most-once is suitable for the cases in which temporary inaccuracy is acceptable. It is important to ask yourself this question when you consider this option: what is the impact when the results are inaccurate temporarily?

The hope

If you want the advantages of at-most-once as well as accurate results, don't lose hope yet. Although it might be too much to expect everything at the same time, there are still a few things we can do to overcome this limitation (to some extent). We will talk about these practical techniques at the end of this chapter, but for now, let's move on and look at the other two delivery semantics.

At-least-once

No matter how convenient the at-most-once semantic is, the flaw is obvious: there is no guarantee that each event will be reliably processed. This is just not acceptable in many cases. Another flaw is that, since the events have been dropped without any trace, there is not much we can do to improve the accuracy.

   Next comes the next delivery semantic—at-least-once—which can be helpful for overcoming the flaws discussed previously. With at-least-once, the streaming engines will guarantee that events will be processed at least one time. A side effect of at-least-once is that events may be processed more than one time. The diagram below shows how events are handled in the Streamwork engine for at-least-once jobs.

   Note that tracking events and making sure each of them is successfully processed might sound easy, but it's not a trivial task in distributed systems. We will look into it in the next few pages.

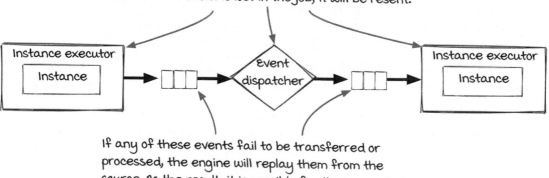

The executors and event dispatchers transfer events to the downstream processes, and the events are tracked. If an event is lost in the job, it will be resent.

If any of these events fail to be transferred or processed, the engine will replay them from the source. As the result, it is possible for these events to be processed more than once.

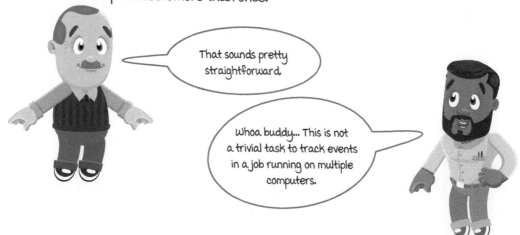

That sounds pretty straightforward.

Whoa buddy... This is not a trivial task to track events in a job running on multiple computers.

At-least-once with acknowledging

A typical approach to support the at-least-once delivery semantic is that each component within a streaming job acknowledges that it has successfully processed an event or experienced a failure. Streaming frameworks usually supply a tracking mechanism for you with a new process *acknowledger*. This acknowledger is responsible for tracking the *current* and *completed* processes for each event. When all processes are completed, and there is no *current* process left for an event, it will report a *success* or *fail* message back to the data source. Let's look at our system usage job running with the at-least-once semantic below.

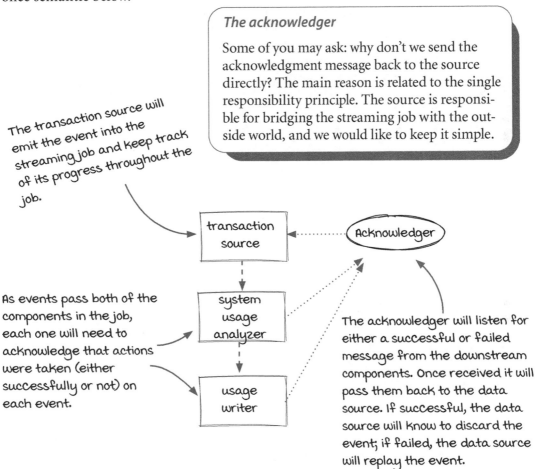

The transaction source will emit the event into the streaming job and keep track of its progress throughout the job.

> ### The acknowledger
>
> Some of you may ask: why don't we send the acknowledgment message back to the source directly? The main reason is related to the single responsibility principle. The source is responsible for bridging the streaming job with the outside world, and we would like to keep it simple.

As events pass both of the components in the job, each one will need to acknowledge that actions were taken (either successfully or not) on each event.

transaction source

Acknowledger

system usage analyzer

usage writer

The acknowledger will listen for either a successful or failed message from the downstream components. Once received it will pass them back to the data source. If successful, the data source will know to discard the event; if failed, the data source will replay the event.

After the source component emits an event, it will keep it in a buffer first. After it receives a *success* message from the acknowledger, it will remove the event from the buffer, since the event has been successfully processed. If the source component receives a *fail* message for the event, it will *replay* that event by emitting it into the job again.

Track events

Let's get closer and see how events are tracked with an example. The engine will wrap the core event in some metadata as it leaves the data source. One of these pieces of meta-data is an event id that is used for tracking the event through the job. Components would report to the acknowledger after the process is completed.

Note that the downstream components are included in acknowledgment data, so the acknowledger knows that it needs to wait for the tracking data from all the downstream components before marking the process *fully processed*.

1. The data source gets a transaction and emits it out with an assigned id 101. It will hold it ready to resend until all components have successfully acknowledged the event has been processed. The acknowledgment might look like:

```
{
  Event id: 101,
  Result: successfully processed,
  Component: transaction source,
  Downstream components: [
    system usage analyzer
  ]
}
```

2. The analyzer would send an acknowledgment on the id once processing has completed on the received event.

```
{
  Event id: 101,
  Result: successfully processed,
  Component: system usage analyzer,
  Downstream components: [
    usage writer
  ]
}
```

4. The acknowledger receives all the needed acknowledgments (from all the "downstream components") and notifies the transaction source that the event with id 101 has been fully processed.

3. The usage writer would send another acknowledgment on the id once the processing has completed.

```
{
  Event id: 101,
  Result: successfully processed,
  Component: usage writer
}
```

Handle event processing failures

In another case, if the event fails to process in any component, the acknowledger will notify the source component to resend.

1. The data source gets a transaction and emits it out with an assigned id 101. It will hold it ready to resend until all components have successfully acknowledged the event has been processed. When a failure is received, the event will be resent with a new assigned event id. The acknowledgment might look like:

```
{
  Event id: 101,
  Result: successfully processed,
  Component: transaction source,
  Downstream components: [
    system usage analyzer
  ]
}
```

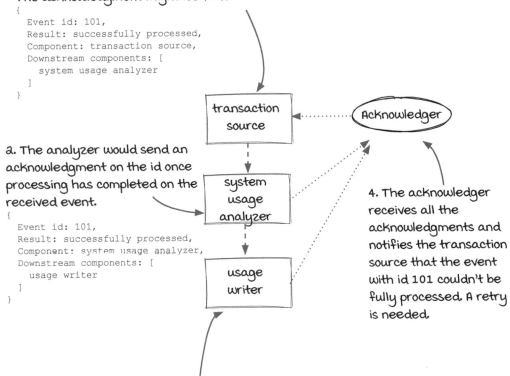

2. The analyzer would send an acknowledgment on the id once processing has completed on the received event.

```
{
  Event id: 101,
  Result: successfully processed,
  Component: system usage analyzer,
  Downstream components: [
    usage writer
  ]
}
```

4. The acknowledger receives all the acknowledgments and notifies the transaction source that the event with id 101 couldn't be fully processed. A retry is needed.

3. The usage writer has an issue to process the event and it would send another acknowledgment on the id once the processing has failed. The acknowledgment might look like:

```
{
  Event id: 101,
  Result: process failed,
  Component: usage writer
}
```

Track early out events

The last case we need to take a look at is when not all events go through all the components. Some events may finish their journey earlier. This is why the downstream component information in the acknowledgment message is important. For example, if the transaction is not valid and won't need to be written to storage, the system usage analyzer will be the last stop of the event, and the process will be completed there.

1. The data source gets a transaction and emits it out with an assigned id 101. It will hold it ready to resend until all components have successfully acknowledged the event has been processed. The acknowledgment might look like:

```
{
  Event id: 101,
  Result: successfully processed,
  Component: transaction source,
  Downstream components: [
    system usage analyzer
  ]
}
```

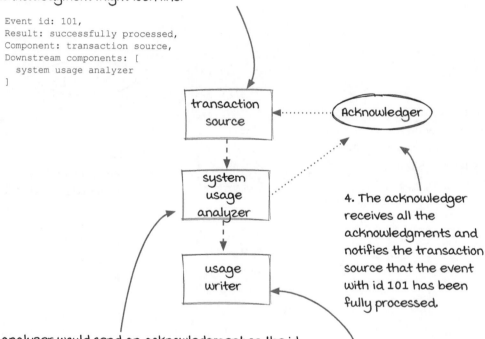

4. The acknowledger receives all the acknowledgments and notifies the transaction source that the event with id 101 has been fully processed.

2. The analyzer would send an acknowledgment on the id once processing has completed on the received event. Note that if this is the last component for the event, there is no downstream component in the acknowledgment data. The acknowledgment might look like:

```
{
  Event id: 101,
  Result: successfully processed,
  Component: system usage analyzer
}
```

3. The usage writer component is not in the downstream component list; hence, the acknowledger won't wait for the acknowledgment from it.

Acknowledging code in components

If you are wondering how the engine will know how a component will pass or fail an event, that is good! Below we have snippets of code that will be implemented in the `SystemUsageAnalyzer` and the `UsageWriter` components.

```
class SystemUsageAnalyzer extends Operator {
  public void apply(Event event, EventCollector collector) {
    if (isValidEvent(event.data)) {
      if (analyze(event.data) == SUCCESSFUL) {
        collector.emit(event);

        collector.ack(event.id);
      } else {
        //signal this event as failure
        collector.fail(event.id);
      }
    } else {
      // signal this event as successful
      collector.ack(event.id);
    }
  }
}
```

An acknowledgment will be sent out when an event is emitted to acknowledge the event as successful.

Analyzing failed. Acknowledge this event as unsuccessful.

The event should be skipped. Acknowledge this event as successful, so the source component won't replay it.

```
class UsageWriter extends Operator {
  public void apply(Event event, EventCollector collector) {
    if (database.write(event) == SUCCESSFUL) {
      //signal this event as successful
      collector.ack(event.id);
    } else {
      // signal this event as unsuccessful
      collector.fail(event.id);
    }
  }
}
```

No need to emit the event out. Manually acknowledge this event as successful.

The database is having issues writing. Acknowledge this event as unsuccessful.

New concept: Checkpointing

Acknowledging works fine for the at-least-once semantic, but it has some drawbacks.

- The acknowledgment logic (aka code change) is needed.

- The order of events processing could be different from the input, which could cause issues. For example, if we have three events [A, B, C] to process, and the processing job has a failure when processing event A, another copy of event A will be replayed later by the source, and eventually four events, [A (failed), B, C, A], are emitted into the job, and event A is successfully processed after B and C.

Luckily, there is another option to support the at-least-once semantic (with tradeoffs, like everything else in the distributed systems): *checkpointing*. It is an important technique in streaming systems to achieve *fault tolerance* (i.e., the system continues operating properly after the failures). Because there are many pieces involved, it is a little messy to explain checkpointing in detail in streaming systems. So let's try a different way. Although the concept of checkpointing sounds technical, it is, in fact, very likely that you have experienced it in real life if you have ever played video games. If you haven't played any, that's OK. You can also think of any text editor software (or maybe you want to try a video game now).

Now, let's play an adventure game fighting all kinds of zombies and saving the world. It is not very common that you will complete the game nonstop from the beginning to the end, unless you are like a superhero and never fail. Most of us will fail occasionally (or more than occasionally). Hopefully, you have saved your progress so you can reload the game and resume where you were instead of starting over from the very beginning. In some games, the progress might be saved automatically at critical points. Now, imagine that you live in the universe of the game. Your time should be continuous without interruption, even though in real life you have been rolled back a few (or many) times to earlier states. The operation of saving a game is very much like checkpointing.

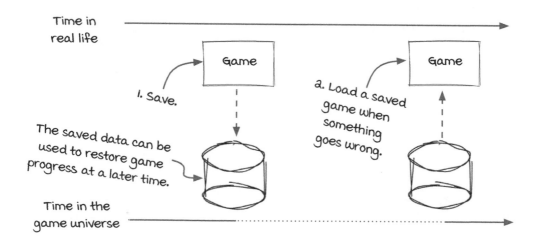

New concept: State

If you play video games, you know how important saved data is. I can't imagine how I can finish any game (or any work) without that functionality. A more formal definition of *checkpoint* is a piece of data, typically persisted in storage, that can be used by an instance to restore to a previous state. We will now cover another related concept: *state*.

Let's go back to the zombie universe and see what data would be needed to restore and continue the adventure. The data could be very different from game to game, but we should be able to imagine that the following data will be needed in the saved games:

- The current score and levels of skills

- The equipment you have

- The tasks that have been finished

One key property that makes the data important is that it changes along with the game-play. The data that doesn't change when you are working hard to save the world, such as the map and the appearance of the zombies, doesn't need to be included in the saved games.

Now, let's go back to the definition of *state* in streaming systems: the internal data inside each instance that changes when events are processed. For example, in the system usage job, each instance of the system usage analyzer keeps track of the count of transactions it has processed. This count changes when a new transaction is processed, and it is one piece of information in the state. When the instance is restarted, the count needs to be recovered.

While the concepts of checkpointing and state are not complicated, we need to understand that checkpointing is not a trivial task in distributed systems like in streaming systems. There could be hundreds or thousands of instances working together to process events at the same time. It is the engine's responsibility to manage the checkpointing of all the instances and make sure they are all synchronized. We will leave it here and come back to this topic later in chapter 10.

Checkpointing in the system usage job for the at-least-once semantic

Before introducing checkpointing for at-least-once, we need to introduce a useful component between the API gateway and the system usage job: an *event log*. Note that the term is used for the purposes of this book and is not widely used, but it shouldn't be hard to get. An event log is a queue of events in which each event is tracked with an offset (or a timestamp). The *reader* (or *consumer*) can jump to a specific offset and start loading data from there. In real life, events might be organized in multiple *partitions,* and offsets are managed independently in each partition, but let's keep things simple here and assume there is only one offset and one transaction source instance.

With an event log in front of the transaction source component, every minute (or other interval) the source instance creates a checkpoint with the current state—the current offset it is working on. When the job is restarted, the engine will identify the right offset for the instance to jump to (a *rollback*) and start processing events from that point. Note that the events processed by the instance from the checkpointing time to the restart time will be processed again, but it is OK under the at-least-once semantic.

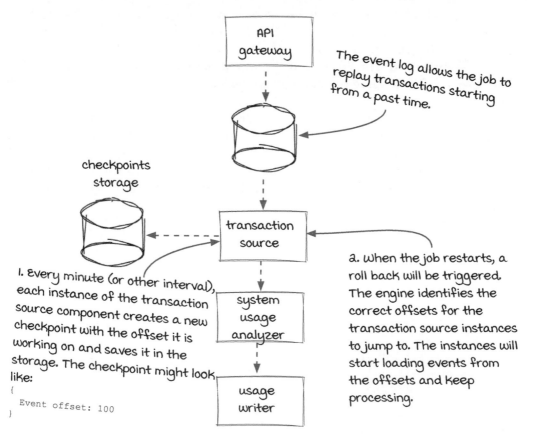

The event log allows the job to replay transactions starting from a past time.

checkpoints storage

1. Every minute (or other interval), each instance of the transaction source component creates a new checkpoint with the offset it is working on and saves it in the storage. The checkpoint might look like:

```
{
    Event offset: 100
}
```

2. When the job restarts, a roll back will be triggered. The engine identifies the correct offsets for the transaction source instances to jump to. The instances will start loading events from the offsets and keep processing.

API gateway

transaction source

system usage analyzer

usage writer

Checkpointing and state manipulation functions

Checkpointing is very powerful. Many things are happening when a job is running with checkpointing enabled. A few major points include:

- Periodically, each source instance needs to create the checkpoint with their current states.

- The checkpoints need be saved into a (hopefully fault-tolerant) storage system.

- The streaming job needs to restart itself automatically when a failure is detected.

- The job needs to identify the latest checkpoints, and each restarted source instance needs to load its checkpoint file and recover its previous state.

- We don't have unlimited storage, so older checkpoints need to be cleaned up to save resources.

It sounds like checkpointing is complicated and a lot of work to implement?...

After looking at all the points above, don't panic! It is true that the whole checkpointing mechanism is a bit complicated, and there are many things happening to make it work. Luckily, most of these are handled by the streaming frameworks, and the stream job owners need to worry about only one thing: the state. More specifically, the two state manipulation functions:

- Get the current state of the instance. The function will be invoked periodically.

- Initialize the instance with a state object loaded from a checkpoint. The function will be invoked during the startup of the streaming job.

As long as the two functions above are provided, the streaming framework will do all the dirty work behind the scenes, such as packing the states in a checkpoint, saving it on disk, and using a checkpoint to initialize instances.

State handling code in the transaction source component

The following is a code example of the `TransactionSource` component with the Streamwork framework:

- The base class is changed from `Source` to `StatefulSource`.

- With this new base class, a new `getState()` function is introduced to extract the state of the instance and return to the engine.

- Another change is that the `setupInstance()` function takes an additional `State` object to set up the instance after it is constructed, which didn't exist for the stateless operators.

Source and StatefulSource classes

```
public abstract class Source extends Component {
  public abstract void setupInstance(int instance);
  public abstract void getEvents(EventCollector eventCollector);
}

public abstract class StatefulSource extends Component {
  public abstract void setupInstance(int instance, State state);
  public abstract void getEvents(EventCollector eventCollector);
  public abstract State getState();
}
```

This new function is used to extract the state of the instance.

A new state object is used to set up the instance.

```
class TransactionSource extends StatefulSource {
  MessageQueue queue;
  int offset = 0;
  ......
  public void setupInstance(int instance, State state) {
    SourceState mstate = (SourceState)state;
    if (mstate != null) {
      offset = mstate.offset;
      log.seek(offset);
    }
  }
```

The data in the state object is used to set up the instance.

```
  public void getEvents(Event event, EventCollector eventCollector) {
    Transaction transaction = log.pull();
    eventCollector.add(new TransactionEvent(transaction));
    offset++;
  }
```

The offset value changes when a new event is pulled from the event log and emitted to the downstream components.

```
  public State getState() {
    SourceState state = new SourceState();
    State.offset = offset;
    return new state;
  }
}
```

The state object of the instance contains the current data offset in the event log.

Exactly-once or effectively-once?

For the system usage job, neither at-most-one nor the at-least-once semantics are ideal because accurate results are not guaranteed, but we need them to make the right decision. To achieve this goal, we can choose the last semantic: *exactly-once*, which guarantees that each event is successfully processed once and only once. Hence, the results are accurate.

First, let's discuss what we mean by *exactly-once*. It is critical to understand the fact that every event is *not* really processed or successfully processed exactly one time like the name suggests. The real meaning is that if you look at the job as a black box—in other words, if you look only at the input and the output and ignore how the job really works internally, it *looks like* each event is processed successfully once and only once. However, if we dive into the system internally, it is possible for each event to be processed more than one time. Now, if you look at the topic of this chapter it is *delivery semantics* instead of *process semantics*. Subtle, right?

When the semantic was briefly introduced earlier in this chapter, we mentioned that it is called *effectively-once* in some frameworks. Technically, effectively-once could be a more accurate term, but exactly-once is widely used; thus, we decided to use the term exactly-once as the standard in this book, so you won't be confused in the future.

It seems that exactly versus effectively are close in meaning. What exactly are the differences?

If you still feel that the *looks like* (or *effectively*) part is tricky, it is totally understandable. To help you understand better what it really is, let's steer away and talk a little about an interesting concept next: *idempotency*. Hopefully, it will be helpful in giving you a better idea about what we mean by *effectively*.

A real exactly-once is extremely difficult in distributed systems—for real.

Bonus concept: Idempotent operation

Idempotent operation seems like a loaded term, right? It is a computational and mathematical term that means no matter how many times a function is given a quantity, the output will always be the same. Another way to think about it is: making multiple identical calls to the operation has the *same effect* as making a single call. Clear as mud? No worries. Let's get into one example in the context of a credit card class.

Let's look at two methods of the class: setCardBalance() and charge().

- The setCardBalance() function sets the card balance to a new value specified as the parameter.

- The charge() function adds the new amount to the balance.

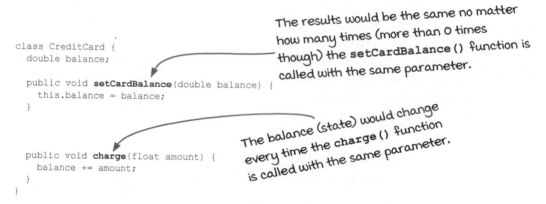

```
class CreditCard {
  double balance;

  public void setCardBalance(double balance) {
    this.balance = balance;
  }

  public void charge(float amount) {
    balance += amount;
  }
}
```

The results would be the same no matter how many times (more than 0 times though) the setCardBalance() function is called with the same parameter.

The balance (state) would change every time the charge() function is called with the same parameter.

One interesting property of the setCardBalance() function is that after it is called once, the state of the credit card object (the card balance) is set to the new value. If the function is then invoked the second time, the balance will still set to the new value again, but the state (the balance) is the same as before. By looking at the card balance, it looks like the function is only called one time because you can't tell if it is called once or more than once. In other words, the function might be called once or more than once, but it is *effectively once*, since the effect is the same. Because of this behavior, the setCardBalance() function is an idempotent operation.

As a comparison, the charge() function is not an idempotent operation. When it is invoked once, the balance will increase by the amount. If the call is repeated for the second time by mistake, the balance will increase again, and the card object will be in a wrong state. Therefore, since the function is not idempotent, it really needs to be called *exactly once* for the state to be correct.

The *exactly-once* semantic in streaming systems works like the setCardBalance() function above. From the states of all the instances in the job, it looks like each event is processed exactly one time, but internally, the event might be processed more than once by each component.

Exactly-once, finally

After learning the real meaning of the semantic and the concept of the idempotent operation, plus knowing the power of returning the accurate results, are you more interested in how exactly-once works now? Exactly-once may sound fancy, but it is really not that complicated. Typically, the exactly-once semantic is supported with checkpointing, which is very similar to the at-least-once support. The difference is that checkpoints are created for both sources and operators, so they can all travel back in time together during a rollback. Note that checkpoints are needed only for the operators with internal states. Checkpoints are not needed for the operators without internal states because there is nothing to recover during a rollback.

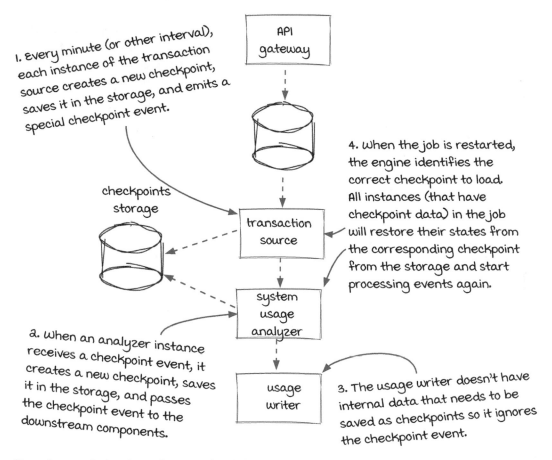

1. Every minute (or other interval), each instance of the transaction source creates a new checkpoint, saves it in the storage, and emits a special checkpoint event.

checkpoints storage

4. When the job is restarted, the engine identifies the correct checkpoint to load. All instances (that have checkpoint data) in the job will restore their states from the corresponding checkpoint from the storage and start processing events again.

2. When an analyzer instance receives a checkpoint event, it creates a new checkpoint, saves it in the storage, and passes the checkpoint event to the downstream components.

3. The usage writer doesn't have internal data that needs to be saved as checkpoints so it ignores the checkpoint event.

Does it sound simple so far? Don't celebrate yet. The state of a source instance is just an offset. But the state of an operator instance could be much more complicated, since it is specific to the logic. For operators, the state could be a simple number, a list, a map, or a complicated data structure. Although streaming engines are responsible for managing the checkpoints data normally, it is important to understand the cost behind the scenes.

State handling code in the system usage analyzer component

With the Streamwork framework, to make the `SystemUsageAnalyzer` component handle the creation and usage of instance state, the changes are similar to the `TransactionSource` we have seen earlier.

- The base class is changed from `Operator` to `StatefulOperator`.

- The `setupInstance()` function takes an extra state parameter.

- A new `getState()` function is added.

```
public abstract class Operator extends Component {
  public abstract void setupInstance(int instance);
  public abstract void getEvents(EventCollector eventCollector);
  public abstract GroupingStrategy getGroupingStrategy();
}
```
A new state object is used to set up the instance.

```
public abstract class StatefulOperator extends Component {
  public abstract void setupInstance(int instance, State state);
  public abstract void apply(Event event, EventCollector eventCollector);
  public abstract GroupingStrategy getGroupingStrategy();
  public abstract State getState();
}
```
This new function is used to extract the state of the instance.

```
class SystemUsageAnalyzer extends StatefulOperator {
  int transactionCount;

  public void setupInstance(int instance, State state) {
    AnalyzerState mstate = (AnalyzerState)state;
    transactionCount = state.count;
    ......
  }
```
When an instance is constructed, a state object is used to initialize the instance.

```
  public void apply(Event event, EventCollector eventCollector) {
    transactionCount++;
```
The count variable changes when events are processed.

```
    eventCollector.add(transactionCount);
  }

  public State getState() {
    AnalyzerState state = new AnalyzerState();
    State.count = transactionCount;
    return state;
  }
}
```
A new state object is created to store instance data periodically.

Note that the API supported by the Streamwork framework is a low-level API to show you how things work internally. Nowadays, most frameworks support higher level APIs, such as functional and declarative APIs. With these new types of APIs, reusable components are designed, so users don't need to worry about the details. You should be able to tell the difference when you start using one in the future.

Comparing the delivery semantics again

All the delivery semantics have their own use cases. Now that we have seen all the delivery semantics, let's compare the differences again (in an overly simplified manner) in one place. We can see from the table that follows it is clear that different delivery semantics have different pros and cons. Sometimes, none of them are perfect for your use case. In those cases, then, you will have to understand the tradeoffs and make the decision accordingly. You may also need to change from one to another when requirements change.

Delivery semantics	At-most-once	At-least-once	Exactly-once
Accuracy	• No accuracy guarantee because of missing events	• No accuracy guarantee because of duplicated events	• (Looks like) accurate results are guaranteed
Latency (when errors happen)	• Tolerant to failures; no delay when errors happen	• Sensitive to failures; potential delay when errors happen	• Sensitive to failures; potential delay when errors happen
Complexity/ resource usage	• Very simple and light weight	• Intermediate (depends on the implementation)	• Complex and heavyweight
Maintenance burden	• Low	• Intermediate	• High
Throughput	• High	• Intermediate	• Low
Code	• No code change is needed	• Some code change is needed	• More code change is needed
Dependency	• No external dependencies	• No external dependencies (with acknowledging)	• Need external storage to save checkpoints

Regarding decisions and tradeoffs, a reasonable concern for people considering choosing at-most-once and at-least-once for benefits like latency and efficiency is that accuracy is not guaranteed. There is a popular technique to avoid this problem that could be helpful to make people feel better: *lambda architecture*. With lambda architecture, a companion batch process is running on the same data to generate accurate results with higher end-to-end latency. Since we have a lot to digest in this chapter, we will talk about it later in more detail in chapter 10.

Summary

In this chapter, we discussed an important new concept in streaming systems: delivery semantics or delivery guarantees. Three types of semantics you can choose for your streaming jobs are:

- *At-most-once*—Each event is guaranteed to be processed no more than once, which means it could be skipped when any failure happens in the streaming jobs.

- *At-least-once*—Events are guaranteed to be processed by the stream jobs, but it is possible that some events will be processed more than once in the face of failures.

- *Exactly-once*—With this semantic, from the results, it looks like each event is processed only once. It is also known as effectively-once.

We discussed the pros and cons of each of these semantics in this chapter and briefly talked about an important technique to support at-least-once and exactly-once in streaming systems: checkpointing. The goal is for you be able to choose the most suitable delivery semantics for your own use cases.

Exercises

1. Which delivery semantic would you choose if you were building the following jobs, and why?

   - Find out the most popular hashtags on Twitter.

   - Import records from a data stream to a database.

2. In this chapter, we have looked at the system usage analyzer component in the system usage job and modified it to be an idempotent operation. What is the usage writer component? Is it an idempotent operation or not?

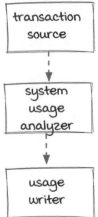

Up next ...

From chapter 2 through chapter 5, quite a few concepts have been introduced. They are the most common and basic concepts you need when you start building streaming systems. In the next chapter, we are going to take a small break and review what we have learned so far. Then, we will jump into more advanced topics like windowing and join operations.

Streaming systems review and a glimpse ahead | 6

In this chapter

- a review of the concepts we've learned

- an introduction of more advanced concepts to be covered in the chapters in part 2

> *Technology makes it possible for people to gain control over everything, except over technology.*
>
> —JOHN TUDOR

After learning the basic concepts in streaming systems in the previous chapters, it is time to take a small break and review them in this chapter. We will also take a peek at the content in the later chapters and get ready for the new adventure.

Streaming system pieces

A *job* is an application that loads incoming data and processes it. All streaming jobs have four different pieces: *event*, *stream*, *source*, and *operator*. Note that these concepts may or may not be named in a similar fashion in different frameworks.

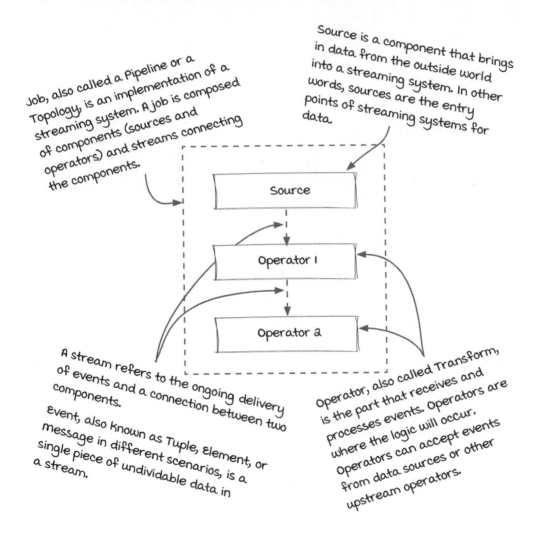

Job, also called a Pipeline or a Topology, is an implementation of a streaming system. A job is composed of components (sources and operators) and streams connecting the components.

Source is a component that brings in data from the outside world into a streaming system. In other words, sources are the entry points of streaming systems for data.

A stream refers to the ongoing delivery of events and a connection between two components.

Event, also known as Tuple, Element, or message in different scenarios, is a single piece of undividable data in a stream.

Operator, also called Transform, is the part that receives and processes events. Operators are where the logic will occur. Operators can accept events from data sources or other upstream operators.

Parallelization and event grouping

Processing events one by one is usually not acceptable in the real world. *Parallelization* is critical for solving problems on a large scale (i.e., it can handle more load). When using parallelization, it is necessary to understand how to route events with a *grouping strategy*.

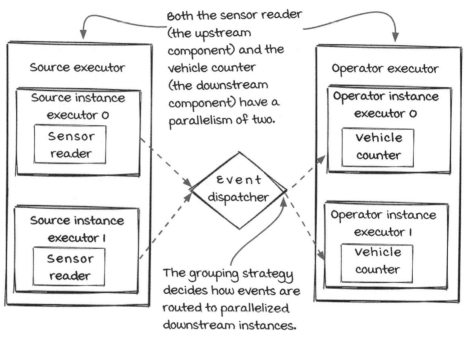

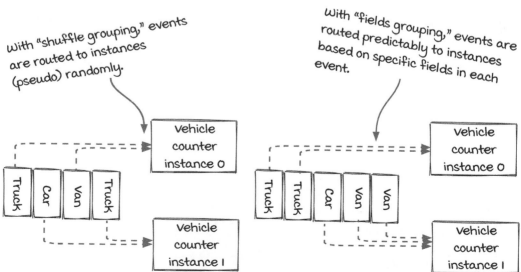

DAGs and streaming jobs

A *DAG*, or directed acyclic graph, is used to represent the logical structure of a streaming job and how data flows through it. In more complicated streaming jobs like the fraud detection system, one component can have multiple upstream components (*fan-in*) and/ or downstream components (*fan-out*).

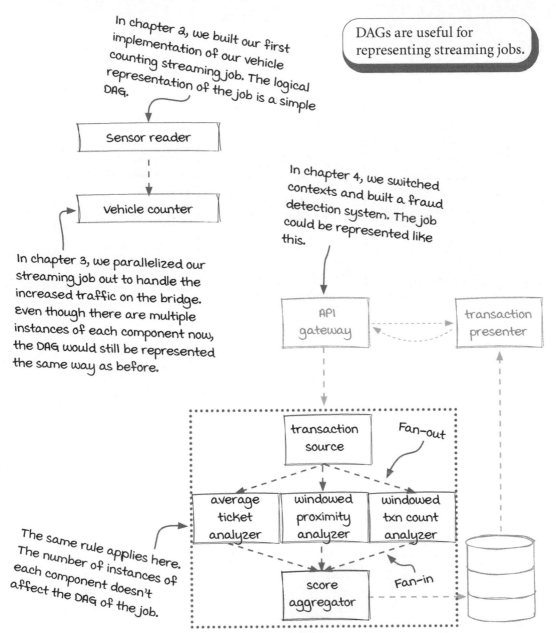

In chapter 2, we built our first implementation of our vehicle counting streaming job. The logical representation of the job is a simple DAG.

DAGs are useful for representing streaming jobs.

In chapter 4, we switched contexts and built a fraud detection system. The job could be represented like this.

In chapter 3, we parallelized our streaming job out to handle the increased traffic on the bridge. Even though there are multiple instances of each component now, the DAG would still be represented the same way as before.

The same rule applies here. The number of instances of each component doesn't affect the DAG of the job.

Sensor reader

vehicle counter

API gateway

transaction presenter

transaction source

Fan-out

average ticket analyzer

windowed proximity analyzer

windowed txn count analyzer

score aggregator

Fan-in

Delivery semantics (guarantees)

After understanding the basic pieces of streaming jobs, we stepped back and looked at the problems to solve again. What are the requirements? What is important for the problem? Throughput, latency, and/or accuracy?

After the requirements are clear, *delivery semantics* need to be configured accordingly. There are three delivery semantics to choose from:

- *At-most-once*—Streaming jobs will process events with no guarantees of being successfully processed at all.

- *At-least-once*—Streaming jobs guarantee that every event will be successfully processed at least once, but there is no guarantee how many times each event will be processed.

- *Exactly-once*—Streaming jobs guarantee that, it *looks like* each event is processed once and only once. It is also known as *effectively-once*.

The exactly-once guarantees accurate results, but there are some costs that can't be ignored, such as latency and complexity. It is important to understand what requirements are essential for each streaming job in order to choose the right option.

Delivery semantics used in the credit card fraud detection system

In chapter 5, a new system usage job was added into the credit card fraud detection system. It gives a real-time view of the usage of the whole system. The fraud detect job and the new job have different requirements:

- Latency is more important for the original fraud detection job.
- Accuracy is more important for the new system usage job.

As a result, different delivery semantics are chosen for them accordingly.

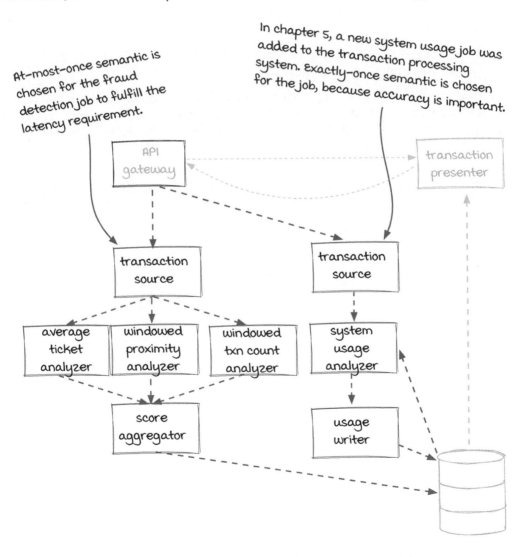

Which way to go from here

The chapters up until now have covered the core concepts of streaming systems. These concepts should get you started building streaming jobs for many purposes in a framework of your choosing.

But they are definitely not all in streaming systems! As you move forward in your career and start to solve bigger, more complex problems, you are likely going to run into scenarios that will require more advanced knowledge of streaming systems. In the following chapters in part 2 of this book, a few more advanced topics will be discussed:

- Windowed computations

- Joining data in real time

- Backpressure

- Stateless and stateful computations

For the basic concepts we have studied in the previous chapters, order is important so far as each chapter built upon the previous. However, in the second part of the book each chapter is more standalone, so you can read the chapters either sequentially or in an order you prefer. To make it easier for you to choose which ones to read first, here is a glimpse ahead of what will be covered in each of the chapters.

Windowed computations

So far, we have been processing events one by one in our examples. However, in the fraud detection job, the analyzers rely on not only the *current* event but also on the information of when, where, and how a card was used *recently* to identify unauthorized card usages. For example, the windowed proximity analyzer identifies fraud by detecting credit cards charged in different locations in a short period of time. How can we build streaming systems to solve these types of problems?

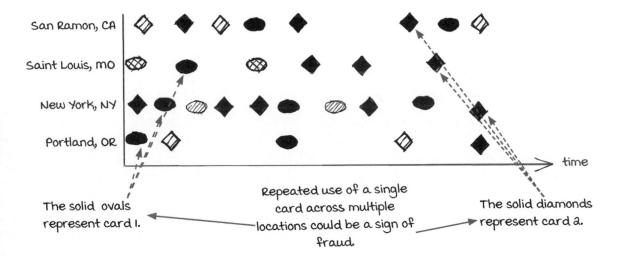

In streaming systems, to slice events into event sets to process, windowed computations will be needed. In chapter 7, we will study different windowing strategies in streaming systems with the windowed proximity analyzer in the fraud detection job.

In addition, windowed computation often has its limitations, and these limitations are important for this analyzer and many other real-world problems. In this chapter, we are also going to discuss a widely used technique: using key-value stores (dictionary-like database systems) to implement windowed operators.

> How do we define what a slice is?

> In streaming systems, windowed operators process event sets instead of individual events.

Joining data in real time

In chapter 8, we will build a new system to monitor the CO_2 emission of all the vehicles in Silicon Valley in real time. Vehicles in the city report their models and locations every minute. These events will be *joined* with other data to generate a real-time CO_2 emission map.

We will keep track of the vehicles going through each zone and aggregate the CO_2 emission results on the fly.

How hard could it be to join data in real-time?

Joining data in real time is harder than you might guess. We will talk about it in chapter 8.

For people who have worked with databases before, *join* shouldn't be a strange concept. It is used when you need to reference data across multiple tables. In streaming systems, there is a similar *join* operator with its own characteristics, and it will be discussed in chapter 8. Note that join is the type of stream fan-in we have mentioned (but skipped) in chapter 4.

Backpressure

After you have a streaming job running to process data, you will (hopefully not too soon) face a problem: computers are not reliable! Well, to be fair, computers are reliable mostly, but typically streaming systems might keep running for years, and many issues can come up.

The team got a request from the banks to review the fraud detection system and provide a report about the reliability of the system. More specifically, will the job stop working when there is any computer or network issue, and will the results be missing or inaccurate? It is a reasonable request, since a lot of money is involved. In fact, even without the request from the banks, it is an important question anyway, right?

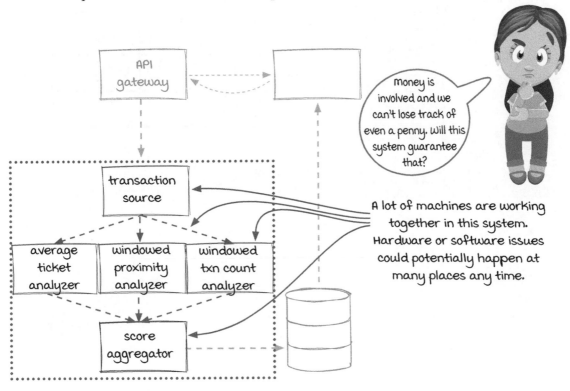

Backpressure is a common self-protection mechanism supported by most streaming frameworks. With backpressure, the processes will slow down temporarily and try to give the system a chance to recover from problems, such as temporary network issues or sudden traffic spikes overloading computers. In some cases, dropping events could be more desirable than slowing down. Backpressure is a useful tool for developers to build reliable systems. In chapter 9, we will see how streaming engines detect and handle issues with backpressure.

Stateless and stateful computations

Maintenance is important for all computer systems. To reduce cost and improve reliability, Sid has decided to migrate the streaming jobs to new and more efficient hardwares. This will be a major maintenance task, and it is critical to proceed carefully to make sure everything works correctly.

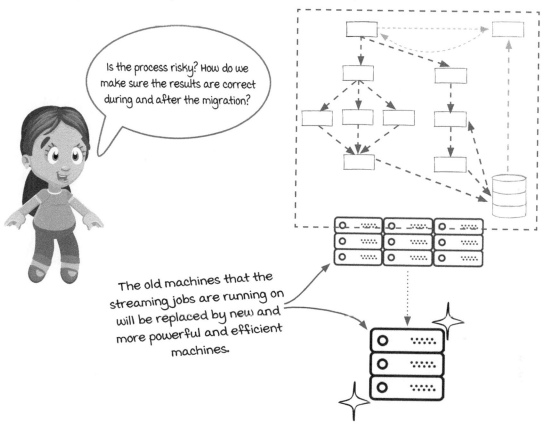

Is the process risky? How do we make sure the results are correct during and after the migration?

The old machines that the streaming jobs are running on will be replaced by new and more powerful and efficient machines.

A debt we have left behind in chapter 5, *delivery semantics,* is stateful component. We have discussed briefly what a stateful component is and how it is used in at-least-once and exactly-once delivery semantics. However, sometimes *less is more*. It is important to understand the tradeoffs to make better technical decisions when building and maintaining streaming systems.

In chapter 10, we will look into how stateful components work internally in greater detail. We will also talk about alternative options to avoid some of the costs and limitations.

Part 2
Stepping up

The second part of this book takes you deep into theory with some framework-agnostic implementations of how streaming systems handle more complex topics. Chapter 7 shows you how to slice never-ending streams of data into meaningful chunks, and chapter 8 lays out the process of joining data in real time. In chapter 9, you find out how streaming systems can help you recover from processing failures, and in chapter 10, you dive into the complexities of managing state in real-time streaming jobs. Finally, chapter 11 quickly recaps the book's content and gives you some guidance on what to do after reading this book.

Windowed computations | 7

In this chapter

- standard windowing strategies

- time stamps in events

- windowing watermark and late events

> ❝ *The attention span of a computer is only as long as its power cord.* ❞
>
> —UNKNOWN

In the previous chapters, we built a streaming job to detect fraudulent credit card transactions. There could be many analyzers that use different models, but the basic idea is to compare the transaction with the previous activities on the same card. Windowing is designed for this type of work, and we are going to learn the windowing support in streaming systems in this chapter.

Slicing up real-time data

As the popularity of the team's new product has grown so has the attention of new types of hackers. A group of hackers has started a new scheme involving gas stations.

Here's how it works: They capture an innocent victim's card information and duplicate it from multiple new physical credit cards. From there, the attackers will send the newly created fraudulent cards out to others in the group and orchestrate spending money on the same credit card from multiple locations across the world at the same time to purchase gas. They hope that by charging the card all at once, the card holder will not notice the charges until it's too late. The result is free gas. Why do they go to a global scale to try and get free tanks of gas? We can consider this a mystery.

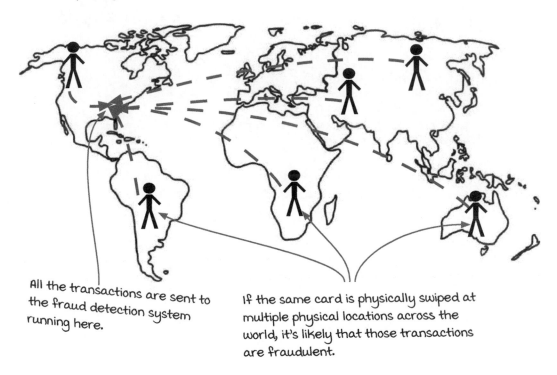

All the transactions are sent to the fraud detection system running here.

If the same card is physically swiped at multiple physical locations across the world, it's likely that those transactions are fraudulent.

How do we prevent this scam?

For the purposes of this book, we are going to use round numbers for easy math calculations. We will also assume that the fastest anyone can travel is 500 miles per hour on a plane. Luckily, the team has already thought of this type of scam.

Breaking down the problem in detail

We have two problems that we are trying to solve here. First, we are looking for large jumps of distance within a single credit card. Second, we are looking for large jumps in card usage across multiple credit cards. In the first scenario, we will be looking to mark specific card transactions as fraudulent; in the second one, we will be looking to flag merchants (gas stations) as under attack by these menacing gas thieves.

Because of the max amount of travel per hour (500 mph), it's safe to assume that someone cannot physically swipe their card in San Ramon, California, then two hours later swipe their card in Saint Louis, Missouri, because the distance traveled in 2 hours is greater than physically possible by a human.

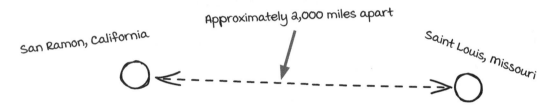

Approximately 2,000 miles apart

San Ramon, California

Saint Louis, Missouri

Here's our formula:

```
final double maxMilesPerHour = 500;
final double distanceInMiles = 2000;
final double hourBetweenSwipes = 2;

if (distanceInMiles > hourBetweenSwipe * maxMilesPerHour) {
  // mark this transaction as potentially fraudulent
}
```

How does the analyzer correlate a current transaction with older transactions in real time?

Breaking down the problem in detail (continued)

This hacker group in particular likes to create massive worldwide attacks—all filling up cars with gas. It's important to look at the behaviors of the entire credit card system as well as one credit card in the system. When these large-scale gas station attacks happen, we need some way to block stores from processing any credit cards that are being attacked to further enhance the security of the system. Study the diagram below that uses a few US cities as examples for locations from which a card could be charged.

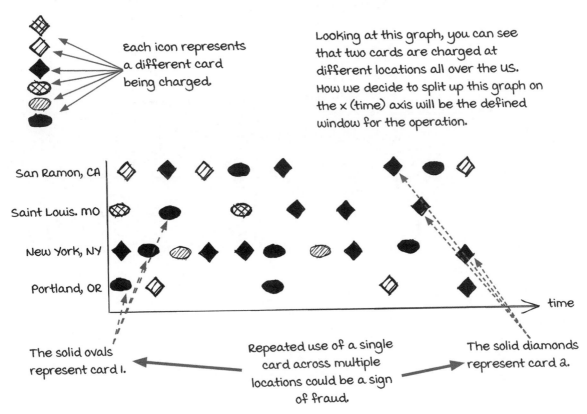

We have two ways to prevent this type of scam:

- We can block individual credit cards from being charged.
- We can block gas stations from processing any credit cards.

But what tools do we have in our streaming systems to help us detect fraudulent activity?

Two different contexts

To address our two different ways of preventing fraud, let's look at the graph from a previous page to further show how we can split up the context. Remember that the windowed proximity analyzer looks for fraud within the context of single credit cards, and the new analyzer works within the context of stores.

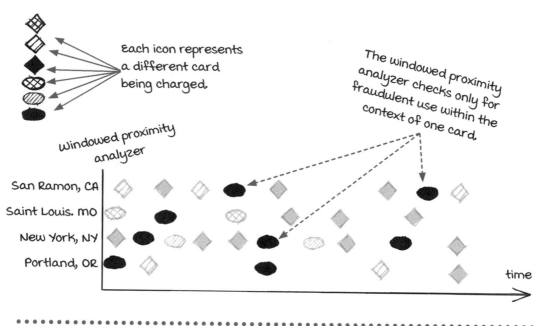

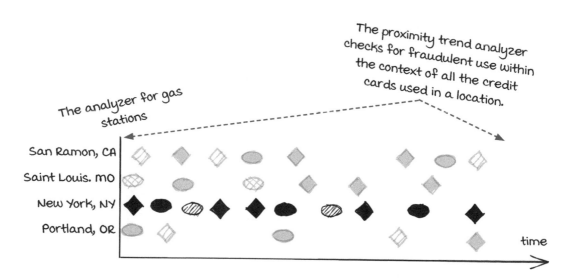

Windowing in the fraud detection job

Most of the analyzer components in the fraud detection job use some type of *window* (we will discuss this next) to compare the current transaction against the previous ones. In this chapter, we are going to focus on the *windowed proximity analyzer*, which detects individual credit cards being swapped in different locations. For the gas stations, we are going to leave it to our smart readers.

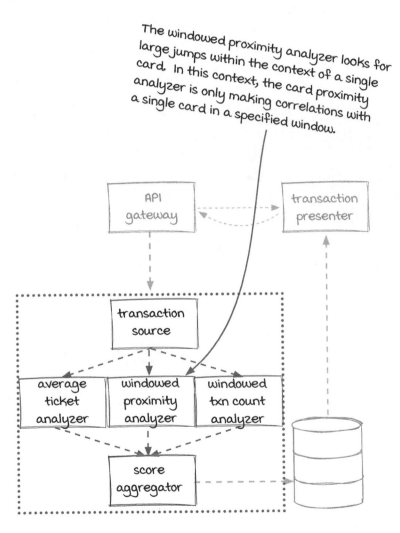

What exactly are windows?

Since the credit card transactions are constantly running through the system, it can be challenging to create cut-off points or segments of data to process. After all, how do you choose an end to something that is potentially infinite, such as a data stream?

Using windows in streaming systems allows developers to slice up the endless stream of events into chunks for processing. Note that the slicing can be either *time-based* (temporal) or *event count-based* in most cases. We are going to use time-based windows in context later, since they fit our scenarios better.

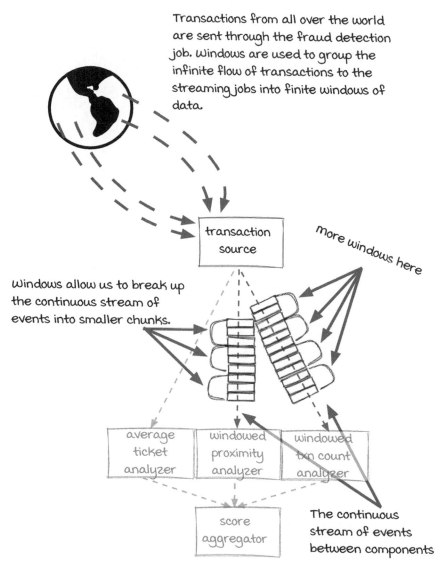

Transactions from all over the world are sent through the fraud detection job. Windows are used to group the infinite flow of transactions to the streaming jobs into finite windows of data.

transaction source

more windows here

Windows allow us to break up the continuous stream of events into smaller chunks.

average ticket analyzer

windowed proximity analyzer

windowed txn count analyzer

score aggregator

The continuous stream of events between components

Looking closer into the window

What we've done with streaming systems so far in this book has been on a per-event, or individual, basis. This method works well for many cases, but it could have some limitations as you start to get into more complex problems. In many other cases, it can be useful to group events via some type of interval to process. Check out the diagrams below to learn a little more about the very basic concept of windowing.

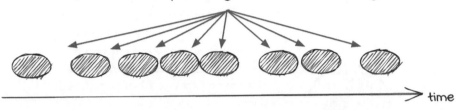

Before, we have been processing each element individually.

time

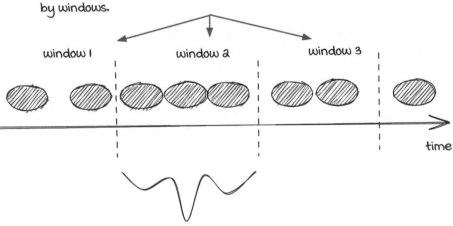

In this chapter, we will process events in groups divided by windows.

window 1   window 2   window 3

time

Note that window size can be defined by a time period or number of elements. It is defined by the developers.

New concept: Windowing strategy

After understanding what windowing is, let's look at how the events are grouped together using a *windowing strategy*. We are going to walk you through three different types of windowing strategies and discuss their differences in the windowed proximity analyzer. The three types of windowing strategies are:

- Fixed window
- Sliding window
- Session window

Often, there is no hard requirement for choosing a *windowing strategy* (how the events are grouped). You will need to talk with other technologists and product owners on your team to make the best decision for the specific problem you are trying to solve.

Fixed windows

The first and most basic window is *fixed window*. Fixed windows are also referred to as *tumbling windows*. Events received from the beginning to the end of each window are grouped as a batch to be processed together. For example, when a *fixed one-minute time window* (also known as a *minutely window*) is configured, all the events within the same one-minute window will be grouped together to be processed. Fixed windows are simple and straightforward, and they are very useful in many scenarios. The question is: do they work for the windowed proximity analyzer?

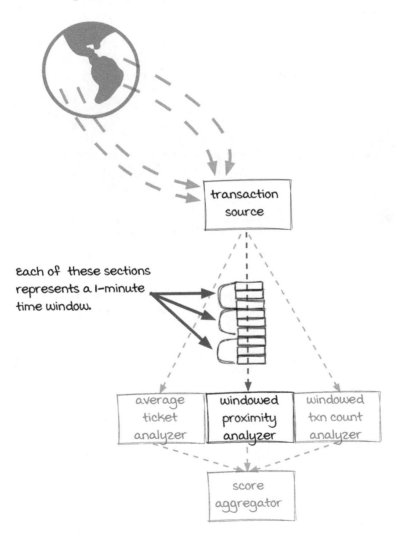

Fixed windows in the windowed proximity analyzer

Here is an example of using a fixed window to look for repeated charges from the same card. To keep things simple, we are just using minutely windows to see what each group of events would look like. The goal is to find out repeated transactions from each card within each one-minute window. We will worry about the other things, such as the 500-miles-per-hour max distance logic later.

It's important to note that using a fixed time window only means the time interval is fixed. It's possible to get more or fewer events in each window based on the number of events flowing through the job.

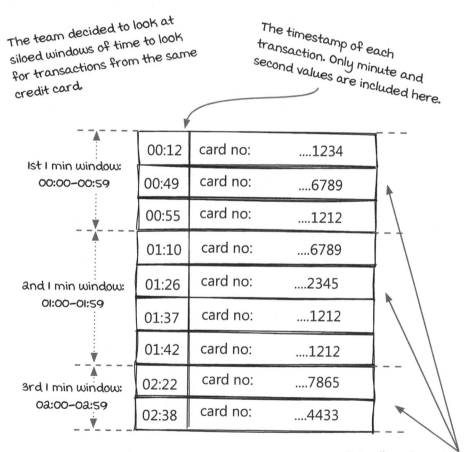

The team decided to look at siloed windows of time to look for transactions from the same credit card.

The timestamp of each transaction. Only minute and second values are included here.

1st 1 min window: 00:00–00:59

00:12	card no:	1234
00:49	card no:	6789
00:55	card no:	1212

2nd 1 min window: 01:00–01:59

01:10	card no:	6789
01:26	card no:	2345
01:37	card no:	1212
01:42	card no:	1212

3rd 1 min window: 02:00–02:59

| 02:22 | card no: | ....7865 |
| 02:38 | card no: | ....4433 |

Even though each window time interval is the same, the number of events per window varies.

Detecting fraud with a fixed time window

Let's look at how the card proximity analyzer would behave using fixed time windows. The amount of transactions per window has been limited to only a few, so we can learn the concepts of windowing most easily.

If you look closely at this diagram, it will hopefully be more clear how fixed time windows would affect potential fraud scores. By running fixed time windows, you are just cutting off other transactions that run through the system, even if they are only a second outside of the window. Do you think this is the windowing type we should use to most accurately detect fraud?

The answer is that a fixed time window is not ideal for our problem. If two transactions on the same card are a just few seconds apart, but they fall into two different fixed windows, such as the two transactions from the card ....6789, we won't be able to run the card proximity function on them.

In this window, there is no repeated card, so no fraud here.

Card ....1212 has a duplicated charge in the same window. Our card proximity function would be run to assess the possibility of fraud.

In this window, there is no repeated card, so no fraud here.

00:12	card no:	1234
00:49	card no:	6789
00:55	card no:	1212
01:10	card no:	6789
01:26	card no:	2345
01:37	card no:	1212
01:42	card no:	1212
02:22	card no:	7865
02:38	card no:	4433

The two transactions on the card ....6789 are 21 seconds apart, but they belong to two different fixed windows.

And these two transactions on the card ....1212 have the same issue.

Looks like the fraud score won't be accurate if we just cut off events from being included in our fixed windows.

Fixed windows: Time vs. count

Before moving forward to the next windowing strategy, let's take a look at two types of fixed windows first:

- Time windows are defined by an unchanging interval of time.
- Count windows are defined by an unchanging interval of number of events processed.

Time Windows. In this case the interval is 3 minutes. The number of events in each window can differ.

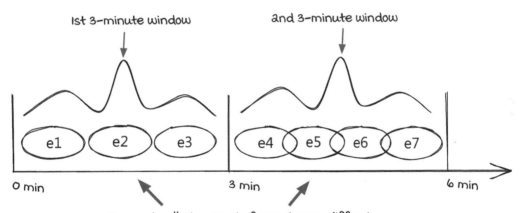

1st 3-minute window

2nd 3-minute window

0 min   3 min   6 min

Remember!! The count of events can differ in time-based windows. It's completely acceptable to have 3 in one window and 4 in another.

With count Windows, the number of events in each window will be the same. The time intervals of each window can differ.

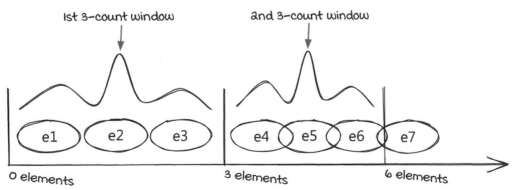

1st 3-count window

2nd 3-count window

0 elements   3 elements   6 elements

Sliding windows

Another widely supported windowing strategy is a *sliding window*. Sliding windows are similar to fixed time windows but different in that they also have a defined *slide interval*. A new window is created every slide interval instead of when the previous window ends. The window interval and slide interval allow windows to overlap, and because of this, each event can be included into more than one window. Technically, we can say that a fixed window is a special case of sliding window in which the window interval equals the slide interval.

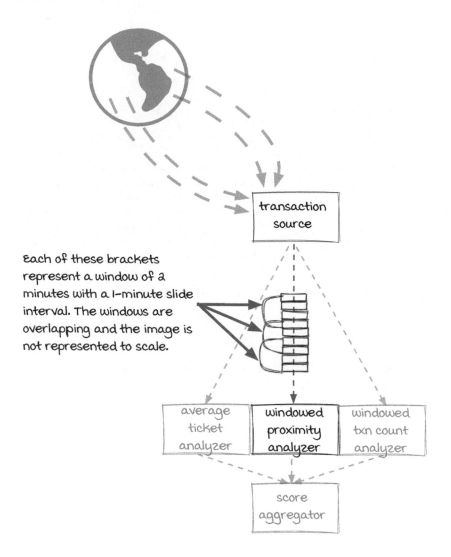

Sliding windows: Windowed proximity analyzer

We could use a sliding window to look for repeated charges from the same card in overlapping windows of time. The diagram below shows one-minute sliding windows with 30-second slide intervals. When using sliding windows it's important to understand that an event may be included in more than one window.

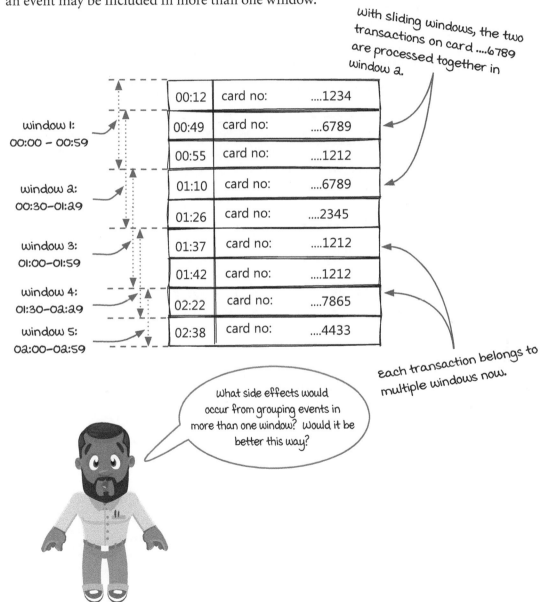

Detecting fraud with a sliding window

Sliding windows differ from fixed windows, as they overlap each other based on the specified interval. The slide provides a nice mechanism for a more evenly distributed aggregation of events to determine whether a transaction is to be marked as fraudulent or not. Sliding windows help with the lopping off of events, as we saw in fixed windows.

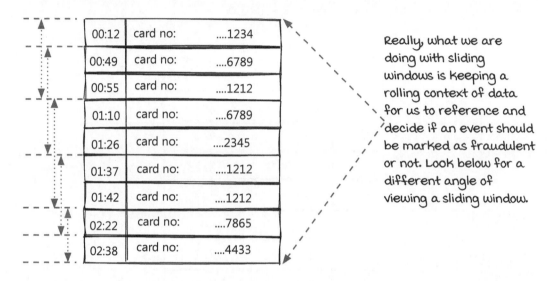

Really, what we are doing with sliding windows is keeping a rolling context of data for us to reference and decide if an event should be marked as fraudulent or not. Look below for a different angle of viewing a sliding window.

As the window slides, the data elements it can make operations on changes. The gradual slide or advance of what data it can reference offers a more gradual and consistent view of data.

Pop Quiz!

Do you think the overlap on sliding windows would be better or worse for calculating averages? Why?

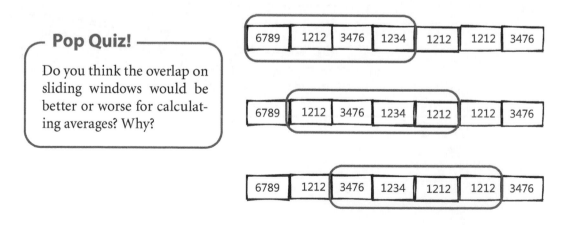

Session windows

The last windowing strategy we would like to cover before jumping into the implementation is the *session window*. A session represents a period of activity separated by a defined gap of inactivity, and it can be used to group events. Typically, session windows are key-specific, instead of global for all events like the fixed and sliding windows.

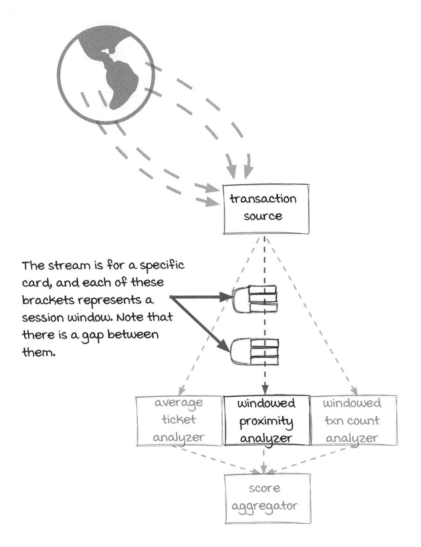

Session windows (continued)

Session windows are typically defined with a timeout, which is the max duration for a
session to stay open. We can imagine there is a timer for each key. If there are no events
under the key received before the timer times out, the session window will be closed.
Next time, when an event under the key is received, a new session will be started. In the
diagram below, let's take look at the transactions from two cards (session windows are
typically key specific, and the key here is the card number). Note that the threshold for
the gap of inactivity is 10 minutes.

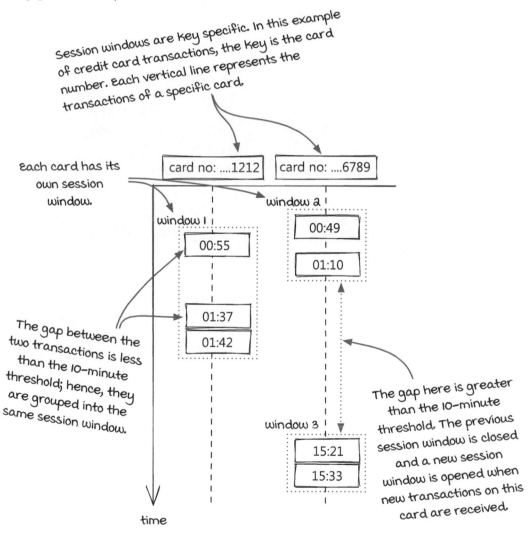

Detecting fraud with session windows

Session windows are relatively less straightforward than fixed and sliding windows. Let's try to see how session windows can potentially be used in the fraud detection job. We don't have an analyzer with this model in the current design; however, it could be a good one to consider and a good example to demonstrate one use case of session windows.

When someone is shopping in a mall, typically they spend some time looking and comparing first. After some time, finally a purchase is made with a credit card. Afterwards, the shopper may visit another store and repeat the pattern or take a break (you know, shopping can be strenuous). Either way, it is likely that there will be a period of time where the card is not swiped.

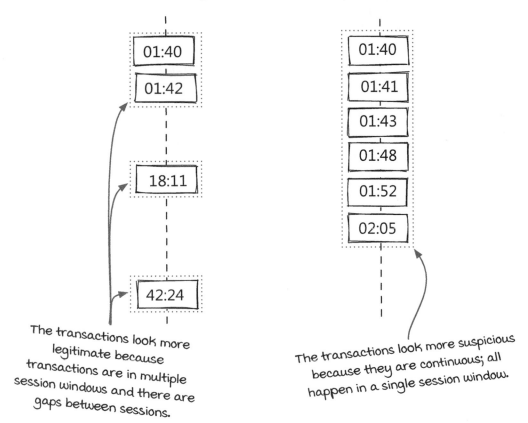

The transactions look more legitimate because transactions are in multiple session windows and there are gaps between sessions.

The transactions look more suspicious because they are continuous; all happen in a single session window.

Therefore, if we look at the two card transaction timelines above, the timeline to the left looks more legitimate than the one to the right, because only one or two transactions happen in each short period of time (session window), and there are gaps between the purchases. In the timeline to the right, the card has been charged many times continuously without a reasonable gap.

Summary of windowing strategies

We have gone through the concepts of three different windowing strategies. Let's put them together and compare the differences. Note that time-based windows are used in the comparison, but fixed and sliding windows can be event count-based as well.

- *Fixed windows* (or tumbling windows) have fixed sizes, and a new window starts when the previous one closes. The windows don't overlap with each other.

- *Sliding windows* have the same fixed size, but a new one starts before the previous one closes. Therefore, the windows overlap with each other.

- *Session windows* are typically tracked for each key. Each window is opened by activity and closed by a gap of inactivity.

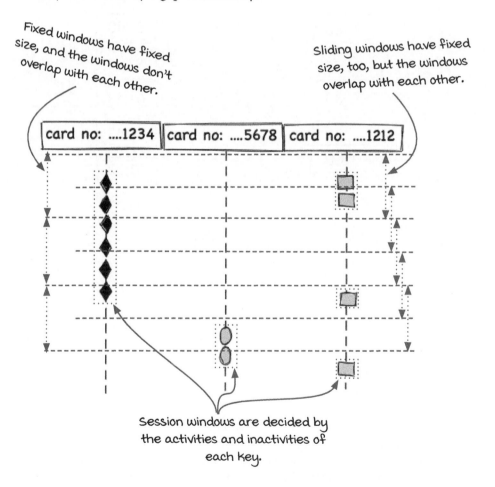

Fixed windows have fixed size, and the windows don't overlap with each other.

Sliding windows have fixed size, too, but the windows overlap with each other.

card no: 1234   card no: 5678   card no: 1212

Session windows are decided by the activities and inactivities of each key.

Slicing an event stream into data sets

After all the concepts, let's move on to the implementation-related topics. With window-ing strategies, events are processed in small sets instead of isolated events now. Because of the difference, the `WindowedOperator` interface is slightly different from the regular `Operator` interface.

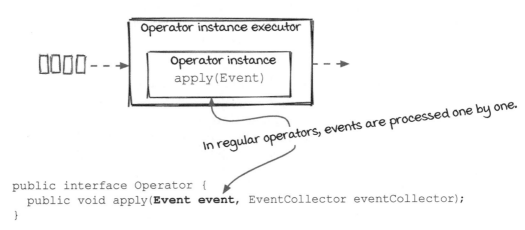

In regular operators, events are processed one by one.

```
public interface Operator {
    public void apply(Event event, EventCollector eventCollector);
}
```

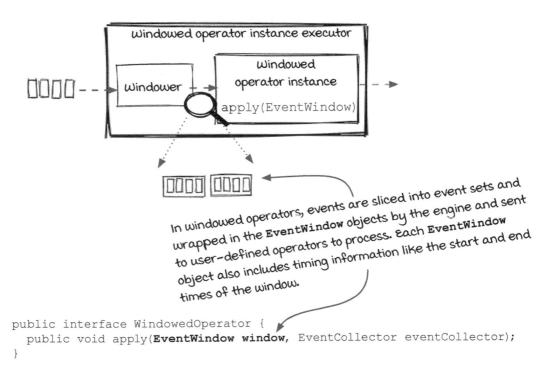

In windowed operators, events are sliced into event sets and wrapped in the `EventWindow` objects by the engine and sent to user-defined operators to process. Each `EventWindow` object also includes timing information like the start and end times of the window.

```
public interface WindowedOperator {
    public void apply(EventWindow window, EventCollector eventCollector);
}
```

Windowing: Concept or implementation

Fundamentally, a windowed operator is a mechanism to reorganize events as event sets, and streaming engines are typically responsible for managing the event sets. Compared to the jobs we have seen before this chapter, the streaming engines need more resources for windowed operators. The more events there are in each window, the more resource the streaming engines need. In other words, stream jobs are more efficient when the window sizes are small. However, real world problems are often not that ideal. *C'est la vie.*

Some of you may have already seen the issues with using windowed operators to implement the windowed proximity analyzer in the fraud detection job:

- In this analyzer, we would like to track transactions far away from each other and compare the distance and the time between them. More specifically, if the distance is greater than 500 miles per hour times the time difference between two transactions in hours, the operator will mark the transaction as *likely fraudulent.* So do we need a multi-hour long sliding window? Hundreds of billions of transactions could be collected in this window, which could be expensive to track and process.

- Things become more complicated when the 20-millisecond latency requirement is taken into consideration. With a sliding window, there is a *slide interval* to determine, and it needs to be short. If this interval is too long (for example, one second), most transactions (those that happened in the first 980 milliseconds in the second) are going to miss the 20-millisecond deadline.

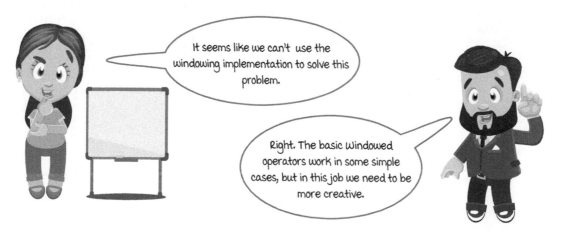

In conclusion, the concepts are useful for us to choose the right strategy for the problem, but to implement the analyzer in the fraud detection job, we need to be more creative than simply relying on the frameworks. Note that this is not a rare case in real-world systems. Streaming frameworks are mainly designed for fast and lightweight jobs, but life is never perfect and simple.

Another look

Now let's see how the team solves the challenge and stops the gas thieves. The first step is to understand how exactly the transactions are processed in the windowed proximity analyzer.

In this operator, we want to track the times and locations of transactions on each card and verify that the time and distance between any two transactions don't violate the rule. However, "any two transactions in the window" isn't really a necessary statement. The problem can be simplified if we look at it in a slightly different way: at any time when a new transaction comes in, we can compare the time and location of the transaction with *the previous transaction on the same card* and apply our equation. The past transactions on the card, before the previous one, and all the transactions on the other cards have no effect on the result and can be ignored.

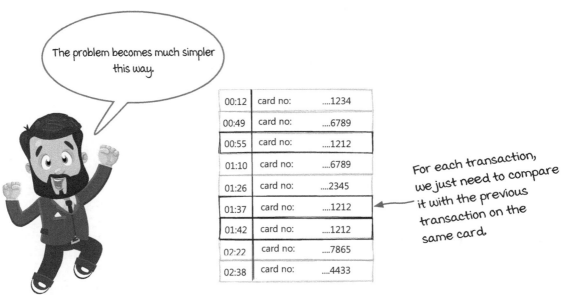

Now since we have the equation already, the problem becomes pretty straightforward: how do we find the previous transaction on the same card?

You might be wondering: what about the sliding window? Good question, and let's take another look at it too. The perimeter of the earth is about 25,000 miles, so 12,500 miles is the max distance between any two places on earth. Based on our 500 miles per hour traveling speed rule, a person can travel to any place on earth within about 25 hours. Therefore, transactions older than 25 hours don't need to be calculated. The updated version of the problem to solve is: *how can we find out the previous transaction on the same card within the past 25 hours?*

Key–value store 101

After thinking about the calculation within the windowed proximity analyzer operator, they decided to use a key–value store system to implement it. This is a very useful technique to build windowed operators without using the standard windowed operator support in streaming frameworks, so let's talk about it here.

A *key–value store* (also known as a *K–V store*) is a data storage system designed for storing and retrieving data objects with keys. It has been a very popular paradigm in the past decade. In case you are not familiar with the term, it works just like a dictionary in which each record can be uniquely identified by a specific key. Unlike the more traditional (and better known) relational databases, the records are totally independent from each other in key–value stores.

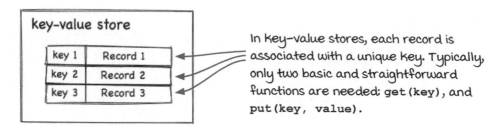

In key-value stores, each record is associated with a unique key. Typically, only two basic and straightforward functions are needed: get(key), and put(key, value).

Why would we want storing systems that have fewer functions? The major advantages are performance and scalability. Because key–value stores don't need to keep track of the relations between different records, rows, and columns, the internal calculations can be a lot simpler than the traditional databases. As a result, operations like reading and writing run much faster. And because the records are independent of each other, it is also much easier to distribute data on multiple servers and make it work together to provide a key–value store service that can handle a huge amount of data. The two advantages are important for the fraud detection system as well as many other data processing systems.

Another interesting feature supported by some key–value stores is *expiration*. An expiration time could be provided when a key–value pair is added into the store. When the expiration time comes, the key–value pair will be removed automatically from the system and the occupied resources will be freed. This feature is very convenient for windowed operators in streaming systems (more specifically, the "within the past 25 hours" part of our problem statement).

Implement the windowed proximity analyzer

With the help of this key–value store, streaming engines don't need to keep and track all the events in the windows in memory. The responsibility has been returned to the system developers. The bad news is: the usage of a key–value store can be different from case to case. There is no simple formula to follow when implementing windowing strategies with key–value stores. Let's take a look at the windowed proximity analyzer as an example.

In the analyzer, we need to compare the time and location of each transaction with the previous transaction on the same card. The current transaction is in the incoming event, and the previous transaction for each card needs to be kept in the key–value store. The key is the card id, and the value is the time and location (to keep it simple, in the source code that follows the whole event is stored as the value).

```
public class WindowedProximityAnalyzer implements Operator {
  final static double maxMilesPerHour = 500;
  final static double distanceInMiles = 2000;
  final static double hourBetweenSwipes = 2;
  final KVStore store;
```

Operator instead of WindowedOperator is used here.

```
  public setupInstance(int instance) {
    store = setupKVStore();
  }
```

Set up the key-value store.

```
  public void apply(Event event, EventCollector eventCollector) {
    TransactionEvent transaction = (TransactionEvent) event;
    TransactionEvent prevTransaction = kvStore.get(transaction.getCardId());
```

The previous transaction is loaded from the key-value store.

```
    boolean result = false;
    if (prevTransaction != null) {
      double hourBetweenSwipe =
          transaction.getEventTime() - prevTransaction.getEventTime();
      double distanceInMiles = calculateDistance(transaction.getLocation(),
          prevTransaction.getLocation());

      if(distanceInMiles > hourBetweenSwipe * maxMilesPerHour) {
        // Mark this transaction as potentially fraudulent.
        result = true;
      }
    }
```

Fraudulent transaction is detected.

```
    eventCollector.emit(new AnazlyResult(event.getTransactionId(), result));
    kvStore.put(transaction.getCardId(), transaction);
  }
}
```

The current transaction is stored into the key-value store using the card id as the key. The previous value is replaced now.

Event time and other times for events

There is one more concept we will cover before wrapping up this chapter. In the code of the windowed proximity analyzer, there is one important piece we would like to zoom in and take a closer look at.

```
transaction.getEventTime();
```

So what is *event time*? Are there other *times*? *Event time* is the time at which the event actually occurs. Most processes on the event don't happen immediately. Instead, after the event has occurred, it is normally collected and sent to some backend systems later, and then even later it is really processed. All these things happen at different times, so yes, there are quite a few other times. Let's use our simple traffic monitoring system as the example and look at the important times related to an event.

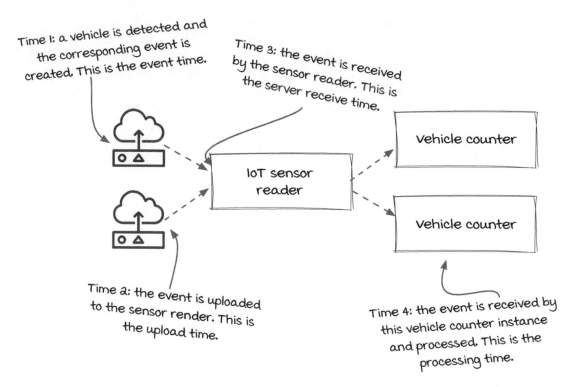

Among all the times, the most important ones for each event are *event time* and *processing time*. Event time for an event is like the birthday for a person. Processing time, on the other hand, is the time at which the event is being processed. In the fraud detection system, what we really care about is the time when the card is swiped, which is the *event time* of the transaction. Event time is typically included in the event objects so that all the calculations on the event have the same time to get the consistent results.

Windowing watermark

Event time is used in many windowed computations, and it is important to understand the gap between event time and processing time. Because of the gap, the windowing strategies we have learned in this chapter aren't as straightforward as they look.

If we look at the traffic monitor system as an example and configure the vehicle counter operator with simple fixed windows to count the number of vehicles detected in each minute, what would be the open and close times for each window? Note that the time for each event to arrive at the vehicle counter operator instances (the processing time) is a little *after* it is created in an IoT sensor (the event time). If the window is closed exactly when the end of the window comes, the events occurring near the end of the window on the IoT sensors will be missing because they haven't been received by the counter instances yet. Note that they can't be put into the next window because, based on the event time, they belong to the already-closed window.

A vehicle might be detected here at the end of the 1-minute time window.

If the window is closed at exactly the end of the time window, some vehicles detected by the IoT sensors could be missing because they haven't arrived here yet.

Vehicle counter

IoT sensor reader

Vehicle counter

The solution to avoid missing events is to keep the window open for a little longer and wait for the events to be received. This extra waiting time is commonly known as the *windowing watermark*.

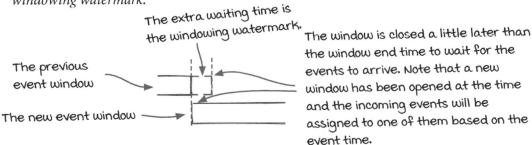

The extra waiting time is the windowing watermark.

The previous event window

The new event window

The window is closed a little later than the window end time to wait for the events to arrive. Note that a new window has been opened at the time and the incoming events will be assigned to one of them based on the event time.

If we look back at the implementation of the windowed proximity analyzer, the watermark is another reason the standard windowed operator is not ideal for the case. Leaving extra time before processing event sets would introduce extra latency and make the 20-millisecond latency requirement even more challenging to meet.

Late events

The windowing watermark is critical for avoiding missing events and generating completed event sets to process. The concept should be easy to understand, but deciding the waiting time isn't as easy.

For example, in the traffic monitoring system, our IoT sensors work very well. As a result, normally, all the vehicle events are collected successfully within one second. In this case, a one second windowing watermark could be reasonable.

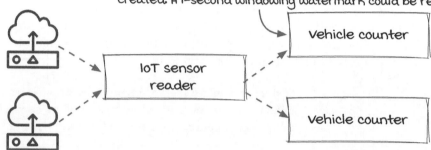

However, the word *normally* might trigger an alert. Earlier in the book, we mentioned a few times that one major challenge in building any distributed system is failure handling. It is often a good habit to ask: what if it doesn't work as expected? Even in a simple system like this one, events could be delayed to be later than one second if something goes wrong—for example, the sensor or the reader could slow down temporarily, or the network could be throttled if the connection is not stable. When this delay happens, the events received after the corresponding window has been closed are known as *late events*. What can we do about them?

Sometimes, dropping these late events could be an option, but in many other cases, it is important for these events to be handled correctly. Most real-world streaming frameworks provide mechanisms to handle these late events, but we will not go into more detail, as the handling is framework-specific. For now, the key takeaway is to keep these late events in mind and not forget about them.

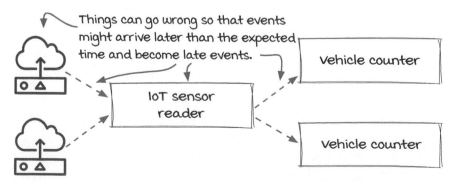

Summary

Windowed computation is critical in streaming systems because it is the way to slice isolated events into event sets to process. In this chapter, we have discussed three standard windowing strategies widely supported by most streaming frameworks:

- Fixed windows
- Sliding windows
- Session windows

The basic support in streaming frameworks has its own limitations and may not work in many scenarios. Therefore, in addition to the concepts and how the streaming frameworks handle the windowed operators, we have also learned how to use a key–value store to simulate a windowed operator and overcome the limitations.

At the end of the chapter, we also covered three related concepts that are important when solving real-world problems:

- Different times related to each event, including event time versus processing time
- Windowing watermarks
- Late events

Exercise

1. At the beginning of the chapter, we mentioned that we have two ways to prevent fraudulent credit card transactions:

   • We can block individual credit cards from being charged.

   • We can block gas stations from processing any credit cards.

   Afterward, we focused on detecting issues on individual credit cards but haven't paid much attention to the second option. The exercise for you is: how can we detect suspicious gas stations, so we can block them from processing credit cards?

In this chapter

* correlating different types of events in real time

* when to use inner and outer joins

* applying windowed joins

> ❝ *An SQL query goes into a bar, walks up to two tables, and asks, can I join you?* ❞
>
> —Anonymous

If you have ever used any SQL (structured query language) database, most likely you have used, or at least learned about, the *join* clause. In the streaming world, the join operation may not be as essential as it is in the database world, but it is still a very useful concept. In this chapter, we are going to learn how join works in a streaming context. We will use the join clause in databases to introduce the calculation and then talk about the details in streaming systems. If you are familiar with the clause, please feel free to skip the introduction pages.

Joining emission data on the fly

Well what do you know? The chief got lucky and fell into an opportunity of tracking the emissions of cars in Silicon Valley, California. Nice, right?

Well, with every great opportunity comes challenges. The team is going to need to find a way to join events from vehicles in specific city locations along with the vehicles' estimated emission rates on the fly. How will they do it? Let's check it out.

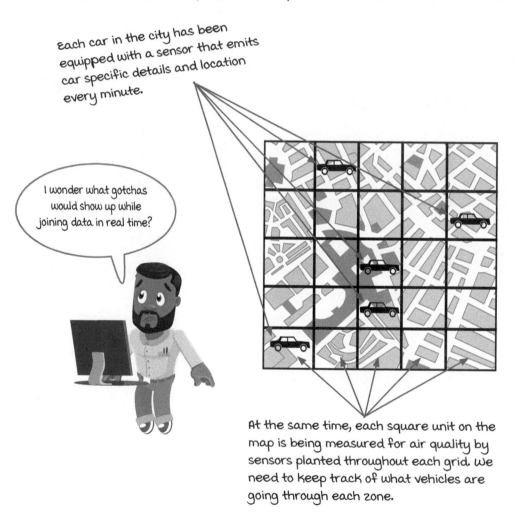

Each car in the city has been equipped with a sensor that emits car specific details and location every minute.

I wonder what gotchas would show up while joining data in real time?

At the same time, each square unit on the map is being measured for air quality by sensors planted throughout each grid. We need to keep track of what vehicles are going through each zone.

The emissions job version 1

They have already implemented a first version of the emissions job. The interesting part of the job is the data store to the right of the emission resolver. It is a static lookup table used by the emission resolver to search for the emission data of each vehicle. Note that we assume that the vehicles with the same make, model, and year have the same emissions in this system.

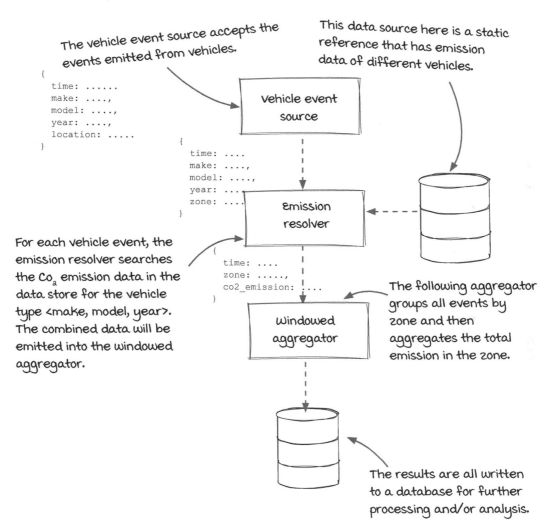

The vehicle event source accepts the events emitted from vehicles.

This data source here is a static reference that has emission data of different vehicles.

```
{
  time: ......
  make: ....,
  model: ....,
  year: ....,
  location: .....
}
```

```
{
  time: ....
  make: ....,
  model: ....,
  year: ...
  zone: ....
}
```

Vehicle event source

Emission resolver

For each vehicle event, the emission resolver searches the CO_2 emission data in the data store for the vehicle type <make, model, year>. The combined data will be emitted into the windowed aggregator.

```
{
  time: ....
  zone: ....,
  co2_emission: ....
}
```

Windowed aggregator

The following aggregator groups all events by zone and then aggregates the total emission in the zone.

The results are all written to a database for further processing and/or analysis.

The emission resolver

The key component in this job is the emission resolver. It takes a vehicle event, looks up the emission data for the vehicle in the data store, and emits an emission event, which contains the zone and emission data. Note that the output emission event contains data from two sources: the incoming vehicle event and the table.

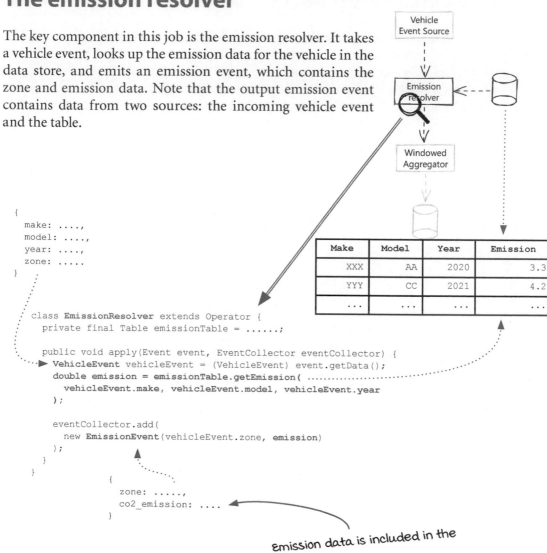

```
{
  make: ....,
  model: ....,
  year: ....,
  zone: .....
}
```

```
class EmissionResolver extends Operator {
  private final Table emissionTable = ......;

  public void apply(Event event, EventCollector eventCollector) {
    VehicleEvent vehicleEvent = (VehicleEvent) event.getData();
    double emission = emissionTable.getEmission( ..................................
      vehicleEvent.make, vehicleEvent.model, vehicleEvent.year
    );

    eventCollector.add(
      new EmissionEvent(vehicleEvent.zone, emission)
    );
  }
}
```

```
{
  zone: .....,
  co2_emission: ....
}
```

Emission data is included in the output event.

Make	Model	Year	Emission
XXX	AA	2020	3.3
YYY	CC	2021	4.2
...	...	...	...

This operator can be considered a very basic *join* operator, which combines data from different data sources based on related data between them (vehicle make, model, and year). However, the emission data is from a table instead of a stream. Join operators in streaming jobs take it one step further by providing real-time data.

Accuracy becomes an issue

The job works OK in general, and it generates real-time emission data successfully. However, one important factor in the equation is missing: temperature (you know, CO_2 emission varies under different temperatures, and there are different seasons in California too). As a result, the emissions per zone reported by the system are not accurate enough. It is too late to add a temperature sensor to the devices installed on each vehicle now, so it becomes the team's challenge to solve in a different way.

The enhanced emissions job

The team added another data source to bring current temperature events into the job for more accurate reporting. The temperature events are joined with the vehicle events using the zone id. The output *emission events* are then emitted to the emission resolver.

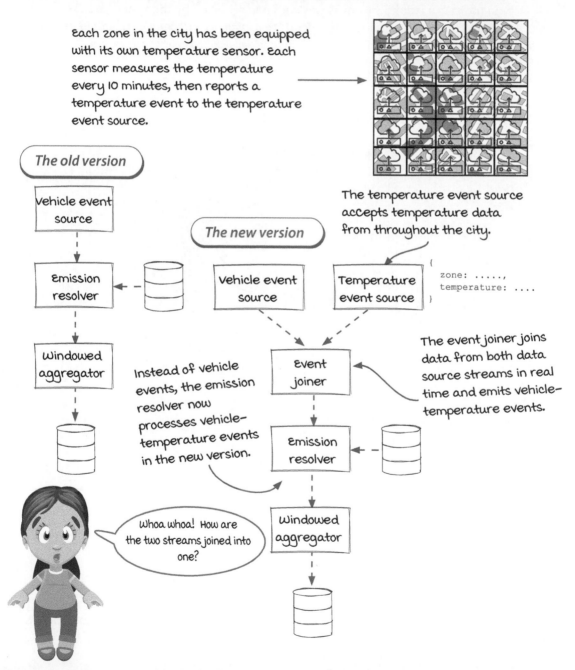

Each zone in the city has been equipped with its own temperature sensor. Each sensor measures the temperature every 10 minutes, then reports a temperature event to the temperature event source.

The old version

Vehicle event source

Emission resolver

Windowed aggregator

The new version

The temperature event source accepts temperature data from throughout the city.

Vehicle event source

Temperature event source

```
{
  zone: .....,
  temperature: ....
}
```

The event joiner joins data from both data source streams in real time and emits vehicle-temperature events.

Event joiner

Emission resolver

Windowed aggregator

Instead of vehicle events, the emission resolver now processes vehicle-temperature events in the new version.

Whoa whoa! How are the two streams joined into one?

Focusing on the join

The major changes in the new version are:

- The extra data source that accepts temperature events into the job
- The event joiner that combines two streams into one

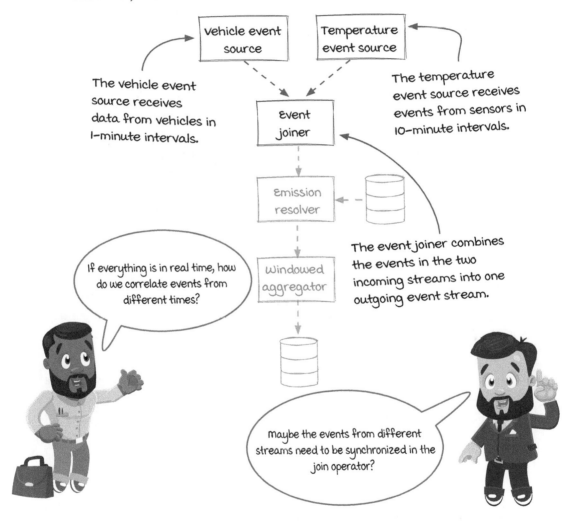

The temperature event source works like normal sources, which are responsible for accepting data into stream jobs. The key change is the newly added event joiner operator, which has two incoming event streams and one outgoing event stream. Events arrive in real time, and it is really rare for the events from the streams to be perfectly synchronized with each other. How should we make different types of events work together in the join operator? Let's dig into it.

What is a join again?

It's probably natural to think of SQL when someone refers to a join operator. After all, *join* is a term that comes from the relational database world.

A join is an SQL clause where you take a certain number of fields from one table and combine them with another set of fields from another table, or tables, to produce consolidated data. The diagram below shows the join operator in terms of relational databases; the streaming join is discussed in the following pages.

Vehicle event table

make	model	year	zone
XXX	AA	2020	3
YYY	CC	2013	1
ZZZ	DD	2017	2
XXX	AA	2008	1
XXX	BB	2014	1
ZZZ	EE	2021	3
ZZZ	EE	2018	5

Temperature table

zone	temperature
1	95.4
2	94.3
3	95.1
4	95.2
5	95.3

The two tables have a common field: zone. It is the relationship between the tables.

```
SELECT v.time, v.make, v.model, v.year, t.zone, t.temperature
FROM vehicle_events v
INNER JOIN temperature t on v.zone = t.zone;
```

The join results of the above tables could look like this.

Joined table

make	model	year	zone	temperature
XXX	AA	2020	3	95.1
YYY	CC	2013	1	95.4
ZZZ	DD	2017	2	94.3
XXX	AA	2008	1	95.4
XXX	BB	2014	1	95.4
ZZZ	EE	2021	3	95.1
ZZZ	EE	2018	5	95.3

How the stream join works

How can we make joins on data that is constantly moving and being updated? The key is to convert the temperature events into a table.

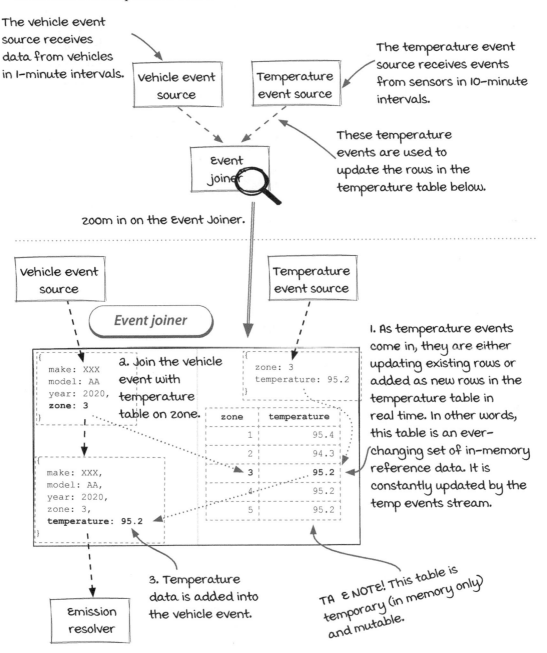

The vehicle event source receives data from vehicles in 1-minute intervals.

The temperature event source receives events from sensors in 10-minute intervals.

These temperature events are used to update the rows in the temperature table below.

zoom in on the Event Joiner.

1. As temperature events come in, they are either updating existing rows or added as new rows in the temperature table in real time. In other words, this table is an ever-changing set of in-memory reference data. It is constantly updated by the temp events stream.

2. Join the vehicle event with temperature table on zone.

3. Temperature data is added into the vehicle event.

TA E NOTE! This table is temporary (in memory only) and mutable.

Stream join is a different kind of fan-in

In chapter 4, we discussed the fraud detection scenario where we aggregated the fraud scores from the upstream analyzers to help determine whether a transaction was fraudulent or not. Is the score aggregator the same type of operator?

The answer is no. In the score aggregator, all the incoming streams have the same event type. The operator doesn't need to know which stream each event is from, and it just applies the same logic. In the event joiner, the events in the two incoming streams are quite different and handled differently in the operator. The score aggregator is a merge operator, and the event joiner is a join operator. They are both *fan-in* operators.

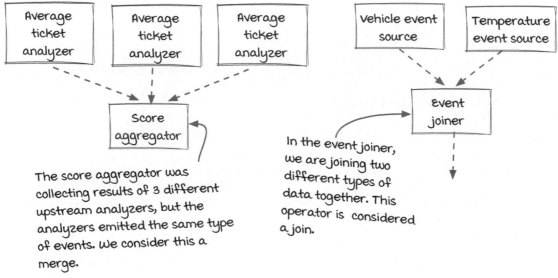

The score aggregator was collecting results of 3 different upstream analyzers, but the analyzers emitted the same type of events. We consider this a merge.

In the event joiner, we are joining two different types of data together. This operator is considered a join.

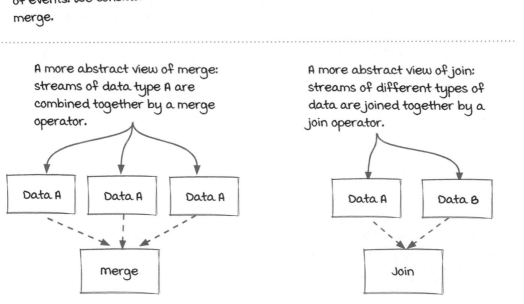

A more abstract view of merge: streams of data type A are combined together by a merge operator.

A more abstract view of join: streams of different types of data are joined together by a join operator.

Vehicle events vs. temperature events

Note that in the join operator, the temperature events are converted into the temporary temperature table, but the vehicle events are processed as a stream. Why convert the temperature events instead of the vehicle events? Why not convert both streams into tables?

These questions can be important when you build your own systems.

First, one outgoing event is expected for each incoming vehicle event. So it makes sense to keep the vehicle events flowing through the operator like a stream. Secondly, it could be more complicated to manage vehicle events as the lookup table. There are many more vehicles than zones in the system, so it would be much more expensive to keep the vehicle events in a temporary in-memory table. Furthermore, only the latest temperature for each zone is important for us, but the vehicle event needs to managed (adding and removing) more carefully, since every event counts.

Anyway, let's put the vehicle events into a table and then join them with the stream of temperature events. There will be multiple rows for each zone in the table, and the results will be event batches instead of individual events.

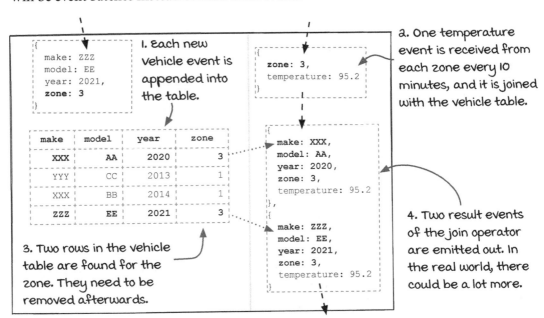

Table: A materialized view of streaming

We are going to be a little more abstract here: what is the relationship between the temperature events and the temperature table? Understanding their relationship could be helpful for us to understand what makes the temperature events special and make better decisions when building new streaming systems.

One important fact about temperature data is that, at any moment, we only need to keep the latest temperature for each zone. This is because we only care about the *latest* temperature of each zone instead of the individual changes or the temperature history. The diagram belows shows the changes of the temperature table before and after two temperature events are received and processed.

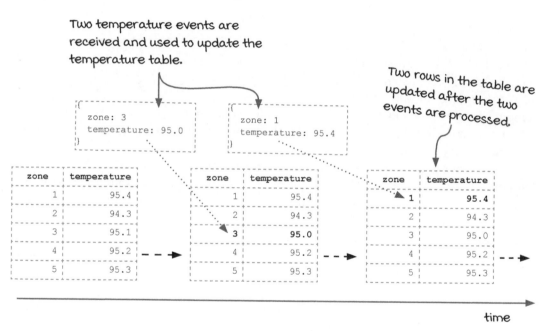

Each temperature event is used to update the table to the latest data. Therefore, each event can be considered a *change* of the data in the table, and the stream of the events is a *change log*.

On the other end, when a join happens, the lookup is performed on the temperature table. At any moment, the temperature table is the result after all the events up to the specific point of time have been applied. Hence, the table is considered a *materialized view* of the temperature events. An interesting effect of a materialized view is that the event interval is not that important anymore. In the example, the interval of temperature events for each zone is 10 minutes, but the system would work the same way whether the interval is one second or one hour.

Vehicle events are less efficient to be materialized

On the other hand, compared to the temperature events, the vehicle events are less efficient to be materialized. Vehicles move around the city all the time, and every single vehicle event for the same vehicle needs to be included in the join instead of the latest one. As a result, the vehicle events table is basically *a list of pending vehicle events* to be processed. Plus, the number of vehicles is likely to be much greater than the number of zones normally. In conclusion, compared to the temperature events, the vehicle events are more complicated and less efficient to be materialized.

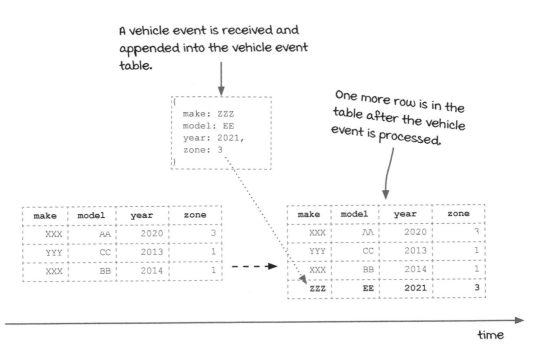

The diagram above shows the vehicle events are *appended* into the table instead of being used to update rows. While there are some things we can do to improve the efficiency, such as adding an extra `count` column and aggregating rows that have the same `make`, `model`, `year`, and `zone` instead of simply appending to the end of the table, it is quite clear that the temperature events are much more convenient to be materialized than the vehicle events. In real-world problems, this property could be an important factor to help decide how the streams should be handled if a join operator is involved.

Data integrity quickly became an issue

The emissions job worked great to help keep track of emissions throughout the area the team planned for. But guess what? People use applications in ways they weren't meant to be used.

Why does this issue happen, and how we can address the issue? We will need to look into different types of join operators.

What's the problem with this join operator?

The key to this join operator is obtaining the temperature for a given `zone`. Let's take a look at a table-centric representation of the operator below. In the diagram, each vehicle event is represented as a row in the table, but keep in mind that the vehicle events are processed one by one like a stream. Another important thing to keep in mind is that the the temperature table is dynamic, and the temperature values could change when new temperature events come in.

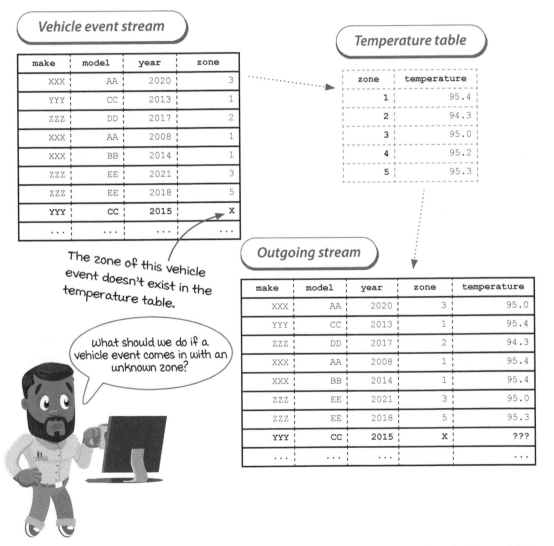

Vehicle event stream

make	model	year	zone
XXX	AA	2020	3
YYY	CC	2013	1
ZZZ	DD	2017	2
XXX	AA	2008	1
XXX	BB	2014	1
ZZZ	EE	2021	3
ZZZ	EE	2018	5
YYY	CC	2015	X
...	...	...	...

Temperature table

zone	temperature
1	95.4
2	94.3
3	95.0
4	95.2
5	95.3

The zone of this vehicle event doesn't exist in the temperature table.

What should we do if a vehicle event comes in with an unknown zone?

Outgoing stream

make	model	year	zone	temperature
XXX	AA	2020	3	95.0
YYY	CC	2013	1	95.4
ZZZ	DD	2017	2	94.3
XXX	AA	2008	1	95.4
XXX	BB	2014	1	95.4
ZZZ	EE	2021	3	95.0
ZZZ	EE	2018	5	95.3
YYY	CC	2015	X	???
...	...	...		...

Now, the data integrity issue is caused by a special case: the zone 7 in the last vehicle event is not in the temperature table. What should we do now? To answer this question, we need to discuss two new concepts first: *inner join* and *outer join*.

Inner join

Inner join processes only vehicle events that have matching zone in the temperature table.

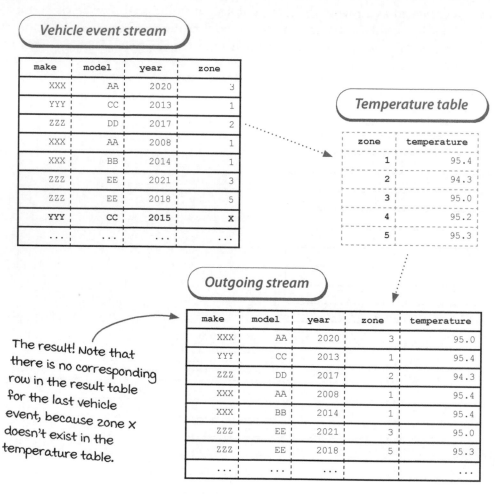

The result! Note that there is no corresponding row in the result table for the last vehicle event, because zone x doesn't exist in the temperature table.

If you look carefully at the above result of the join operator, you will see that there is no row in the result associated with zone 7. This is because inner joins only return rows of data that have matching values, and there is no zone 7 in the temperature table.

With inner join, emission in these unknown zones will be missed, since the vehicle events are dropped. Is this a desirable behavior?

Outer join

Outer joins differ from inner, as they *include* the matching and non-matching rows on a specified column or data. Therefore, no event will be missing, although there could be some incomplete events in the result.

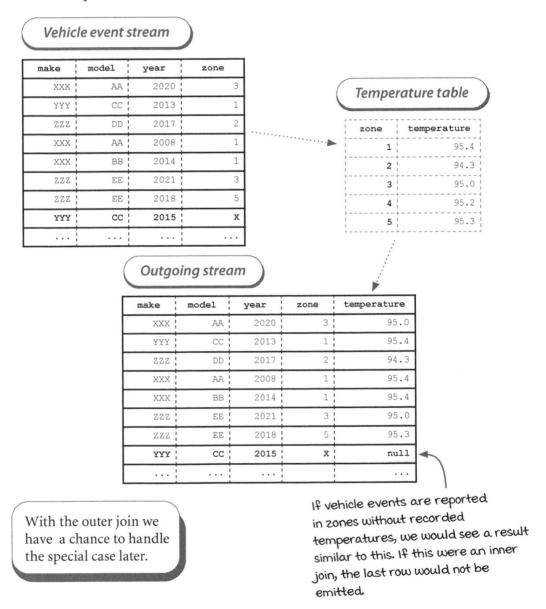

Vehicle event stream

make	model	year	zone
XXX	AA	2020	3
YYY	CC	2013	1
ZZZ	DD	2017	2
XXX	AA	2008	1
XXX	BB	2014	1
ZZZ	EE	2021	3
ZZZ	EE	2018	5
YYY	**CC**	**2015**	**x**
...	...	...	...

Temperature table

zone	temperature
1	95.4
2	94.3
3	95.0
4	95.2
5	95.3

Outgoing stream

make	model	year	zone	temperature
XXX	AA	2020	3	95.0
YYY	CC	2013	1	95.4
ZZZ	DD	2017	2	94.3
XXX	AA	2008	1	95.4
XXX	BB	2014	1	95.4
ZZZ	EE	2021	3	95.0
ZZZ	EE	2018	5	95.3
YYY	**CC**	**2015**	**x**	**null**
...	...	...		...

With the outer join we have a chance to handle the special case later.

If vehicle events are reported in zones without recorded temperatures, we would see a result similar to this. If this were an inner join, the last row would not be emitted.

The team decided to do an outer join to capture non-matching rows and handle them later.

The inner join vs. outer join

Vehicle events that have no matching data in the temperature table are handled differently with inner and outer joins. Inner joins only return results that have matching values on both sides, but outer joins return results whether or not there is matching data.

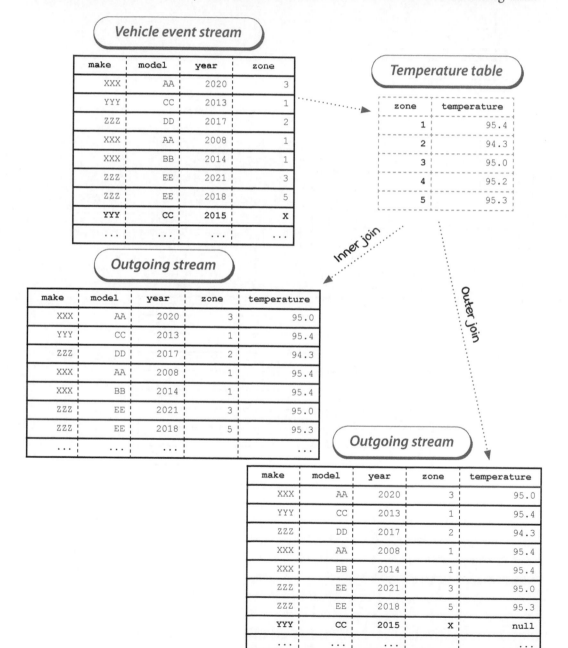

Different types of joins

If you are familiar with the join clause in databases, you will remember that there are a few different types of outer joins: *full outer joins* (or *full joins*), *left outer joins* (or *left joins*), and *right outer joins* (or *right joins*). All join operators are included in the diagrams that follow to illuminate the differences in the context of an SQL database.

Inner joins only return results that have matching values in both tables.

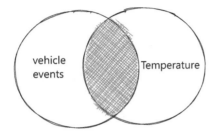

Full outer joins return all results in both tables.

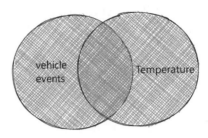

Left outer joins return all results in the vehicle events table and only matching rows from the temperature table.

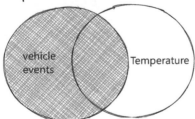

Right outer joins return all results in the temperature table and only matching rows from the vehicle events table.

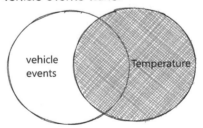

Outer joins in streaming systems

Now we know the inner and outer joins in SQL databases. Overall, things are pretty similar in the streaming world. One difference is that, in many cases (such as the CO_2 emission job), events in one of the incoming streams are processed *one by one*, while the other streams are materialized into tables to be joined. Usually, the special stream is treated as the *left stream*, and the streams to be materialized are the *right streams*. Therefore, the join used in the event joiner is a left outer join

 With left outer join, the team can identify the vehicles that are moving outside of the planned area and improve the data integrity issue by filling in the average temperature into the resulting vehicle-temperature events instead of dropping them. The results are more accurate now.

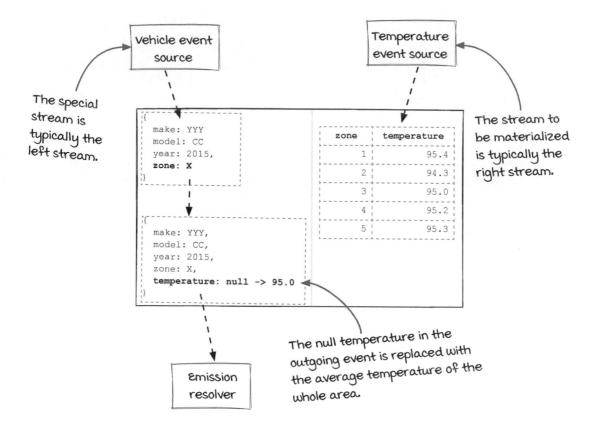

Note that in more complicated (hence, interesting) cases, there could be more than one *right* stream, and different types of joins can be applied to them.

A new issue: Weak connection

After fixing the data integrity issue, the team noticed another problem a few weeks later: some values in the temperature table look strange. After investigating, they found the root cause: one sensor has connection issues, and sometimes it reports temperature successfully every few hours instead of every 10 minutes. The issue can be fixed by repairing the device and its connection, but at the same time, can we make the system more resilient to the connection issues?

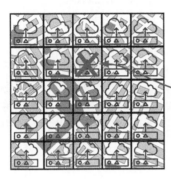

The connection of this sensor is not reliable, and this temperature value in the table is outdated because it hasn't been updated for a few hours.

zone	temperature
1	95.4
2	94.3
3	**91.2**
4	95.2
5	95.3

> In general, streaming systems have to account for the possibility that some of their event sources might be unreliable.

Windowed joins

A new concept can be very helpful for making the job handle the unreliable connection issue: *windowed joins*. The name explains itself well: a windowed join is an operator that combines both windowing and join. In the previous chapter, we discussed windowed computation in detail. The details are not required here, so don't worry if you picked this chapter to read first.

With windowed joins, the job works similarly to the original version: the vehicle events are handled one by one, and the temperature events are materialized into a lookup table. However, the materialization of the temperature events is based on a fixed time window instead of the continuous events. More specifically, temperature events are collected into a buffer first and materialized into an empty table as a batch every 30 minutes. If all the sensors report data successfully in the window, the calculation should work just fine. However, in case no temperature event is received from a sensor within the window, the corresponding row in the lookup table will be empty, and the event joiner can then estimate the current value from the neighbor zones. In the diagram below, the temperatures in zone 2 and 4 are used to estimate the temperature of zone 3. By using a windowed join, we can make sure all the temperature data in the table is up-to-date.

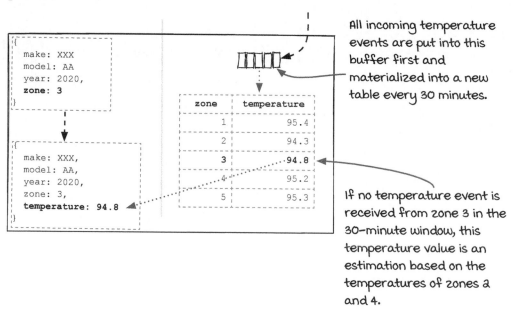

By changing from a continuous materialization to a window-based materialization, we sacrifice the latency of temperature changes a little (temperatures are updated every 30 minutes instead of 10 minutes), but in return, we get a more robust system that can detect and handle some unexpected issues automatically.

Joining two tables instead of joining a stream and table

Before wrapping up the chapter, as an example, let's take a look at the option in which both streams are converted to tables first and then the two tables are joined together using the CO_2 emission monitor system. With this solution, the overall process in the component has two steps: materialization and join. First, the two incoming streams are materialized into two tables. Then, the join logic is applied on the tables, and the results are emitted out to the downstream components. Usually, windowing is used in the materialization step, and the join operation is very similar to the join clause in SQL databases. Note that a different windowing strategy can be applied to each incoming stream.

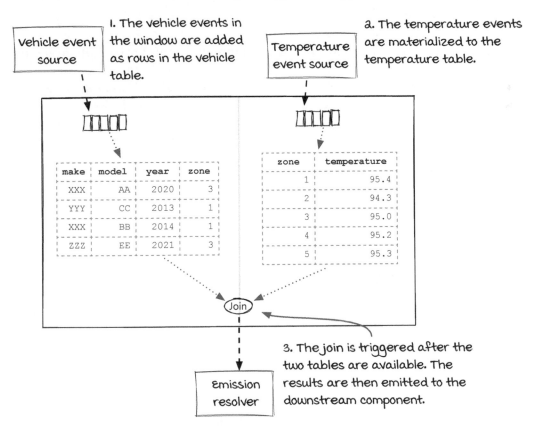

Because the overall process is rather standard, developers can focus on the join calculation without worrying about handling streams differently. This could be an advantage when building more complicated join operators; hence, this option is important to know. On the other hand, the latency might not be ideal because the events are processed in small batches instead of continuously. Remember that it is up to the developers to choose the best option according to the requirements.

Revisiting the materialized view

We have discussed that the temperature events are more efficient to be materialized than the vehicle events, and we have also discussed that, typically, the events in one special stream are processed one by one, and the other streams are materialized into temporary tables, but we can also materialize all streams and join the tables. I bet some curious readers will ask: can we join with the raw temperature events instead of the materialized view?

```
zone: 3
temperature: 95.0
```

zone	temperature
1	95.4
2	94.3
3	95.0
4	95.2
5	95.3

Let's try to keep all the temperature events as a list and avoid the temporary table. To avoid running out of memory, we will drop the temperature events that are older than 30 minutes. For each vehicle event, we need to search for the last temperature of the zone in the temperature list by comparing the zone id in the vehicle event with the zone id of each temperature in the list. The final results will be the same, but with a lookup table which could be a hash map, a binary search tree, or a simple array with the zone id as the index, the searching would be much more efficient. From the comparison, we can tell that the materialized view can be considered an *optimization*. In fact, the materialized view is a popular optimization pattern in many data processing applications.

> The materialized view is a popular pattern to optimize data processing applications.

Since it is an optimization, we can be more creative about how to manage the events if there are ways to make the operator more efficient. For example, in the real world a lot more information, such as noise level and air quality, can be collected by these sensors. Because we only care about the real-time temperature in each zone in this job, we can drop all other information and only extract the temperature data from the events and put them into the temporary lookup table. In your systems, if it makes your jobs more efficient, you can also try to create multiple materialized views from a single stream or create one materialized view from multiple streams to build more efficient systems.

Summary

In this chapter, we discussed the other type of fan-in operator: join. Similar to merge operators, join operators have multiple incoming streams. However, instead of applying the same logic to all events from different streams, events from different streams are handled differently in join operators.

Similar to the join clause in SQL databases, there are different types of joins. Understanding the joins is important for solving the data integrity issue:

- *Inner joins* only return results that have matching values in both tables.

- *Outer joins* return results whether or not there is matching data in both tables. There are three types of outer joins: full outer joins (or full joins), left outer joins (or left joins), and right outer joins (or right joins).

In the CO_2 emission monitoring system, the vehicle events are processed like a stream, and the temperature events are used as a lookup table. A table is a materialized view of a stream. At the end of the chapter, we also learned that windowing can be used together with join and a different option to build join operators: materializing all the incoming streams into tables and then joining them together.

In this chapter

- an introduction to backpressure

- when backpressure is triggered

- how backpressure works in local and
  distributed systems

Be prepared for unexpected events is a critical rule when building any distributed systems, and streaming systems are not exceptions. In this chapter, we are going to learn a widely supported failure handling mechanism in streaming systems: *backpressure*. It is very useful for protecting a streaming system from breaking down under some unusual scenarios.

Reliability is critical

In chapter 4, the team built a stream processing system to process transactions and detect credit card fraud. It works well, and customers are happy so far. However, the chief has a concern—a very good one.

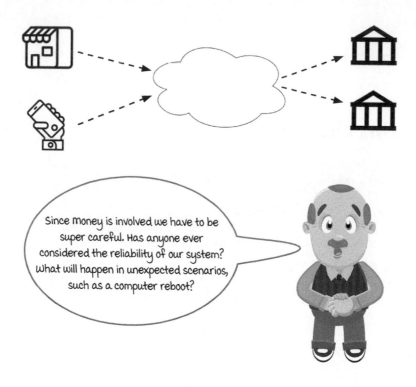

Review the system

Before moving forward, let's review the structure of the system to refresh our memory.

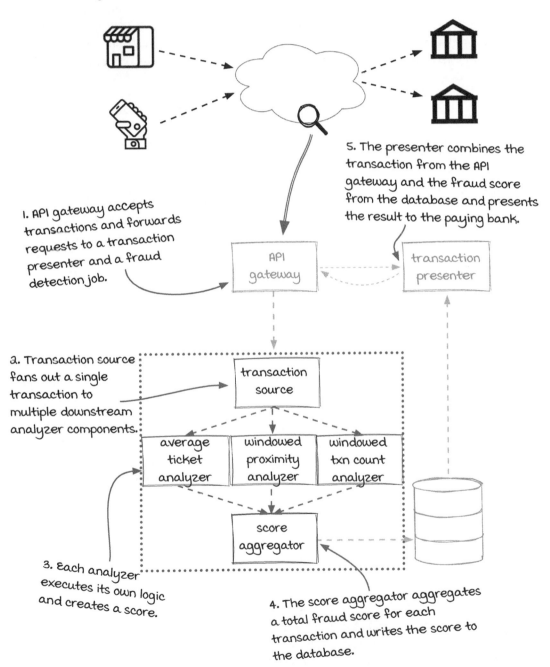

1. API gateway accepts transactions and forwards requests to a transaction presenter and a fraud detection job.

5. The presenter combines the transaction from the API gateway and the fraud score from the database and presents the result to the paying bank.

2. Transaction source fans out a single transaction to multiple downstream analyzer components.

3. Each analyzer executes its own logic and creates a score.

4. The score aggregator aggregates a total fraud score for each transaction and writes the score to the database.

Streamlining streaming jobs

The reason streaming systems are increasingly being used is the need for on-demand data, and on-demand data can be unpredictable sometimes. Components in a streaming system or a dependent external system, such as the score database in the diagram, might not be able to handle the traffic, and they also might have their own issues occasionally. Let's look at a few potential issues that could arise in the fraud detection system.

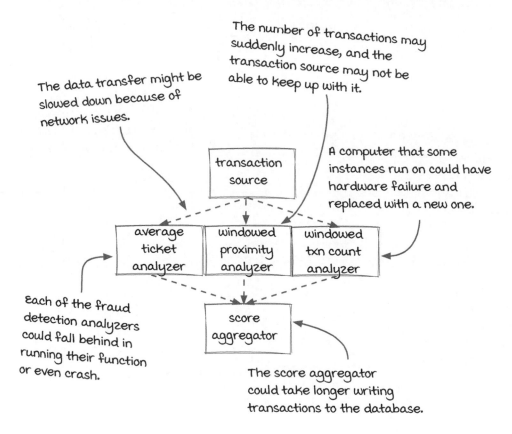

After all, failure handling is an important topic in all distributed systems, and our fraud detection system is no different. Things can go wrong, and some safety nets are important for preventing problems from arising.

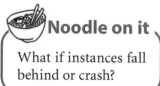

Noodle on it

What if instances fall behind or crash?

New concepts: Capacity, utilization, and headroom

Familiarize yourself with these related concepts, which will be helpful in discussing backpressure:

- *Capacity* is the maximum number of events an instance can handle. In the real world, capacity is not that straightforward to measure; hence, CPU and memory utilization are often used to estimate the number. Keep in mind that in a streaming system, the number of events that various instances can handle could be very different.

- *Capacity utilization* is a ratio (in the form of a percentage) of the actual number of events being processed to the capacity. Generally speaking, higher capacity utilization means higher resource efficiency.

- *Capacity headroom* is the opposite of capacity utilization—the ratio represents the extra events an instance can handle on top of the current traffic. In most cases, an instance with more headroom could be more resilient to unexpected data or issues, but its efficiency is lower because more resources are allocated but not fully used.

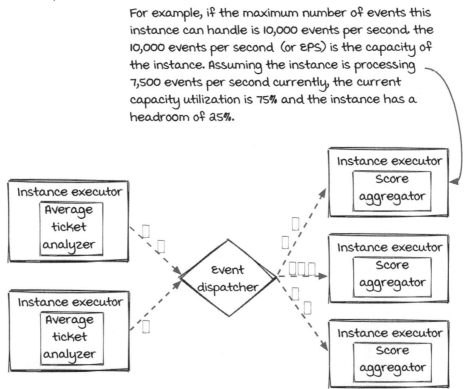

For example, if the maximum number of events this instance can handle is 10,000 events per second, the 10,000 events per second (or EPS) is the capacity of the instance. Assuming the instance is processing 7,500 events per second currently, the current capacity utilization is 75% and the instance has a headroom of 25%.

More about utilization and headroom

In real-world systems, something unexpected could occasionally happen, causing the capacity utilization to spike. For example:

- The incoming events could suddenly spike from time to time.

- Hardware could fail, such as a computer restarting because of a power issue, and the network performance might be poor when bandwidth is occupied by something else.

It is important to take these potential issues into consideration when building distributed systems. A resilient job should be able to handle these temporary issues by itself. In streaming systems, with enough headroom, the job should be running fine without any user intervention.

However, headroom can't be unlimited (plus, it is not free). When utilization capacity reaches 100%, the instance becomes *busy,* and backpressure is the next front line.

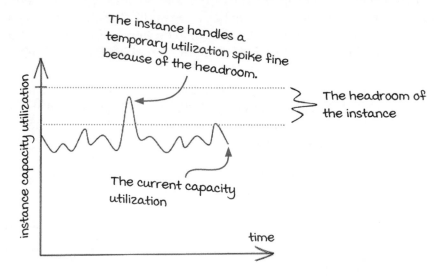

- In a streaming job, the headroom could be different from one instance to another. Generally speaking, the headroom of a component is the minimal headroom of all the instances of the component; and the headroom of a job is the minimal headroom of all the instances in the job. Ideally, the capacity utilization of all the instances in a job should be at a similar level.

- For critical systems, like the fraud detection system, it's a good practice to have enough headroom on every instance, so the job is more tolerant to unexpected issues.

New concept: Backpressure

When the capacity utilization reaches 100%, things become more interesting. Let's dive into it using the fraud detection job as an example.

1. Instances of the analyzer emit events

2. The events in the queues are waiting to be processed.

Instance executor

Instance executor

Instance executor

The dispatcher moves events between queues.

Instance executor

Instance executor

Instance executor

3. All instances of the score aggregator process the events normally, except the last instance is having issues and processing events at a lower speed.

average ticket analyzer

score aggregator

4. Some time passes ......

Instance executor

Instance executor

Instance executor

Instance executor

Instance executor

Instance executor

5. Because the downstream instance lags behind, the intermediate queue backs up with events to be processed. Backpressure needs to kick in.

When the instance becomes busy and can't catch up with the incoming traffic, its incoming queue is going to grow and run out of memory eventually. The issue will then propagate to other components, and the whole system is going to stop working. Backpressure is the mechanism to protect the system from crashing.

Backpressure, by definition, is a pressure that is opposite to the data flowing direction—from downstream instances to upstream instances. It occurs when an instance cannot process events at the speed of the incoming traffic, or, in other words, when the capacity utilization reaches 100%. The goal of the *backwards* pressure is to slow down the incoming traffic when the traffic is more than the system can handle.

Measure capacity utilization

Backpressure should trigger when the capacity utilization reaches 100%, but capacity and capacity utilization are not very easy to measure or estimate. There are many factors that determine the limit of how many events an instance can handle, such as the resource, the hardware, and the data. CPU and memory usage is useful but not very reliable for reflecting capacity, either. We need a better way; luckily, there is one.

We have learned that a running streaming system is composed of processes and event queues connecting them. The event queues are responsible for transferring events between the instances, like the conveyor belts between workers in an assembly line. When the capacity utilization of an instance reaches 100%, the processing speed can't catch up with the incoming traffic. As a result, the number of events in the incoming queue of the instance starts to accumulate. Therefore, the length of the incoming queue

for an instance can be used to detect whether the instance has reached its capacity.

Normally, the length of the queue should go up and down within a relatively stable range. If it keeps growing, it is very likely the instance has been too busy to handle the traffic.

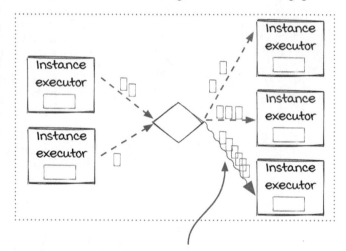

After too many events are accumulated in the queue, a backpressure event should happen to "slow down" events from the upstream components.

In the next few pages, we will discuss backpressure in more detail with our local Streamwork engine first to get some basic ideas, then we will move to more general distributed frameworks.

Note that backpressure is especially useful for the temporary issues, such as instances restarting, maintenance of the dependent systems, and sudden spikes of events from sources. The streaming system will handle them gracefully by temporarily slowing down and resuming afterwards without user intervention. Therefore, it is very important to understand what backpressure can and cannot do, so when system issues happen, you have things under control without being panicky.

Backpressure in the Streamwork engine

Let's start from our own Streamwork engine first, since it is more straightforward. As a local system, the Streamwork engine doesn't have complicated logic for backpressure. However, the information could be helpful for us to learn backpressure in real frameworks next.

In the Streamwork engine, *blocking queues* (queues that can suspend the threads that try to append more events when the queue is full or take elements when the queue is empty) are used to connect processes. The lengths of the queues are not unlimited. There is a maximum capacity for each queue, and the capacity is the key for backpressure. When an instance can't process events fast enough, the consuming rate of the queue in front of it would be lower than the insertion rate. The queue will start to grow and become *full* eventually. Afterward, the insertion will be blocked until an event is consumed by the downstream instance. As the result, the insertion rate will be slowed down to the same as the event processing speed of the downstream instance.

In the Streamwork, blocking queues with a specified capacity are used to connect processes.

1. The last instance of the component can't keep up with the incoming traffic.

2. When this queue is full, the incoming transactions will be blocked until the downstream instance consumes more elements from the queue. As a result, the processing speed of the event dispatcher process is slowed down to the speed of the slow instance.

Backpressure in the Streamwork engine: Propagation

Slowing down the event dispatcher isn't the end of the story. After the event dispatcher is slowed down, the same thing will happen to the queue between it and the upstream instances. When this queue is full, all the instances of the upstream component will be affected. In the diagram below, we need to zoom in a little more than normal to see the blocking queue in front of the event dispatcher that is shared by all the upstream instances.

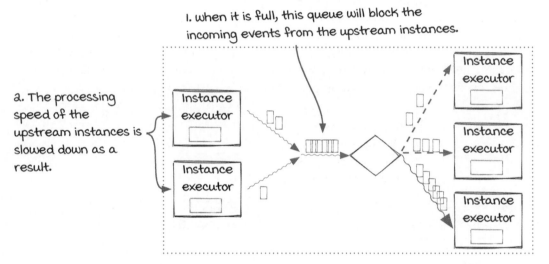

1. when it is full, this queue will block the incoming events from the upstream instances.

2. The processing speed of the upstream instances is slowed down as a result.

When there is a fan-in in front of this component, which means there are multiple direct upstream components for the downstream component, all these components will be affected because the events are blocked to the same blocking queue.

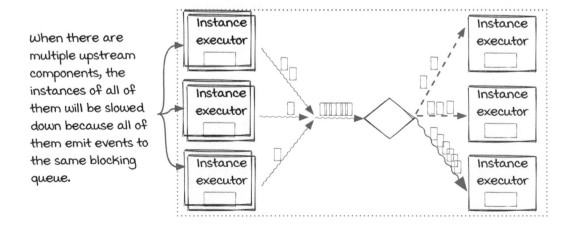

When there are multiple upstream components, the instances of all of them will be slowed down because all of them emit events to the same blocking queue.

Our streaming job during a backpressure

Let's look at how the fraud detection job is affected by backpressure with our Streamwork engine when one score aggregator instance has trouble catching up with the incoming traffic. At the beginning, only the score aggregator runs at a lower speed. Later, the upstream analyzers will be slowed down because of the backpressure. Eventually, the backpressure will bog down all your processing power, and you'll be stuck with an underperforming job until the issue goes away.

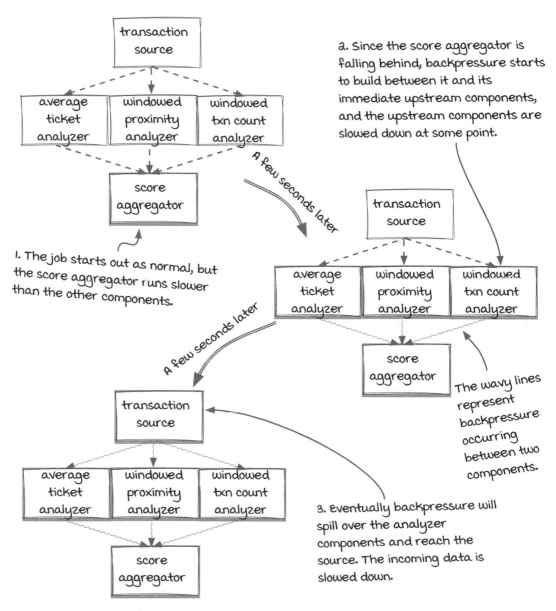

Backpressure in distributed systems

Overall, it is fairly straightforward in a local system to detect and handle backpressure with blocking queues. However, in distributed systems, things are more complicated. Let's discuss these potential complications in two steps:

1. Detecting busy instances

2. Backpressure state

Detecting busy instances

As the first step, it is important to detect busy instances, so the systems can react proactively. We mentioned in chapter 2 that the event queue is a widely used data structure in streaming systems to connect the processes. Although normally unbounded queues are used, monitoring the size of the queues is a convenient way to tell whether an instance can keep up with the incoming traffic. More specifically, there are at least two different units of length we can use to set the threshold:

• The number of events in the queue

• The memory size of the events in the queue

When the number of events or the memory size reaches the threshold, there is likely an issue with the connected instance. The engine declares a backpressure state.

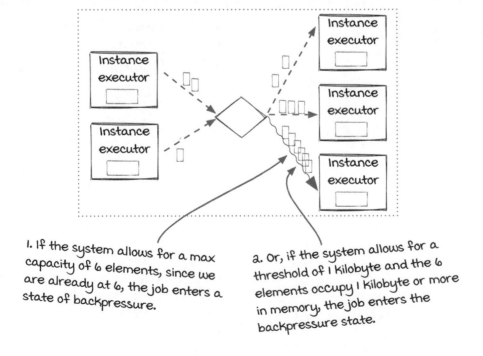

1. If the system allows for a max capacity of 6 elements, since we are already at 6, the job enters a state of backpressure.

2. Or, if the system allows for a threshold of 1 kilobyte and the 6 elements occupy 1 kilobyte or more in memory, the job enters the backpressure state.

Backpressure state

After a backpressure state is declared, similar to the Streamwork engine, we would want to slow down the incoming events. However, this task could often be much more complicated in distributed systems than in local systems, because the instances could be running on different computers or even different locations. Therefore, streaming frameworks typically stop the incoming events instead of slowing them down to give the busy instance room to breathe temporarily by:

- Stopping the instances of the upstream components, or
- Stopping the instances of the sources

Although much less popular, we would also like to cover another option later in this chapter: dropping events. This option may sound undesirable, but it could be useful when end-to-end latency is more critical and losing events is acceptable. Basically, between the two options, there is a tradeoff between accuracy and latency.

The two options are explained in the diagram below. We've added a source instance to help with explanations, and left out the details of some intermediate queues and event dispatchers for brevity.

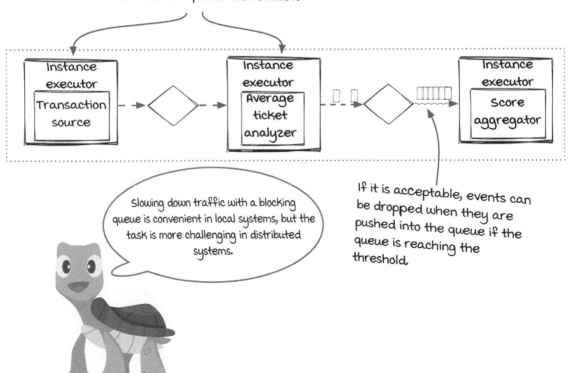

Backpressure handling: Stopping the sources

Performing a stop at the source component is probably the most straightforward way to relieve backpressure in distributed systems. It allows us to drain the incoming events to the slow instance as well as all other instances in a streaming job, which could be desirable when it is likely that there are multiple busy instances.

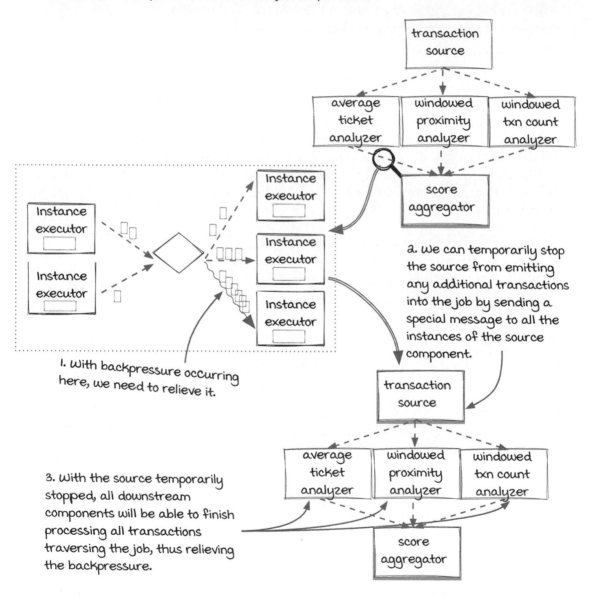

1. With backpressure occurring here, we need to relieve it.

2. We can temporarily stop the source from emitting any additional transactions into the job by sending a special message to all the instances of the source component.

3. With the source temporarily stopped, all downstream components will be able to finish processing all transactions traversing the job, thus relieving the backpressure.

Backpressure handling: Stopping the upstream components

Stopping the incoming event could also be implemented at the component level. This would be a more fine-grained way (to some extent) than the previous implementation. The hope is that only specific components or instances are stopped instead of all of them and that the backpressure can be relieved before it is propagated widely. If the issue stays long enough, eventually the source component will still be stopped. Note that this option can be relatively more complicated to implement in distributed systems and has higher overhead.

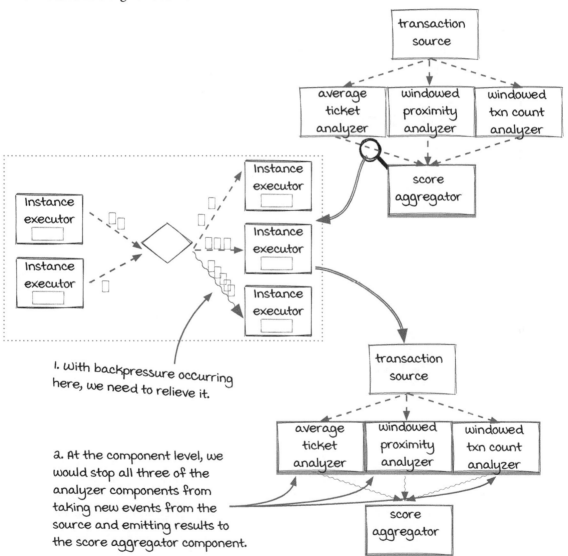

1. With backpressure occurring here, we need to relieve it.

2. At the component level, we would stop all three of the analyzer components from taking new events from the source and emitting results to the score aggregator component.

Relieving backpressure

After a job is in a backpressure state for a while and the busy instance has recovered (hopefully), the next important question is: what is the end of a backpressure state, so the traffic can be resumed?

The solution shouldn't be a surprise, as it is very similar to the detection step: monitoring the size of the queues. Opposite to the detection in which we check whether the queue is *too full*, this time we check whether the queue is *empty enough*, which means the number of events in it has decreased to be below a low threshold, and it has enough room for new events now.

Note that relieving doesn't mean the slow instance has recovered. Instead, it simply means there is room in the queue for more events.

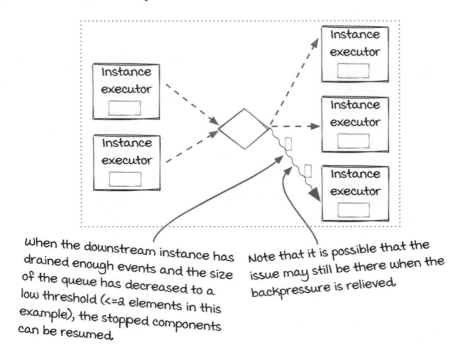

When the downstream instance has drained enough events and the size of the queue has decreased to a low threshold (<=2 elements in this example), the stopped components can be resumed.

Note that it is possible that the issue may still be there when the backpressure is relieved.

Here, one important fact to keep in mind is that backpressure is a *passive* mechanism designed for protecting the slow instance and the whole system from more serious problems (like crashing). It doesn't really address any problem in the slow instance and make it run faster. As a result, backpressure could be triggered again if the slow instance still can't catch up after the incoming events are resumed. We are going to take a closer look at the thresholds for detecting and relieving backpressure first and then discuss the problem afterward.

New concept: Backpressure watermarks

The sizes of the intermediate queues are examined and compared with the thresholds for the declaration and relieving of the backpressure state. Let's take a closer look at these two thresholds together with a new concept: *backpressure watermarks*. They are typically the configurations provided by streaming frameworks:

- Backpressure watermarks represent the high and low utilizations of the intermediate queues between the processes.

- When the size of the data in a queue is higher than the high backpressure watermark, backpressure state should be declared if it hasn't been already.

- When a backpressure is present, and the size of the data in the queue that triggered backpressure is lower than the low backpressure watermark, the backpressure can be relieved. Note that it is not ideal for this low backpressure watermark to be zero because that means the previously busy instance won't have work to do between the relieving of backpressure and new events reaching the queue.

The data sizes in the queues go up and down when a job is processing events. Ideally, the numbers are always between the low and high backpressure watermarks, so the events are processed in full speed.

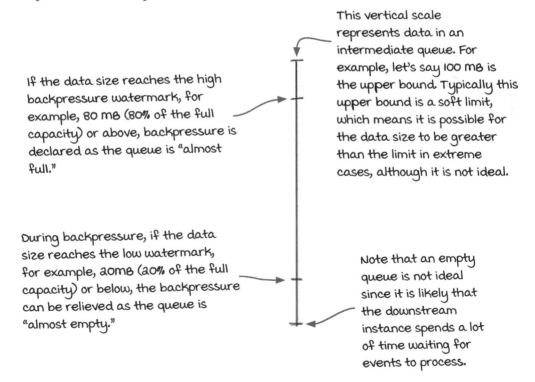

This vertical scale represents data in an intermediate queue. For example, let's say 100 mB is the upper bound. Typically this upper bound is a soft limit, which means it is possible for the data size to be greater than the limit in extreme cases, although it is not ideal.

If the data size reaches the high backpressure watermark, for example, 80 mB (80% of the full capacity) or above, backpressure is declared as the queue is "almost full."

During backpressure, if the data size reaches the low watermark, for example, 20mB (20% of the full capacity) or below, the backpressure can be relieved as the queue is "almost empty."

Note that an empty queue is not ideal since it is likely that the downstream instance spends a lot of time waiting for events to process.

Another approach to handle lagging instances: Dropping events

Backpressure is useful for protecting systems and keeping things running. It works well in most cases, but in some special cases you also have another option: simply dropping events.

In this approach, when a lagging instance is detected, instead of stopping and resuming the incoming events, the system would just discard the new events emitted into the incoming queue of the instance.

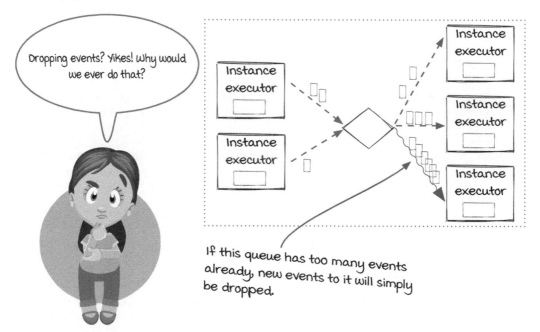

If this queue has too many events already, new events to it will simply be dropped.

The option might sound scary because the results will be inaccurate. You are definitely right about that. If you remember the delivery semantics we talked about in chapter 5, you will notice that this option should only be used in the *at-most-once* cases.

However, it may not be as scary as it sounds. The results are inaccurate *only* when an instance can't catch up with the traffic, which should be rare if the system is configured correctly. In other words, the results should be accurate *almost* all the time. We have mentioned a few times that backpressure is a self-protection mechanism for the extreme scenarios to prevent the systems from crashing. The backpressure state is not an ideal state for streaming jobs. If it happens too often to your streaming job, you should take another look at the system and try to find the root causes and address them.

Why do we want to drop events?

Why would we ever want to throw away an event in a system? You are not alone if you are wondering. Well, that's a question to definitely ask yourself when designing your jobs: are you willing to trade away accuracy for end-to-end latency in case any instance fails to catch up with the work load?

Let's take social media platforms as an example and track the number of user interactions, such as *likes*, in real time. With the second option, the count is always the latest, although it is not 100% accurate. In the case that 1 instance in 100 is affected, we can expect the error to be less than 1%. If backpressure is applied to stop events, the count will be accurate, but you won't get the latest count during the backpressure state, because the system is slowed down. After the backpressure state is relieved, it also needs time to catch up to the latest events. In the case that the issue is permanent, you won't have the latest count until the issue is addressed, which could likely be worse than the < 1% error. Basically, with the dropping events approach, you get a *more real-time* system with *likely accurate enough* results.

Back to the fraud detection job—the deadline is critical to us. Pausing the data processing for a few minutes and missing the deadline until the backpressure is addressed would not be acceptable to us. Comparatively speaking, it may be more desirable to keep the process going without delay, although the accuracy is sacrificed slightly. Engineers should definitely be notified, so the underlying issue is investigated and fixed as soon as possible. Monitoring the number of dropped events is critical for us to understand the current state and the accuracy level of the results.

> Event dropping is a common design consideration when you're balancing the tradeoff between accuracy and overall latency.

Backpressure could be a symptom when the underlying issue is permanent

Backpressure is an important mechanism in streaming systems for handling temporary issues, such as instance crashing and sudden spikes of the incoming traffic, to avoid more serious problems. The streaming systems can resume a normal state automatically after the underlying issue is gone without user intervention. In other words, with backpressure, the stream systems are more resilient to unexpected issues, which is generally desirable in distributed systems. In theory, it would be ideal if backpressure never happened in a streaming system, but as you well know, life is not perfect, and it never will be. Backpressure is a necessary safety net.

While we hope that the issue is temporary and backpressure can handle it for us, it all depends on the underlying situation. It is totally possible that the instance won't recover by itself and owners' interventions will be required to take care of the root cause. In these cases, permanent backpressure becomes a symptom. Typically, there are two permanent cases that should be treated differently:

- The instance simply stops working, and backpressure will never be relieved,

- The instance is still working, but it can't catch up with the incoming traffic. Backpressure will be triggered again soon after it is relieved.

Instance stops working, so backpressure won't be relieved

In this case, no events will be consumed from the queue, and the backpressure state will never be relieved at all. This is relatively straightforward to handle: fixing the instance. Restarting the instance could be an immediate remediation step, but it could be important to figure out the root cause and address accordingly. Often, the issue leads to bugs to be fixed.

Instance can't catch up, and backpressure will be triggered again

It is more interesting when an instance can't catch up with the traffic. In this case, the data processing can resume temporarily after the data in the queue has been drained, but backpressure will be declared again soon. Let's take a closer look at this case.

Backpressure is efficient for temporary issues but not for permanent issues.

Stopping and resuming may lead to thrashing if the issue is permanent

Now, let's take a look at an effect that we will term *thrashing*. If the underlying issue is permanent, when the job declares a state of backpressure, the events in the queues are drained by all instances; then, as soon as the backpressure state is relieved, as new data events flood the instance once again, the state is declared again shortly. Thrashing is a cycle of declaring and relieving backpressure.

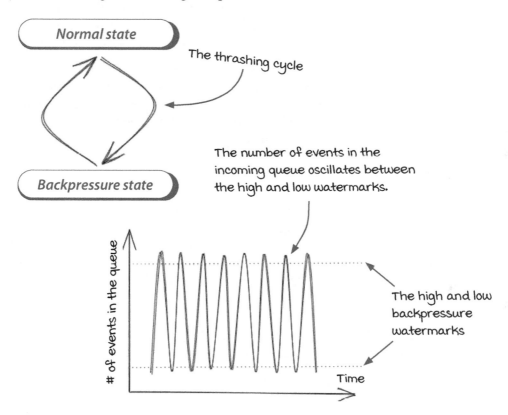

Thrashing is expected if the situation doesn't change. If the same instance still can't catch up with the traffic, the data size in the queue will increase again until it reaches the high watermark and triggers a backpressure again. And after the next time the backpressure is relieved, it is likely to happen again. The number of events in the incoming queue of the instance looks like the chart above. To recover from a thrashing, we need to find the root cause and address it.

Handle thrashing

If you see the thrashing, you will likely need to consider why the instance doesn't process fast enough. For example, is there an internal issue that makes the instance slow down, or is it time to scale up your system? Typically, this kind of issue comes from two sources—the traffic and the components:

- The event traffic from the source might have increased permanently to a level that is more than the job can handle. In this case, it is likely the job needs to be scaled up to handle the new traffic. More specifically, the parallelisms (the number of instances of a specific component—read chapter 3 for more details) of the slow components in the job may need to be increased as the first step.

- The processing speed of some components could be slower than before for some reason. You might need to look into the components and see if there is something to optimize or tune. Note that the dependencies used by the components should be taken into consideration as well. It is not rare that some dependencies can run slower when the pattern of traffic changes.

It is important to understand the data and the system

Backpressure occurs when an instance can't process events at the speed of the incoming traffic. It is a powerful mechanism to protect the system from crashing, but it is important for you, the owner of the systems, to understand the data and the systems and figure out what causes backpressure to be triggered. Many issues might happen in real-world systems, and we can't cover all of them in this book. Nevertheless, we hope that understanding the basic concepts will be helpful for you to start your investigation in the right direction.

Backpressure is important for the systems to be more resilient, but it is more important for us to understand the root causes.

Summary

In this chapter, we discussed a widely supported mechanism: backpressure. More specifically:

- When and why backpressure happens
- How stream frameworks detect issues and handle them with backpressure
- Stopping incoming traffic or dropping events—how they work and the tradeoffs
- What we can do if the underlying issues don't go away.

Backpressure is an important mechanism in stream systems. We hope and believe that understanding the details about it could be helpful for you to maintain and improve your systems.

Stateful computation | **10**

- -

In this chapter

- an introduction to stateful and stateless components

- how stateful components work

- related techniques

- -

66 *Have you tried turning it off and on again?* **99**

—The IT Crowd

We talked about *state* in chapter 5. In most computer programs, it is an important concept. For example, the progress in a game, the current content in a text editor, the rows in a spreadsheet, and the opened pages in a web browser are all *states* of the programs. When a program is closed and opened again, we would like to recover to the desired *state*. In streaming systems, handling states correctly is very important. In this chapter, we are going to discuss in more detail how states are used and managed in streaming systems.

The migration of the streaming jobs

System maintenance is part of our day-to-day work with distributed systems. A few examples are: releasing a new build with bug fixes and new features, upgrading software or hardware to make the systems more secure or efficient, and handling software and hardware failures to keep the systems running.

AJ and Sid have decided to migrate the streaming jobs to new and more efficient hardware to reduce cost and improve reliability. This is a major maintenance task, and it is important to proceed carefully.

Stateful components in the system usage job

Stateful components are very useful for the components that have internal data. We talked about them briefly in chapter 5 in the context of the system usage job. It is time take a closer look now and see how they really work internally.

> We have discussed stateful components briefly in previous chapters. They are needed at a few places in our streaming job.

In order to resume the processing after a streaming job is restarted, each instance of a component needs to persist its key internal data, the state, to external storage beforehand as a checkpoint. After an instance is restarted, the data can be loaded back into memory and used to set up the instance before resuming the process.

The data to persist varies from component to component. In the system usage job:

- The transaction source needs to track the processing offsets. The offsets denote the positions that the transaction source component is reading from the data source (the event log).

- The transaction counts are critical for the system usage analyzer and need to be persisted.

- The usage writer doesn't have any data to save and restore.

Therefore, the first two components need to be implemented as *stateful components*, and the last one is a *stateless component*.

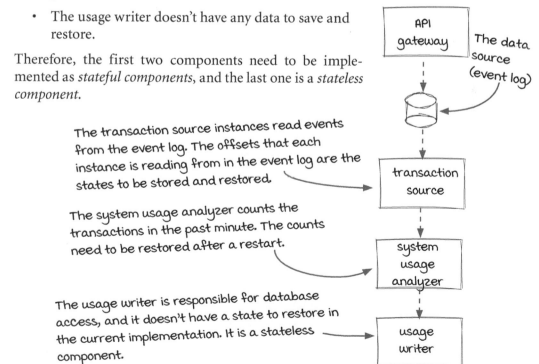

The transaction source instances read events from the event log. The offsets that each instance is reading from in the event log are the states to be stored and restored.

The system usage analyzer counts the transactions in the past minute. The counts need to be restored after a restart.

The usage writer is responsible for database access, and it doesn't have a state to restore in the current implementation. It is a stateless component.

Revisit: State

Before going deeper, let's pause here and revisit a very basic concept: *what is a state?* As we explained in chapter 5, state is the internal data inside each instance that changes when events are processed. For example, the state of the transaction source component is where each instance is loading from the data source (aka the offset). The offset moves forward after new events are loaded. Let's look at the state changes of a transaction source instance before and after two transactions are processed.

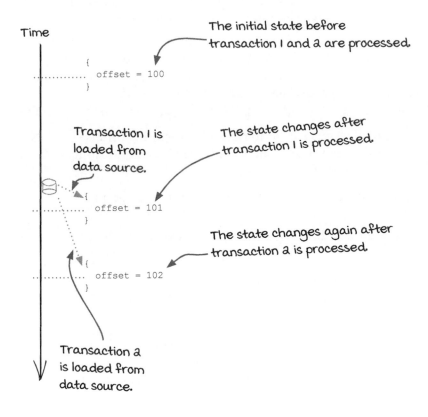

The states in different components

Things become interesting when we look at states in different components together. In chapter 7 about windowed computation, we said that the processing time of an event is different for different instances because the event flows from one instance to another. Similarly, for the same event, in different instances, the state changes happen at different times. Let's look at the state changes of a transaction source instance and a system usage analyzer instance together before and after two transactions are processed.

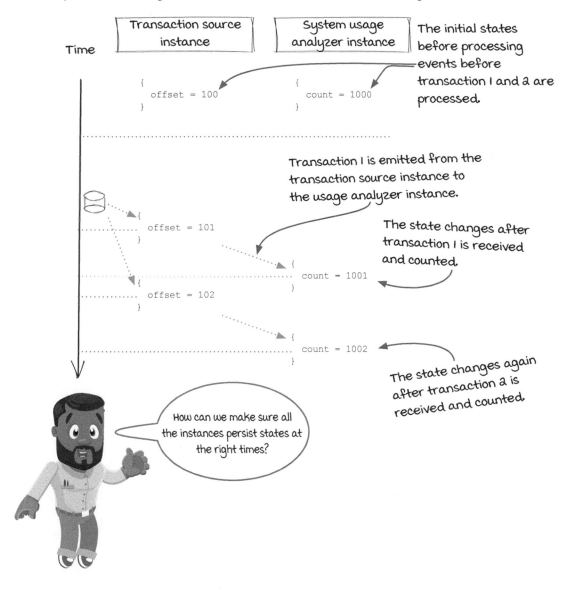

State data vs. temporary data

So far, the definition of *state* is straightforward: the internal data inside an instance that changes when events are processed. Well, the definition is true, but some state data could be *temporary* and doesn't need to be recovered when an instance is restored. Typically, temporary data is *not* included in the state of an instance.

For example, *caching* is a popular technique to improve performance and/or efficiency. Caching is the process of a component sitting in front of an expensive or slow calculation (e.g., a complex function or a request to a remote system) and storing the results, so the calculation doesn't need to be executed repetitively. Normally, caches are not considered to be instance state data, although they could change when events are processed. After all, an instance should still work correctly with a brand new cache after being restarted. The database connection in each usage writer instance is also temporary data, since the connection will be set up again from scratch after the instance is restarted.

Another example is the transaction source component in the fraud detection job. Internally, each instance has an offset of the last transaction event it has loaded from the data source. However, like we have discussed in chapter 5, because latency is critical for this job, it is more desirable to skip to the latest transaction instead of restoring to the previous offset when an instance is restarted. The offset is temporary in this job, and it should not be considered to be state data. Therefore, the component is a *stateless component* instead of a stateful one.

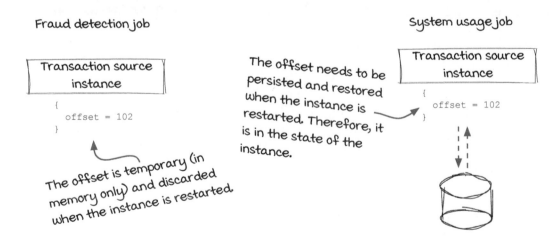

In conclusion, instance state includes only the key data, so the instance can be rolled back to a previous point and continue working from there correctly. Temporary data is typically not considered to be state data in stream systems.

Stateful vs. stateless components: The code

The transaction source component exists in both the system usage job and the fraud detection job, and it works in a similar way. The only difference is that it is stateful in the system usage job and stateless in the fraud detection job. Let's put their code together to look at the changes in the stateful component:

- The `setupInstance()` function has an extra `state` parameter.

- There is a new `getState()` function.

```
class TransactionSource extends StatefulSource {          The stateful version in the
  EventLog transactions = new EventLog();                 system usage job
  int offset = 0;
  ......
  public void setupInstance(int instance, State state) {
    SourceState mstate = (SourceState)state;              The data in the state object is
    if (mstate != null) {                                 used to set up the instance.
      offset = mstate.offset;
      transactions.seek(offset);
    }
  }

  public void getEvents(Event event, EventCollector eventCollector) {
    Transaction transaction = transactions.pull();
    eventCollector.add(new TransactionEvent(transaction));
    offset++;
    system.out.println("Reading from offset %d", offset);
  }

public State getState() {
    SourceState state = new SourceState();
    State.offset = offset;
    return new state;                    The state object of the instance
  }                                       contains the current data offset in
}                                         the event log.


class TransactionSource extends Source {       The stateless version in
  EventLog transactions = new EventLog();      the fraud detection job
  int offset = 0;
  ......
  public void setupInstance(int instance) {
    offset = transactions.seek(LATEST);
  }

  public void getEvents(Event event, EventCollector eventCollector) {
    Transaction transaction = transactions.pull();
    eventCollector.add(new TransactionEvent(transaction));
    offset++;
    system.out.println("Reading from offset %d", offset);
  }
}
```

The stateful source and operator in the system usage job

In chapter 5, we have read the code of the `TransactionSource` and the `SystemUsageAnalyzer` classes. Now, let's put them together and compare. Overall, the state handling is very similar between stateful sources and operators.

```
class TransactionSource extends StatefulSource {
  MessageQueue queue;
  int offset = 0;
  ......
  public void setupInstance(int instance, State state) {
    SourceState mstate = (SourceState)state;
    if (mstate != null) {
      offset = mstate.offset;          ◄── The data in the state object is
      log.seek(offset);                     used to set up the instance.
    }
  }


  public void getEvents(Event event, EventCollector eventCollector) {
    Transaction transaction = log.pull();
    eventCollector.add(new TransactionEvent(transaction));
    offset++;                ◄──  The offset value changes when a new
  }                               event is pulled from the event log and
  public State getState() {       emitted to the downstream components.
    SourceState state = new SourceState();
    State.offset = offset;
    return new state;       ◄── The state object of the instance
  }                             contains the current data offset in
}                              the event log.


class SystemUsageAnalyzer extends StatefulOperator {
  int transactionCount;

  public void setupInstance(int instance, State state) {
    AnalyzerState mstate = (AnalyzerState)state;
    transactionCount = state.count;     ◄── When an instance is constructed,
  }                                          a state object is used to initialize
                                             the instance.

  public void apply(Event event, EventCollector eventCollector) {
    transactionCount++;
                         ◄── The count variable changes when
                             events are processed.

    eventCollector.add(transactionCount);
  }

  public State getState() {
    AnalyzerState state = new AnalyzerState();
    State.count = transactionCount;     ◄── A new state object is created to
    return state;                            store instance data periodically.
  }
}
```

States and checkpoints

Compared to stateless components we have seen before, two functions are added in stateful components and need to be implemented by developers:

- The getState() function, which translates the instance data to a state object.

- The setupInstance() function, which uses a state object to reconstruct an instance.

Now, let's look at what really happens behind the scenes to connect the dots. This information could be useful for you to build efficient and reliable jobs and investigate when issues happen.

In chapter 5, we defined *checkpoint* as "a piece of data that can be used by an instance to restore to a previous state." The streaming engine, more specifically, the *instance executor* and the *checkpoint manager* (remember the single responsibility principle?), is responsible for calling the two functions in the following two cases, respectively:

- The getState() function is called periodically by the instance executor to get the latest state of each instance, and the state object is then sent to the checkpoint manager to create a checkpoint.

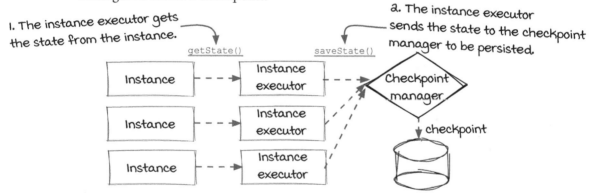

- The setupInstance() function is called by the instance executor after the instance is created, and the most recent checkpoint is loaded by the checkpoint manager.

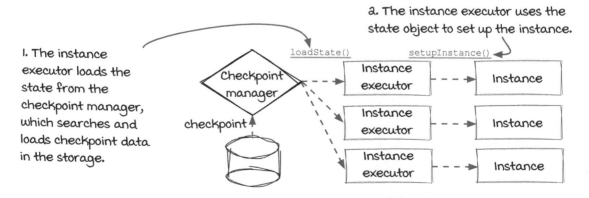

Checkpoint creation: Timing is hard

The instance executors are responsible for calling the instances' `getState()` function to get the current states and then sending them to the checkpoint manager to be saved in the checkpoint. An open question is how the instance executors know the right time to trigger the process.

An intuitive answer might be triggering by clock time. All instance executors trigger the function at exactly the same time. A *snapshot* of the whole system can be taken just like when we put a computer into hibernation mode in which everything in memory is dumped to disk, and the data is reloaded back into memory when the computer is woken up.

However, in streaming systems this technique doesn't work. When a checkpoint creation is started, some events have been processed by some components but not processed by the downstream components yet. If a checkpoint is created this way and used to reconstruct instances, the states of different instances would be *out of sync*, and the results will be incorrect afterwards.

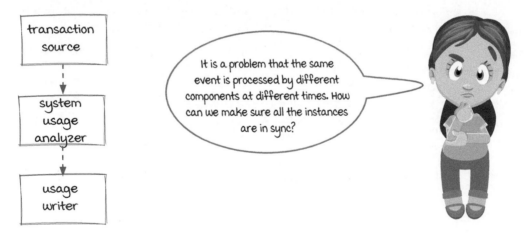

For example, in a working streaming job, each event is processed by an instance of the source component (the transaction source in the system usage job), and then sent to the right instance of the downstream component (the system usage analyzer in the system usage job). The process repeats until there is no downstream component left. Therefore, each event is processed at a different time in different components, and at the same time, different components are working on different events.

To avoid the out-of-sync issue and keep the results correct, instead of dumping states at the same clock time, the key is for all the instances to dump their states at the same *event-based time*: right after the same transaction is processed.

Event-based timing

For checkpointing in streaming systems, time is measured by event id instead of clock time. For example, in the system usage job, the transaction source would be at the time of *transaction #1001* when transaction #1001 has just been processed by it and emitted out. The system usage analyzer would be at the time of *after transaction #1000* at the same moment and reaches the time of transaction #1001 after transaction #1001 is received, processed, and emitted out. The diagram below shows the clock time and the event-based time in the same place. To keep things simple, we are assuming that each component has only one instance. The multiple instance case will be covered later when we discuss the implementation.

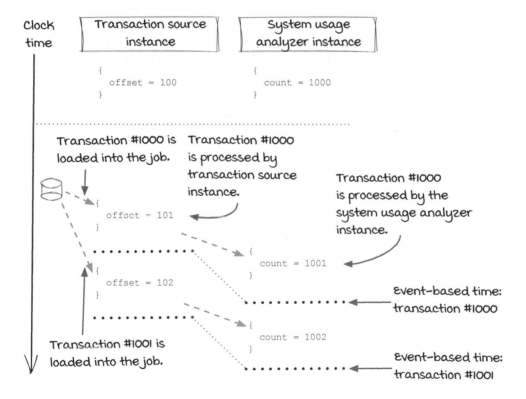

With this event-based timing, all instances can dump their states at the same time to create a valid checkpoint.

Creating checkpoints with checkpoint events

So how is event-based timing implemented in streaming frameworks? Like events, the timing is built in a streaming context we have been talking about throughout this book. Sound interesting?

Event-based timing sounds straightforward overall, but there is a problem: typically, there are multiple instances created for each component, and each event is processed by one of them. How are the instances synchronized with each other? Here, we would like to introduce a new type of events, *control events*, which have a different routing strategy than the data events.

So far, all our streaming jobs have been processing *data events*, such as vehicle events and credit card transactions. Control events don't contain data to process. Instead, they contain data for all modules in a streaming job to communicate with each other. In the checkpoint case, we need a *checkpoint event* with the responsibility of notifying all the instances in a streaming job that it is time to create a checkpoint. There could be other types of control events, but the checkpoint event is the only one in this book.

Periodically, the checkpoint manager in the job issues a checkpoint event with a unique id and emits it to the source component, or more accurately, the instance executors of the instances of the source component. The instance executors then insert the checkpoint event into the stream of regular data events, and the journey of the checkpoint event starts.

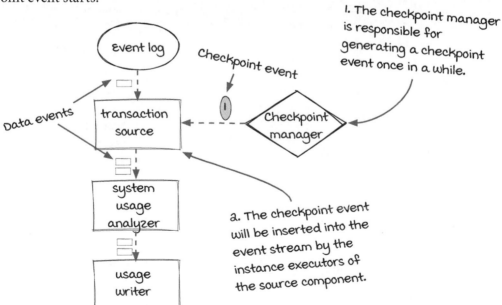

Note that the instances of the source component that contain user logic don't know the existence of the checkpoint event. All they know is that the `getState()` function is invoked by the instance executor to extract the current states.

A checkpoint event is handled by instance executors

Each instance executor repeats the same process:

- Invoking the `getState()` function and sending the state to the checkpoint manager
- Inserting the checkpoint event into its outgoing stream

If you look at the diagram below closely, you will find that each checkpoint event also contains a *checkpoint id*. The checkpoint id can be considered an event-based time. When an instance executor sends the state object to the checkpoint manager, the id is included, so the checkpoint manager knows that the instance is in this state at this time. The id is included in the checkpoint object, as well, for the same purpose.

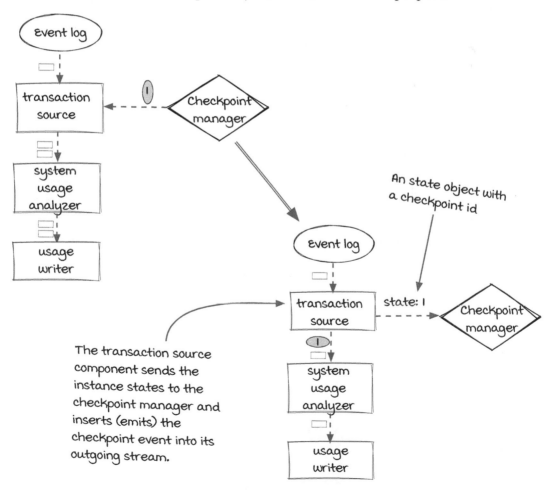

A checkpoint event flowing through a job

After the checkpoint event is inserted into the event stream by the source instance executors, it is going to flow through the job and visit the instance executors of all the operators in the job. The two diagrams below show that the checkpoint event with id 1 is processed by the transaction source and the system usage analyzer components one after the other.

The last component, usage writer, doesn't have a state, so it notifies the checkpoint manager that the event has been processed without a state object. The checkpoint manager then knows that the checkpoint event has visited all the components in the job, and the checkpoint is finally *completed* and can be persisted to storage.

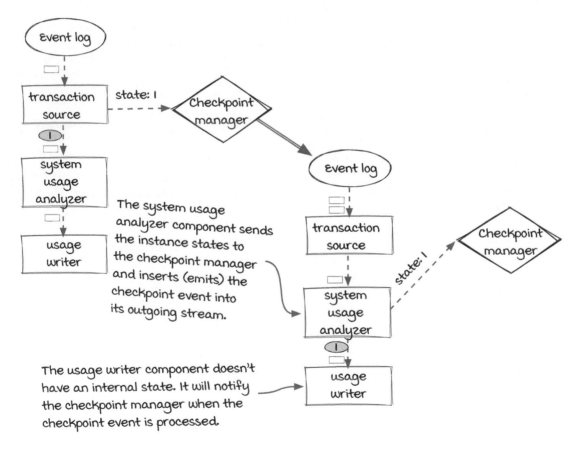

Overall, the checkpoint event flows through the job similarly to a regular event but not in exactly the same way. Let's look one level deeper.

Creating checkpoints with checkpoint events at the instance level

The checkpoint event flows from component to component. State objects are sent to the checkpoint manager one by one by the instance executors when the checkpoint event is received. As a result, all the states are created between the same two events (200 and 201) for every single component in the example shown here.

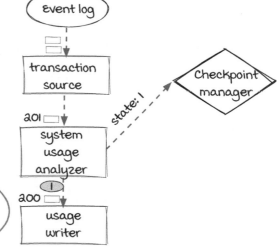

I remember there could be multiple instances for each component? Will it still work correctly?

One thing we shouldn't forget is that there could be multiple instances for each component. We learned in chapter 4 that each event is routed to a specific instance based on a grouping strategy. The checkpoint event is routed quite differently; let's take a look. (Note that this page and the next might be a little too detailed for some readers. If you have this feeling, please feel free to skip them and jump to the checkpoint loading topic.)

The simple answer is that *all the instances* need to receive the checkpoint event to trigger the `getState()` call correctly. In our Streamwork framework, the event dispatcher is responsible for *synchronizing* and *dispatching* the checkpoint event. Let's start with the dispatching first (since it is simpler) and talk about the synchronizing in the next page.

When an event dispatcher receives a checkpoint event from the upstream component, it will emit one copy of the event to *each* instance of the downstream component. For comparison, for a data event, typically only one instance of the downstream component will receive it.

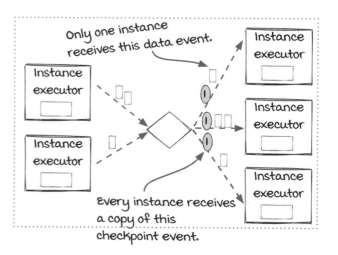

Only one instance receives this data event.

Every instance receives a copy of this checkpoint event.

Checkpoint event synchronization

While the checkpoint event dispatching is fairly straightforward, the synchronization part is a little trickier. Checkpoint event synchronization is the process for the event dispatcher to receive the incoming checkpoint events. Each event dispatcher receives events from multiple instances (in fact, it could also receive events from instances of multiple components), so one checkpoint event is expected from each upstream instance executor. These checkpoint events rarely arrive at the same time like in the example in the diagram shown here. So what should it do in this case?

The checkpoint events arrive at different times and need to be synchronized.

If we look at the diagram above and take the event-based timing into consideration, the *time* that the checkpoint event #1 represents is *between data events #200 and #201*. A checkpoint event is received by all the instance executors, so it is possible that the checkpoint event is processed by one instance earlier than the others like in the diagram above. In this case, after receiving the first checkpoint event, the event dispatcher will *block* the event stream that the checkpoint event came from, until the checkpoint event is received from all the other incoming connections. In other words, the checkpoint event is treated like a *barrier,* or a *blocker.* In the example above, the checkpoint event arrives from the bottom connection first. The event dispatcher will block the process of data event #201 and keep processing events (the data events #200 and the one before it) from the upper incoming connection until the checkpoint event is received.

After the checkpoint event #1 is received from both connections, since there are no other incoming connections to wait for, the event dispatcher emits the checkpoint event to all the downstream instance executors and starts consuming data events. As a result, data event #200 is dispatched before checkpoint event #1 and data event #201 by the event dispatcher.

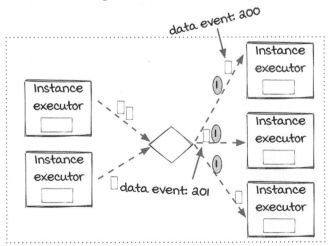

data event: 200

data event: 201

Checkpoint loading and backward compatibility

Now that we have discussed how checkpoints are created, let's take a look at how checkpoints are loaded and used. Unlike the creation process, which happens repetitively, checkpoint loading happens only once in each life cycle of a stream job: at the start time.

When a streaming job is started (e.g., something has happened, like an instance has just crashed, and the job needs to be restarted on the same machines; the job instances moved to different machines like the migration AJ and Sid are working on), each instance executor requests the state data for the corresponding instance from the checkpoint manager. The checkpoint manager in turn accesses the checkpoint storage, looks for the latest checkpoint, and returns the data to the instance executors. Each instance executor then uses the received state data to set up the instance. After all the instances are constructed successfully, the stream job starts processing events.

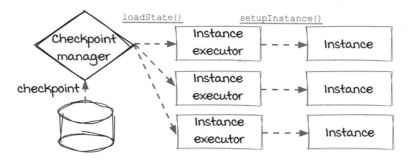

The whole process is fairly straightforward, but there is a catch: *backward compatibility*. The checkpoint was created in the *previous* run of the job, and the state data in the checkpoint is used to construct the *new* instances. If the job is simply restarted (manually or automatically), there shouldn't be any problem, as the logic of the instances is the same as before. However, if the logic of the existing stateful components has changed, it is important for developers to make sure that the new implementation works with the old checkpoints, so the instances' states can be restored correctly. If this requirement is not met, the job might start from a bad state, or it might stop working.

Some streaming frameworks manage the checkpoints between deployments as a special type of checkpoints: *savepoints*. These savepoints are similar to regular checkpoints, but they are triggered manually, and developers have more control. This can be a factor to consider when developers choose streaming frameworks for their systems.

Checkpoint storage

The last topic related to checkpoints is storage. Checkpoints are typically created period-ically with a *monotonically increasing* checkpoint id, and this engine-managed process continues until the streaming job is stopped.

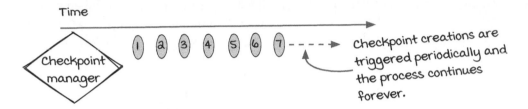

When instances are restarted, only the *most recent* checkpoint is used to initialize them. In theory, we can keep only one checkpoint for a stream job and update it in place when a new one is created.

However, life is full of ups and downs. For exam-ple, the checkpoint creation can fail if some instances are lost and the checkpoint is not com-pleted, or the checkpoint data can be corrupted because of disk failures and can't be loaded. In order to make the streaming systems more reliable, typically the most recent N checkpoints are kept in the storage and the older checkpoints can be dropped and the N is typically configurable. In case the most recent checkpoint is not usable, the checkpoint manager will fall back to the second latest checkpoint and try to use it to restore the streaming job. The fall back can happen again if needed until a good one is loaded successfully.

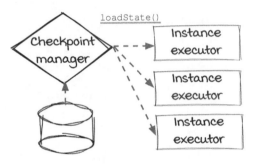

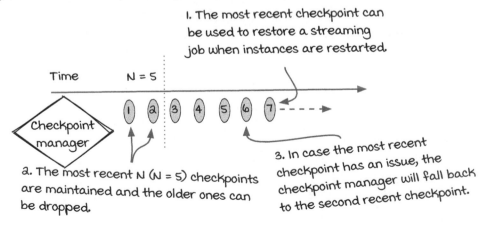

Stateful vs. stateless components

We have read enough about the details of stateful components and checkpoints. It is time to take a break, look at the bigger picture, and think about the pros and cons of stateful components. After all, stateful components are not free. The real question is: should I use stateful components or not?

The fact is that only you, the developer, have the final answer. Different systems have different requirements. Even though some systems have similar functionality, they may run totally differently because the incoming event traffic has different patterns, such as the throughput, data size, cardinality, and so on. We hope that the brief comparison below can be helpful for you to make better decisions and build better systems. In the rest of this chapter, we are going to talk about two practical techniques to support some useful features of stateful components with stateless components.

	Stateful component	Stateless component
Accuracy	• Stateful computation is important for the exactly-once semantic, which guarantees accuracy (effectively).	• There is no accuracy guarantee because instance states are not managed by the framework.
Latency (when errors happen)	• Instances will roll back to the previous state after errors happen.	• Instances will keep working on the new events after errors happen.
Resource usage	• More resources are needed to manage instance states.	• No resource is needed to manage instance states.
Maintenance burden	• There are more processes (e.g., checkpoint manager, checkpoint storage) to maintain and backward compatibility is critical.	• There is no extra maintenance burden.
Throughput	• Throughput could drop if checkpoint management is not well tuned.	• There is no overhead to handle high throughput.
Code	• Instance state management is needed.	• There is no extra logic.
Dependency	• Checkpoint storage is needed.	• There is no external dependency.

> We use stateful components only when they are necessary. We do this to keep the job as simple as possible to reduce the burden of maintenance.

Manually managed instance states

From the comparison, it is clear that accuracy is the advantage of stateful components. When something happens, and some instances need to be restarted, streaming engines help to manage and rollback the instance states. In addition to the burden, the engine-managed states also have some limitations. One obvious limitation is that the checkpoint shouldn't be created too frequently because the extra burden would be higher, and the system would become less efficient. Furthermore, it could be more desirable for some components to have different intervals, which is not feasible with engine-managed states. Therefore, sometimes, it is a valid option to consider is managing instance states manually. Let's use the system usage job as an example to study how it works.

> Are there any other options to manage state?

The diagram below shows the system usage job with a state storage hooked up. Different instances store their states in the storage independently. Like we discussed earlier, absolute time won't really work because different instances are working on different events. And since we are managing states manually, now we don't have the checkpoint events to provide event-based timing. What should we do to synchronize different instances?

The key is to have something in common that can be used by all components and instances to sync up with each other. One solution is to use transaction id. For example, transaction source instances store offsets, and system usage analyzer instances store transaction ids and current counts in the storage every minute. When the job is restarted, transaction source instances load the offset from storage, and then they *go back a little* (a number of events or a few minutes back) and restart from there. The system usage analyzer instances load the most recent transaction ids and counts from the storage. Afterwards, the analyzer instances can skip the incoming events until the transaction ids in the states are found and then the regular counting can be resumed. In this solution, transaction source and system usage analyzers can manage their instance states in different ways because the two components are not tightly coupled by the checkpoint ids anymore. As a result, the overhead could be lower, and we also get more flexibility, which could be important for some real-world use cases.

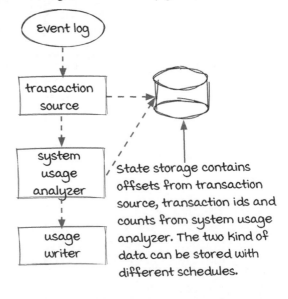

State storage contains offsets from transaction source, transaction ids and counts from system usage analyzer. The two kind of data can be stored with different schedules.

Lambda architecture

Another popular and interesting technique is called *lambda architecture*. The name sounds fancy, but take it easy; it is not that complicated.

To understand this technique, we will need to recall a concept from chapter 1 about the comparison of batch and stream processing systems. While streaming processing systems can generate results in real time, batch processing systems are normally more failure tolerant because if things go wrong, it is easy to drop all the temporary data and reprocess the event batch from the beginning. In consequence, the final results are accurate because each event is calculated exactly once toward the final results. Also, because batch processing systems can be more efficient to process a huge number of events, in some cases more complicated calculations that are hard to do in real time can be applied.

The idea of lambda architecture is rather simple: running a streaming job and a batch job in parallel on the same event data. In this architecture, the streaming job is responsible for generating the real-time results that are mostly accurate but provides no guarantee when bad things happen; the batch job, on the other hand, is responsible for generating accurate results with higher latency.

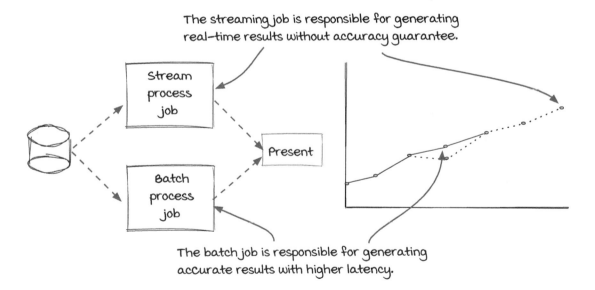

With lambda architecture, there will be two systems to build and maintain, and the presentation of the two sets of results can be more complicated. However, the accuracy requirement of the streaming job can be much less strict, and the streaming job can focus on what it is designed for and good at: processing events *in real time*.

Summary

In this chapter, we revisited the instance state and took a closer look. Then, we dived into more details of how instance states and checkpoints are managed in streaming jobs, including:

- Checkpoint creation via checkpoint events
- Checkpoint loading and the backward compatibility issue
- Checkpoint storage

After briefly comparing stateful and stateless components, we also learned two popular techniques that can be used to archive some benefits of stateful components without the burdens:

- Manually managed instance states
- Lambda architecture

Exercises

1. If the system usage job is converted into a stateless job, what are the pros and cons? Can you improve it by manually managing the instance states? And what would happen if a hardware failure occurred and the instances were restarted on different machines?

2. The fraud detection job is optimized for real-time processing because of the latency requirement. What are the tradeoffs, and how can it be improved with lambda architecture?

Wrap-up: Advanced concepts in streaming systems | **11**

In this chapter

- reviewing the more complex topics in streaming systems

- understanding where to go from here

> *It's not whether you get knocked down; it's whether you get up.*
>
> —VINCE LOMBARDI

You did it! You have reached the end of part two of this book, and we have discussed quite a few topics in more detail. Let's review them quickly to strengthen your memory.

Is this really the end?

Well, we authors think it's safe to say this is the end of the book, but you can count on having many more years of learning and experimenting in front of you. As we sit and write this chapter, we're reflecting on the long journey of learning. What an adventure it has been for us! Hopefully, after reading this book, you feel that you benefited from it—we certainly have.

What you will get from this chapter

There have been many complex topics covered in the second half of the book. We'd like to recap the main points. You may not need to know all of these topics in depth in the beginning of your career, but knowing them will help you establish yourself in the upper echelon of technologists in the field when it comes to real-time systems. After all, learning these topics well is not a trivial task.

Windowed computations

We learned that not all streaming jobs want to handle events one at a time. It can be useful to group events together in some cases, whether that is time- or count-related.

Before, we had been processing each element individually.

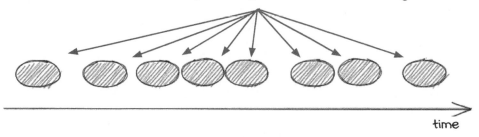

time

In chapter 7, we learned how to process events in groups divided by windows.

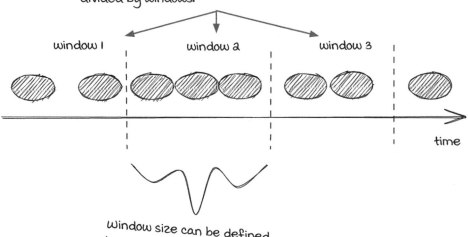

window 1   window 2   window 3

time

Window size can be defined by a time period or number of elements. It is defined by the developers.

The major window types

Creating or defining a window is entirely up to the developer. We showed three different base window types, using the fraud detection job as an example. Note that time-based windows are used in the diagrams below.

Fixed Windows

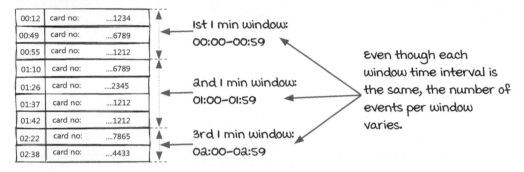

Sliding Windows

With sliding windows, you simply keep a rolling context of data to reference and decide if an event should be marked as fraudulent.

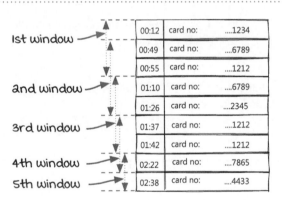

Session Windows

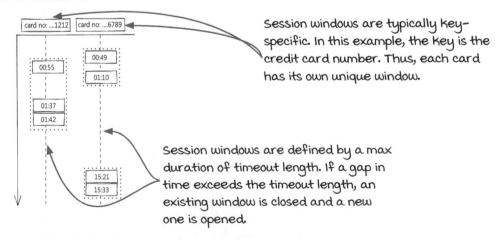

Joining data in real time

In chapter 8, we covered joining data in real time. In this scenario, we had two different types of events being emitted from the same geographic region. We needed to decide how to join events that are in two different event types and coming at different intervals.

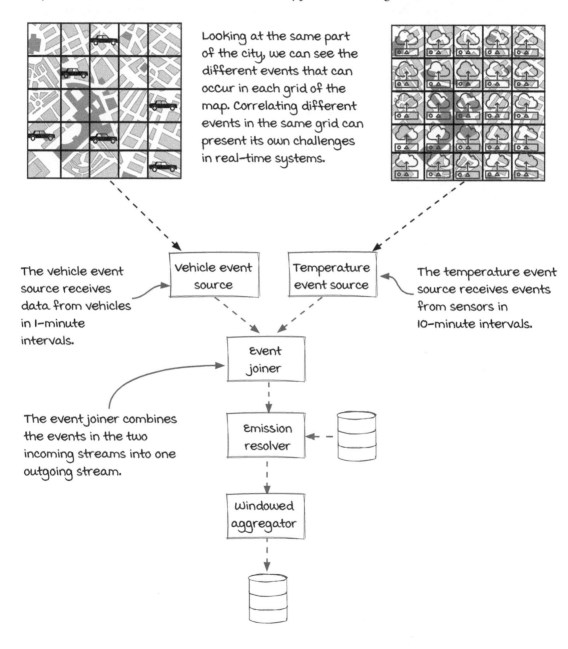

Looking at the same part of the city, we can see the different events that can occur in each grid of the map. Correlating different events in the same grid can present its own challenges in real-time systems.

The vehicle event source receives data from vehicles in 1-minute intervals.

The temperature event source receives events from sensors in 10-minute intervals.

The event joiner combines the events in the two incoming streams into one outgoing stream.

SQL vs. stream joins

Most of us are familiar (enough) with the join clause in SQL. In streaming systems, it is similar but not quite the same. In one typical solution, one incoming stream works like a stream, and the other stream is (or streams are) converted into a temporary in-memory table and used as reference data. The table can be considered to be a materialized view of a stream.

There are two things to remember:

1. Stream join is another type of fan-in.
2. A stream can be materialized into a table continuously or using a window.

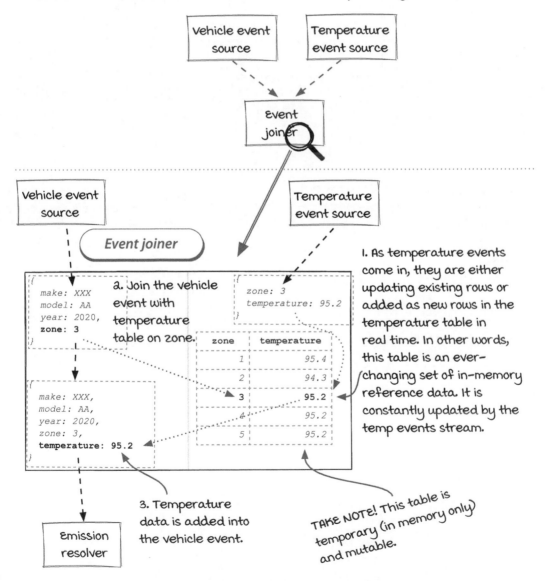

Inner joins vs. outer joins

Like the join clause in SQL, there are four types of joins in streaming systems as well. You need to choose the right one for your own use case.

Inner joins only return results that have matching values in both tables.

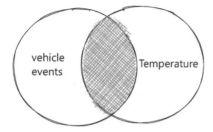

Full outer joins return all results in both tables.

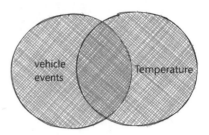

Left outer joins return all results in the vehicle events table and only matching rows from the temperature table.

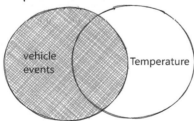

Right outer joins return all results in the temperature table and only matching rows from the vehicle events table.

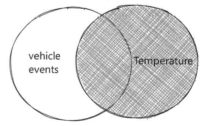

Unexpected things can happen in streaming systems

Building reliable distributed systems is challenging and interesting. In chapter 9, we explored common issues that can occur in streaming systems and cause some instances to lag behind, as well as a widely supported technique for temporary issues: backpressure.

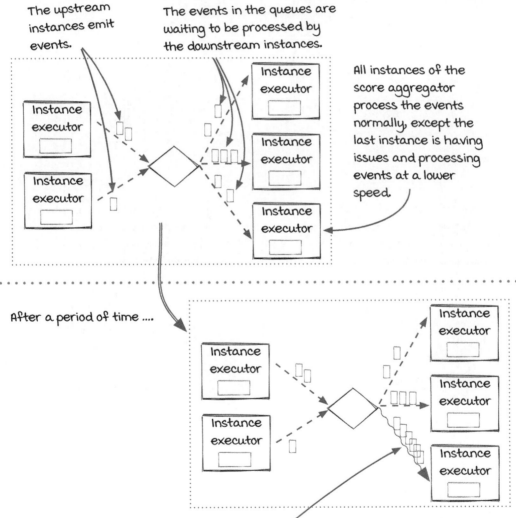

The upstream instances emit events.

The events in the queues are waiting to be processed by the downstream instances.

All instances of the score aggregator process the events normally, except the last instance is having issues and processing events at a lower speed.

After a period of time ....

Because the downstream instance lags behind, the intermediate queue backs up with events to be processed. Eventually, when the queue becomes full, the system might become unstable.

Backpressure: Slow down sources or upstream components

Backpressure is a force opposite to the data flow direction that slows down the event traffic. Two methods we covered for addressing backpressure were stopping the sources and stopping the upstream components.

Stopping the sources

1. We can temporarily stop the source from emitting any additional transactions into the job by sending a special message to all the instances of the source component.

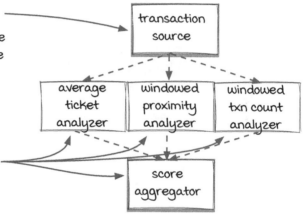

2. With the source temporarily stopped, all components will be able to finish processing all transactions traversing the job and then the source can be resumed.

Stopping the upstream components

At the component level, we would stop all three of the analyzer components from taking new events from the source and emitting results to the score aggregator component temporarily. The score aggregator will be able to finish processing the pending events and the analyzers will be resumed.

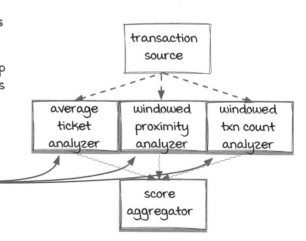

Another approach to handle lagging instances: Dropping events

In this approach, when an instance is lagging behind, instead of stopping and resuming the processing of the source or the upstream components, the system will just throw away the new events being routed to the instance.

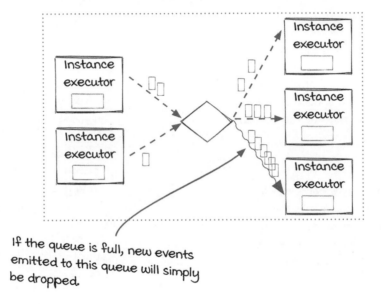

If the queue is full, new events emitted to this queue will simply be dropped.

It is certainly reasonable to be cautious when choosing this option, as the events will be lost. However, it may not be as scary as it sounds. The results are not accurate *only* when backpressure is happening, which should be rare in theory. So, they should still be accurate *almost* all the time. On the other side, dropping events could be desirable in the cases in which end-to-end latency is more important than accuracy. Don't forget that dropping events is much more lightweight than pausing and resuming the event processing.

Backpressure can be a symptom when the underlying issue is permanent

We have mentioned a few times that backpressure is a self-protection mechanism for avoiding more serious issues in extreme scenarios. While we hope that the issue that causes some instances to lag behind is temporary and backpressure can handle it automatically, it is possible that the instance won't recover and the owner's interventions will be required to take care of the root cause. In these cases, permanent backpressure is a symptom, and developers need to address the root causes.

The instance stops working, so backpressure won't be relieved

In this case, no events will be consumed from the queue, and the backpressure state will never be relieved at all. This is relatively straightforward to handle: by fixing the instance. Restarting the instance could be an immediate remediation step, but it could be important to figure out the root cause and address it accordingly. Often, the issue leads to bugs that need to be fixed.

The instance can't catch up, and backpressure will be triggered again: Thrashing

If you see the thrashing, you will likely need to consider why the instance doesn't process quickly enough. Typically, this kind of issue comes from two causes: the traffic and the components. If the traffic has increased or the pattern has changed, it could be necessary to tune or scale up the system. If the instance runs slower, you will need to figure out the root cause. Note that it is important to take the dependencies into consideration as well. After all, it is important for you, the owner of the systems, to understand the data and the systems and figure out what is causing the backpressure to be triggered.

Stateful components with checkpoints

In chapter 10, we learned how we could stop and start a streaming job without losing data. Stateful components allow for the recreation of a context, so the components resume the processing from the state where it stopped previously. In our specific case, AJ and Miranda needed a way to stop and restart the system usage job on new machines transparently.

A checkpoint, a piece of data that can be used by an instance to restore to a previous state, is the key for persisting and restoring instance states.

- The getState() function is called periodically by the instance executor to get the latest state of each instance, and the state object is then sent to the checkpoint manager to create a checkpoint.

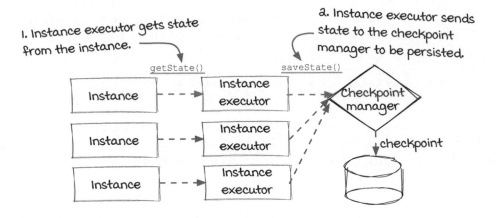

- The setupInstance() function is called by the instance executor after the instance is created, and the most recent checkpoint is loaded by the checkpoint manager.

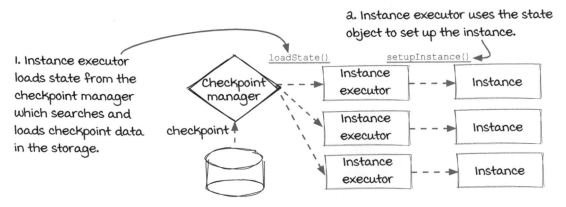

Event-based timing

Every instance in a streaming job needs to get its state at the same *time*, so a job can be restored to a previous time when needed. However, the time here isn't the *clock time*. Instead, it needs to be *event-based time*.

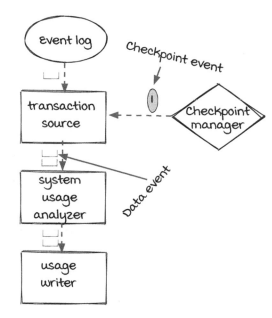

The checkpoint manager is responsible for generating a checkpoint event periodically and emitting it to all the source instances. The event then flows through the whole job to notify each instance that it is time to send the internal state to the checkpoint manager. Note that, unlike the regular data events, which are routed to one instance of a downstream component, the checkpoint event is routed to all the instances of a downstream component.

At the instance level, each event dispatcher connects to multiple upstream instances and multiple downstream instances. The incoming checkpoint events of the event dispatcher may not arrive at the same time, and they need to be synchronized before sending out to the downstream instances.

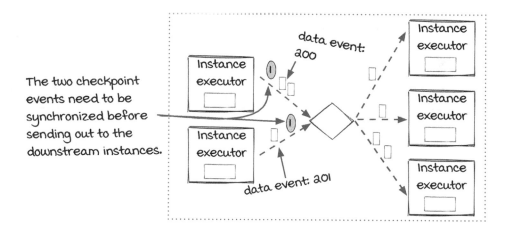

Stateful vs. stateless components

As a creator or maintainer of streaming jobs, you will need to decide when to use a stateless or a stateful component. This is where you will need to go with your gut instinct or collaborate with a team to make this decision. It is not clear-cut when to use a stateful or stateless component in every scenario, so in times like these, you really become the artist. The following table compares several aspects of stateful and stateless components.

	Stateful component	Stateless component
Accuracy	• Stateful computation is important for the exactly-once semantic, which guarantees accuracy (effectively).	• There is no accuracy guarantee because instance states are not managed by the framework.
Latency (when errors happen)	• Instances will roll back to the previous state after errors happen.	• Instances will keep working on the new events after errors happen.
Resource usage	• More resources are needed to manage instance states.	• No resource is needed to manage instance states.
Maintenance burden	• There are more processes (e.g., checkpoint manager, checkpoint storage) to maintain, and backward compatibility is critical.	• There is no extra maintenance burden.
Throughput	• Throughput could drop if checkpoint management is not well tuned.	• There is no overhead to handle high throughput.
Code	• Instance state management is needed.	• There is no extra logic.
Dependency	• Checkpoint storage is needed.	• There is no external dependency.

Stateful components are fantastic in terms of adding reliability to a streaming job, but remember to keep things simple at first. As soon as you introduce state into your streaming jobs, the complexity of planning, debugging, diagnosing, and predicting could make them much more cumbersome. Make sure you understand the cost before making each decision.

You did it!

Pat yourself on the back; that was a lot of material to cover. You have made it through about 300 pages of how streaming systems work! So, what's next? Well, you can start working hard to increase your knowledge and experience on the subject. Don't have a degree? Don't worry; you don't need one. With a little dedication you can definitely master streaming systems (and your tech career). We've listed a few ideas for you to consider. Again, you don't necessarily have to work on them in the same order.

Pick an open source project to learn

Try to rebuild the problems you've worked through in the book in a real open source streaming framework. See if you can recognize the parts that make up our Streamwork engine in real streaming frameworks. What are instances, instance executors, and event dispatchers called in the frame you picked?

Start a blog, and teach what you learn

The best way to learn something is to teach it. Start to build your own brand, and be ready for some critical reviewers to come your way, too. It is interesting to see people interpret the same concept from many different angles.

Attend meetups and conferences

There are many details and real-world use cases in stream systems and other event processing systems. You can learn a lot from other people's stories in related meetups and conferences. You can also go further by speaking and holding virtual presentations and discussions as well!

Contribute to open source projects

If there is one thing we can say will work for you most in this list, it's this one. In our experience, nothing has increased our technology and people skills more than this strategy. Contributing to open source projects exposes you to advanced technologies and allows you to plan, design, and implement features with real-life professionals across the world. Most importantly, we would bet that working on open source projects will fulfill you more than anything you've ever been paid for. There is something about contributing to a cause being driven by purpose that will pay more than any paycheck can for years to come.

Don't quit, ever

Obtaining any extraordinary goal comes with walking through failure over and over. Be okay with failure. It is what will make you better.

Key concepts covered
in this book

index